HENRY IV

PART ONE

BROADVIEW / INTERNET SHAKESPEARE EDITIONS

Broadview Editions Series Editor
L.W. Conolly
Internet Shakespeare Editions Coordinating Editor
Michael Best
Internet Shakespeare Editions Textual Editor
Eric Rasmussen

HENRY IV

PART ONE

William Shakespeare

EDITED BY

Rosemary Gaby

BROADVIEW / INTERNET SHAKESPEARE EDITIONS

Library and Archives Canada Cataloguing in Publication

Shakespeare, William, 1564-1616, author
  Henry IV. Part one / William Shakespeare ; edited by
Rosemary Gaby.

(Broadview/Internet Shakespeare editions)
Includes bibliographical references.
ISBN 978-1-55481-051-2 (pbk.)

  I. Gaby, Rosemary, editor II. Internet Shakespeare Editions
III. Title. IV. Series: Broadview Internet Shakespeare editions

PR2810.A2G33 2013   822.3'3   C2013-903536-2

Broadview Press is an independent, international publishing house, incorporated in 1985.

We welcome comments and suggestions regarding any aspect of our publications—please feel free to contact us at the addresses below or at broadview@broadviewpress.com / www.broadviewpress.com.

North America	UK, Europe, Central Asia, Middle East, Africa, India and Southeast Asia	Australia and New Zealand
Post Office Box 1243 Peterborough, Ontario Canada K9J 7H5		NewSouth Books c/o TL Distribution 15-23 Helles Ave. Moorebank, NSW Australia 2170
2215 Kenmore Ave. Buffalo, New York USA 14207 tel: (705) 743-8990 fax: (705) 743-8353 customerservice @broadviewpress.com	Eurospan Group 3 Henrietta St., London WC2E 8LU, UK tel: 44 (0) 1767 604972 fax: 44 (0) 1767 601640 eurospan @turpin-distribution.com	tel: (02) 8778 9999 fax: (02) 8778 9944 orders@tldistribution.com. au

Copy-edited by Denis Johnston
Book design by Michel Vrana

For Alex, Johanna and Ari

CONTENTS

FOREWORD

The Internet Shakespeare Editions (http://internetshakespeare. uvic.ca) and Broadview Press are pleased to collaborate on a series of Shakespeare Editions in book form, creating for each volume an "integrated text" designed to meet the needs of today's students.

The texts, introductions, and other materials for these editions are drawn from those prepared by leading scholars for the Internet Shakespeare editions, modified to suit the demands of publication in book form. The print editions are integrated with the fuller resources and research materials that are available electronically on the site of the Internet Shakespeare Editions. Consistent with other volumes in the Broadview Editions series, each of these Shakespeare editions includes a wide range of background materials, providing information on the staging of the play, as well as on its historical and intellectual context, in addition to the text itself, introduction, chronology, and bibliography; all these will be found in more complex form on the website.

The Internet Shakespeare Editions, a non-profit organization founded in 1996, creates and publishes works for the student, scholar, actor, and general reader in a form native to the medium of the Internet: scholarly, fully annotated texts of Shakespeare's plays, multimedia explorations of the context of Shakespeare's life and works, and records of his plays in performance. The Internet Shakespeare Editions is affiliated with the University of Victoria.

The Broadview Editions series was founded in 1992 under the title "Broadview Literary Texts." Under the guidance of executive editors Julia Gaunce and Marjorie Mather, of series editors Eugene Benson and Leonard Conolly, and of managing editors Barbara Conolly and Tara Lowes, it has grown to include several hundred volumes— lesser-known works of cultural significance as well as canonical texts. Designed with the needs of undergraduate students in mind, the series has also appealed widely to scholars—and to readers in general.

Michael Best, Coordinating Editor, University of Victoria
Eric Rasmussen, General Textual Editor, University of Nevada, Reno
Don LePan, President, Broadview Press

ACKNOWLEDGEMENTS

I owe a huge debt of thanks to Michael Best, Coordinating Editor of the Internet Shakespeare Editions, for his thoughtful and patient guidance through every stage of preparing this text for the ISE/ Broadview series. It is a great privilege to be part of the community of ISE editors and I am grateful to the many people associated with the ISE who have supported this project. I have received invaluable feedback from Don Bailey, Eric Rasmussen, and James Mardock, and I am indebted to the pioneering work of David Bevington and John Cox whose outstanding editions of *As You Like It* and *Julius Caesar* precede mine in this series. It has been a pleasure to work with Broadview Press toward the preparation of this print edition and I would like to thank Denis Johnston for his rigorous copy-editing and Leonard Conolly, Tara Lowes, and Marjorie Mather for their help in bringing this volume and the series into existence.

Financial support for academic study leave from the University of Tasmania enabled me to visit the Huntington and Folger Shakespeare libraries and I am beholden to the staff at those libraries for the opportunity to view the 1598 quarto of *Henry IV, Part One* and the Dering manuscript. Thanks are also due to library staff at the University of Tasmania, to Ralph Crane and my colleagues at Utas for their support and encouragement, and to Luke Hortle for his efficient research assistance. I would also like to acknowledge my early mentors in the task of editing *Henry IV, Part One*: Adrian Colman, John Golder, and the late Richard Madelaine.

Shakespeare's Globe Theatre kindly granted permission to reproduce John Haynes's photo of Roger Allam as Falstaff, and images from the 2005 National Theatre production of *Henry IV, Part One* are courtesy of the National Theatre Archive and photographer Catherine Ashmore. I am indebted to Rob Conkie, photographer Tanya Tuffrey, and the Australian Research Council Centre of Excellence for the History of Emotions for the image of *Henry IV, Part One* on the New Fortune Stage. The brief essays on Shakespeare's life and Shakespeare's theater are reprinted from the Broadview edition of *As You Like It*, courtesy of David Bevington. Quotations from Shakespeare's plays other than *Henry IV, Part One* are from David Bevington's *Complete Works*, 6th edition (NewYork: Pearson Longman, 2009). Biblical quotations are taken from *The Geneva Bible: A Facsimile of the 1560 Edition* (Madison, Milwaukee, and London: U of Wisconsin P, 1969).

INTRODUCTION

THE HISTORY PLAY

Historical fiction is so pervasive today on stage, television, film, and in the novel that it is easy to overlook how much our appetite for the genre owes to Shakespeare and the Elizabethan history play. Shakespeare has played a key role in building an audience for stories about English history and through the centuries his fictionalized versions of historical figures and events have, rightly or wrongly, helped to shape the way we imagine the past.

In 1623, when Shakespeare's actor-friends John Heminges and Henry Condell gathered together 36 of his plays for publication in what we now call the First Folio, the plays were grouped as comedies, histories, and tragedies. The ten plays described as histories were based on the reigns of English kings from King John (1199–1216) to Henry VIII (1509–47). Although some of these plays were also described elsewhere as tragedies, Shakespeare's contemporaries clearly thought they were significantly different from plays about more remote political figures such as Julius Caesar, or legendary English kings such as Cymbeline or Lear.

Nearly all of Shakespeare's history plays were written in the 1590s, and it seems that the vogue for staged histories, established by Shakespeare, was largely limited to this decade. The history play's popularity at this time has been associated with numerous factors, including an increased sense of nationhood and patriotism after the defeat of the Spanish Armada (1588), anxieties about the nation's political future during the final decade of Elizabeth's reign, and rapidly evolving ideas about historiography. However, Shakespeare's personal interests and influence are also obviously important: while he was not the only Tudor writer of history plays, he certainly dominated the field. Shakespeare's histories can be viewed as experimental works, drawing upon chronicle-history materials and morality-play traditions to present a new dramatic form.

AN ONGOING SAGA

Henry IV, Part One was written sometime around 1596–97. It was one of a sequence of four plays, written between 1595 and 1599, covering the consecutive reigns of Richard II, Henry IV, and Henry V. *Richard II* focuses on the deposition of Richard II and Henry Bolingbroke's rise to the throne; the two parts of *Henry IV* chart both the dissension that accompanied Henry's reign and the preparations of Prince Hal for a more effective style of kingship; and *Henry V* shows what happened when Hal became king and made war against the French. Shakespeare's earlier history plays—the three *Henry VI* plays and *Richard III*—actually chronicle events *after* the reign of Henry V. Together, the two groups of plays (now often called "tetralogies") dramatize the fortunes of the English monarchy from, roughly, 1398 to 1485.

The success of his first group of histories probably influenced Shakespeare's decision to embark on a second sequence. It was a particularly sound move: Shakespeare's histories were good box office material. *Henry IV, Part One* became his most published play, appearing in seven solo "quarto" editions before the publication of his complete works in the First Folio. Perhaps the success of *Henry IV, Part One* led to the writing of its sequel: we simply do not know how Shakespeare planned the sequence, or even whether *Henry IV* was intended as one play or two from the start. It was never called *Part One* during Shakespeare's lifetime. In its first edition, the title page announces: *The History of Henrie the Fourth; With the battell at Shrewsburie, betweene the King and Lord Henry Percy, surnamed Henrie Hotspur of the North. With the humorous conceits of Sir John Falstalffe.* This title gives no indication that this is the first of three plays about Prince Hal; instead, attention is drawn to the more popular characters, Hotspur and Falstaff, and to the battle that forms the climax of the play.

The history plays inevitably have many characters in common, and it is interesting to trace the fortunes of various figures from one play to another. Often the dialogue refers back to the material of earlier plays (in *Henry IV* the rebels are constantly harking back to the fact that Henry "put down" Richard II) and sometimes situations that develop in later plays are anticipated earlier. Toward the end of *Richard II*, the newly crowned Henry IV asks, "Can no man tell me of my unthrifty son?" (*R2* 5.3.1, TLN 2497), and Harry Percy ("Hotspur" in *Henry IV*) tells him about a recent meeting he had with the wayward Prince. Throughout *Henry IV, Part One* the audience is made aware of the impending rejection of Falstaff that concludes *Part Two*, and at certain moments *Henry IV, Part Two* looks ahead to the war with France that is dramatized in *Henry V*.

Henry IV, Part Two continues the story begun in *Part One*. It begins with the delivery of conflicting reports about the battle of Shrewsbury, delivered to Hotspur's "crafty-sick" father, Northumberland, and goes on to chart the quelling of further rebellion, the death of Henry IV, and Prince Hal's assumption of the crown. In many ways *Part Two* seems to repeat the material of *Part One*, but in a minor key. Hal spends less time on stage with Falstaff in *Part Two*, but his dying father still sees him as a rebellious prince until their climactic reconciliation scene toward the end of the play. Falstaff rushes to London from the Gloucestershire home of his friend, Justice Shallow, to greet the newly-crowned Henry V, but Hal publicly affirms his reformation by denying Falstaff and leaving him in the charge of the Lord Chief Justice. At the end of *Part Two* the epilogue promises to continue the story "with Sir John in it"; instead, *Henry V* simply reports Falstaff's death, then moves on to dramatize Hal's campaign in France.

Obviously, the Henry plays are closely linked in terms of characters, tone, and narrative. Nevertheless, *Part One* can be happily read and performed on its own. Like many modern films with sequels that expand and develop the plot, the play works well as an individual entertainment *and* as a part of a larger story.

AN UNPREDICTABLE GENRE

In the histories the tone of the drama—whether comic or tragic—depends largely on the events being staged. *Henry IV, Part One* encompasses the tragic pathos of Hotspur's death, the thrill of Hal's battlefield valor, the intrigue of power politics, and the broad humor of the tavern scenes, not to mention a few more lyrical moments. Some history plays—including *Richard II* which was written before *Henry IV, Part One*—adhered largely to the conventions of tragedy, telling "sad stories of the death of kings" (R2 3.2.156, TLN 1516). The stories of kings such as Henry IV and Henry V did not suit tragedy, however, and instead Shakespeare produced what has been described as "hybrid histories" (Grene 191) to dramatize their reigns. These plays shift from verse to prose and from scenes based on serious historical events to scenes of anarchic comic fiction. For Shakespeare and his audience, the history play was new dramatic territory where anything might happen.

The openness of the genre in comparison with other forms is particularly evident with regard to the gargantuan figure of Falstaff. His irreverent roguish spirit spilled over into another two histories and one comedy, *The Merry Wives of Windsor* (supposedly written so that Queen Elizabeth could see Falstaff in love). In the history plays, Falstaff is a powerful and unpredictable force. Irrepressible in *Henry IV, Part One*, a potentially tragic figure at the end of *Henry IV, Part Two*, and recalled with pathos in *Henry V*, he can re-direct our responses to the historical story in many interesting ways. In *The Merry Wives of Windsor*, however, Falstaff's role is limited by the conventions of its comic genre. His roguish activities are contained within a smaller context and, although he retains some of his history-play incorrigibility, he is made to suffer gross indignities to meet the demands of comic justice. In *Henry IV, Part One* Falstaff has more room to move: the history play provided an environment that could accommodate his sprawl.

The English history plays defied some of the limitations of other genres, but they were based on a relatively limited pool of stories. When the genre was revisited in later years, in plays such as Shakespeare's *Henry VIII* (1613) and John Ford's *Perkin Warbeck* (1634), it was to dramatize events of the Tudor period that might not have been safely staged while Elizabeth I (the last Tudor monarch) was still on the throne. While the genre enjoyed a relatively brief heyday, Shakespeare's history plays have retained enormous popularity from the 1590s to the present day. *Richard III* and *Henry V* have been frequently filmed, and all the histories have fared well in the theater.

With their overt political focus, the history plays have attracted contrasting readings and met diverse cultural expectations for different times and places. Laurence Olivier's *Henry V*, filmed near the end of World War II, and Kenneth Branagh's *Henry V*, filmed 45 years later, convey very different perspectives on war. Outside England, the histories are much less likely to engender the kind of nationalistic pride with which they are often associated, but French, German, and Japanese directors have found occasion to produce them nevertheless. The openness of the history play genre seems to have had a lot to do with the plays' durability. History plays raise questions about the construction of identity, about how social groups are formed and organized, about image-making and ideological control, and about how power is exerted, contested, and manipulated at personal, local, and national levels. Approaches to these issues constantly change, but they remain of enduring and urgent concern.

Shakespeare's history plays are not a good place to go for an accurate rendering of historical events. The details of place, time, and personality are all subject to a great deal of artistic license (much like most modern Hollywood versions of the past). Shakespeare did, however, research his materials in some depth. Close studies have shown that *Henry IV, Part One* draws on a surprising range of disparate sources.

The most obvious source for *Henry IV, Part One* is the 1587 edition of Raphael Holinshed's *Chronicles of England, Scotland, and Ireland* (see Appendix A1). Holinshed's style of history focuses on the personalities and motivations of significant historical figures and much of the detail of Henry IV's struggle with the Percys comes from here. Another important source is the third book of Samuel Daniel's *The First Four Books of the Civil Wars between the Two Houses of Lancaster and York* (1595; see Appendix A4). Daniel's poem differs significantly from Holinshed in the emphasis it places on the Prince of Wales and his rivalry with Hotspur. Shakespeare followed Daniel in making Hotspur a much younger man at the time of the rebellion (historically he was older than King Henry) and in both Daniel and Shakespeare the battle of Shrewsbury becomes an occasion for the prince to prove his valor and martial prowess.

Other probable sources include John Stow's *Chronicles of England* (1580) and *Annales of England* (1592) and an anonymous play from the 1580s, *The Famous Victories of Henry the Fifth* (see Appendices A2 and A9). *The Famous Victories* survives in an edition from 1598, which may not accurately reflect the play that Shakespeare knew, but it does provide an example of the "wild prince" legend and some comic play-acting moments that might have inspired Shakespeare's tavern scenes. *The Famous Victories* and *Henry IV, Part One* are strikingly different nevertheless. *The Famous Victories* is primarily about the prince and his progress from thief to victorious king. He is much more reckless and irresponsible than Shakespeare's relatively level-headed Prince Hal and his unplanned reformation occurs miraculously within the space of a few lines. In the *Henry IV* plays Shakespeare constructed a much wider story.

Invented scenes of revelry are offset by more serious scenes, closely based on historical writings, and this skillful balancing of one kind of scene against another creates the impression of a rich and complex historical world. While many other possible literary source-materials for *Henry IV* have been recognized, including chronicles, ballads, and morality plays, what is striking about all these sources of inspiration is their huge distance from Shakespeare's play. In Shakespeare's hands, history becomes the product of a complex chain of interwoven events, dynamic personality clashes, and complex personal motives.

THE HISTORICAL STORY

Although characters such as Falstaff, Poins, and Bardolph are fictive creations, most of the figures in this play are based on real people. The broad outlines of character and destiny were already familiar to Shakespeare's audience, and so too were many details of the political context, if only through other history plays such as *Richard II*. An understanding of the historical background can make the play more intelligible to modern audiences and readers too.

The first character we hear from in the play is King Henry IV. He launches into a long speech about the end of England's civil strife and his plan to organize a crusade against the Turks. His words are addressed to his closest advisers, and are charged with the weight of weary emotion. At the end of his speech Henry abruptly announces that the proposed crusade is *not* the purpose of the present meeting and instead we hear various accounts about battles against the Welsh and the Scots. We hear that "the noble Mortimer" has been captured by the Welsh leader Glendower, and that the young Harry Percy, or "Hotspur," while victorious against the Scots, is refusing to give up his prisoners (and hence their valuable ransom) to the king, probably at his uncle Worcester's suggestion. It appears that internal strife is continuing to thwart Henry's plans.

Behind this scene lies a complicated chain of events. Henry IV came to power in 1399 by forcing his cousin, Richard II, to abdicate. Five months later Richard died in prison, probably murdered. Richard had become king by direct line of succession after the deaths of his father, Edward the "Black Prince," in 1376 and his grandfather, Edward III, in 1377. Henry was the son of Edward III's fourth son, John of Gaunt, the Duke of Lancaster. In taking the crown from Richard, Henry violated the normal laws of succession. Henry, in effect, was a usurper, depending for his power on his personal popularity and the support of his nobles. Foremost amongst the nobles who helped Henry to power were the Percys: the Earl of Northumberland, his brother the Earl of Worcester, and Northumberland's son Hotspur. The Percys were soon dissatisfied with the king they had helped to make.

Henry's problems were aggravated by the fact that Richard had nominated Edmund Mortimer, the Earl of March, as his heir in 1398. The real Earl of March was kept under lock and key during Henry's reign. Shakespeare, however, follows Holinshed in confusing the Earl with his uncle, Sir Edmund Mortimer, who married Glendower's daughter and joined the rebels in 1403. Holinshed claims that Mortimer was taken prisoner by Glendower after leading an English power against him, and that Henry was "not hasty to purchase the deliverance of the Earl March, because his title to the crown was well enough known." Mortimer, meanwhile, decided "to take part" with Glendower.

The issue of Mortimer's ransom is what ignites the rebellion in Shakespeare's play. Hotspur is married to Mortimer's sister (Kate in the play). He wants Henry to ransom his brother-in-law in return for the Scottish prisoners captured at Holmedon. Henry responds by labeling the Earl a traitor, citing the Welsh marriage as evidence that Mortimer never did attempt to confront Glendower. Hotspur is incensed at this insult to his family, and at Henry's apparent ingratitude to those who helped him gain the throne. When he learns that Richard had proclaimed Mortimer heir to the throne, he leaps at the idea of rebellion and readily falls in with the plan put forward by his uncle and his father to join forces with the Scots, the Archbishop of York, Glendower, and Sir Edmund Mortimer against the king.

INTERPRETING HISTORY

In recent years Shakespearean critics have paid increasing attention to the difficulties associated with interpreting the past. The need to contextualize Shakespeare's plays—to see how they feed from and into the culture that produced them—has been emphasized by many scholars, and there has been a great deal of debate about how this should be done. One thing that the debate has consistently illustrated is the extent to which our interpretations of the past are subject to the preoccupations, beliefs, and assumptions of our own time and place. Whenever we attempt to enter the minds of an earlier time, we inevitably do so through the lens of our own cultural contexts.

In the twentieth century many critics sought to elucidate Shakespeare's interpretation of historical events in *Henry iv, Part One* by discussing the play in the context of the whole sweep of Shakespeare's history plays. Arguably the most influential mid-twentieth century study was E.M.W. Tillyard's *Shakespeare's History Plays* (1944), which described a conservative Elizabethan world-view reflected in Shakespeare's histories. In subsequent decades Tillyard's work was frequently criticized for its insistence on Shakespeare's adherence to the thought-idiom of his age, and the idea that the history tetralogies enact the working out of the "Tudor myth": that by deposing Richard ii, Henry Bolingbroke established a long period of political instability that would only be resolved by the divinely-sanctioned intervention of Henry Tudor. Later critics have emphasized the diversity inherent in Elizabethan thinking about the past, noting the uneasy relationship between the stage and the Elizabethan state, and finding subversive voices within and outside the drama.

Most recent critics have accepted the idea that Elizabethan thinking about the past encompassed many diverse viewpoints and political agendas and it has been frequently asserted that Shakespeare's plays reflect readings of history no less complex and contradictory than our own (see, for example, Holderness et al. 1988). Phyllis Rackin describes Renaissance ideas about history as developing in two main directions: one explained historical events in terms of providence, the other in the more pragmatic terms of Machiavellian power politics (6–7). The providential view of historical causation would explain Henry iv's troubles as divine retribution for the act of usurping the throne from the rightful king, Richard ii. The pragmatic view would explain events as the result of human rather than divine will, with an emphasis on the personal conflicts and tactical errors that create political instability (43–46). Rackin argues that the conflict between these two early modern interpretations of history is an integral part of Shakespeare's staged history. Both interpretations are made available to us, as they were to their first audiences, provoking ongoing debate and dramatic tension.

Henry IV, Part One frequently draws attention to the existence of multiple versions of past events. Characters tend to reinterpret the past in the context of their present desires. The deposition of Richard II is reworked by an angry Hotspur into a shameful and unjust act so that Richard becomes "that sweet and lovely rose" as opposed to "this thorn, this canker Bolingbroke." Henry tells a different story when he describes the "skipping king" Richard, and compares himself at Ravenspurgh to Hotspur now. The most obvious re-telling, of course, is Falstaff's marvelously embroidered account of the Gadshill robbery: the details rapidly fly further and further from the truth.

Hotspur, disgusted at Glendower's fantastic account of his "nativity" advises: "Tell truth, and shame the devil" (3.1.57, TLN 1584), but truth is a rare commodity in the world of this play. The Shrewsbury battlefield is filled with counterfeit kings, suggesting the masking that has become habitual for Henry IV. The rebels, too, are prone to deceit, most obviously in Worcester and Vernon's failure to deliver the king's offers before the battle. Prince Hal's first soliloquy presents a plan that involves misrepresenting himself to everyone, and on more than one occasion he finds himself compelled to "gild" a lie for Falstaff's sake. Falstaff, of course, makes an art of lying—so much so that he can be seen as the most honest character in the play: he, at least, finds any pretense at virtue an intolerable burden.

This emphasis on the elusive nature of truth is one of the ways in which the play engages its audience in the business of interpreting historical events. There are many sides to the struggles that take place within *Henry IV, Part One*, and many possible explanations of events and actions are made available to us. The play itself is a kind of counterfeit history: the actors are not real kings or corpses after all. This knowledge seems to haunt the edges of the play, reminding us that this "history" is far from real and that from this distance the puzzles it presents can never be fully resolved.

FATHERS, SONS, AND SUBJECTS

It has been frequently noted that the basic outlines of character in *Henry IV, Part One* are etched by a clever and intricate series of parallels and contrasts. The comparisons begin in 1.1 when King Henry complains that he envies Northumberland's being father to "so blest a son" as Hotspur, and wishes that "some night-tripping fairy" had exchanged their children: "Then would I have his Harry, and he mine" (1.1.89, TLN 93). Here a minor parallel—two fathers who, as time proves, both undervalue their sons—is linked with one of the play's most important structural pairings of Henry Percy (Hotspur) and Prince Hal, the future Henry v. As the play progresses we are drawn into the game of comparing these two "Henries." They are acutely conscious of the game themselves, frequently mocking each other's predilections and debating each other's worth. On its simplest level *Henry IV, Part One* is a competitive quest between Hal and Hotspur to become "the theme of honor's tongue" (1.1.80, TLN 84).

Another important parallel is set up between Hal's father-substitute, Falstaff, and King Henry. Henry is a stern parent, prone to giving long-winded lectures and making unfair public comparisons between his own son and other people's children. It is little wonder that Hal has more fun with "that father Ruffian," Falstaff. A yawning generation gap is evident between Hal and his real father. Henry has no idea of what Hal is really like. He shows in his interview with Hal that his feelings toward his eldest son are all tangled up with his guilt over the murder of Richard II. As Henry cannot help equating Hal's wild behavior with Richard's, it is all too easy to view his heir's debauchery as punishment for the murder of his cousin-king. If Henry cannot rely on his son to take over the kingdom, then his own grab for power loses its point. Falstaff provides Hal with a very different kind of parenting. He is indulgent, affectionate, and body-focused. It is sometimes suggested that he takes on a maternal, nurturing role in the very masculine world that Hal inhabits, and some recent productions have added a homoerotic dimension to their relationship.[1] Certainly Falstaff and Hal share a different kind of language to that of the court: their battles are battles of wit conducted in prose. By exchanging insults with Falstaff, Hal can relieve some of his filial angst.

Both Hal and Hotspur rebel against Henry IV: the father-son relationship mirrors that of king and subject. In fact Henry sarcastically expresses his surprise that Hal has not joined the rebels under Percy's pay (3.2.126, TLN 1946). By such means, personal family relationships

---

1 Taken to extremes in Benedict Andrews's heavily abridged version of the play for Sydney Theatre Company's 2009 "Wars of the Roses" during which Prince Hal (Ewen Leslie) performed fellatio on Falstaff (John Gaden).

are linked to the wider political situation throughout *Henry IV, Part One*. The struggles depicted in the history plays are dynastic, and the marriages, quarrels, habits, and obsessions of the country's most powerful families are of national significance. Like Hal, Hotspur is subjected to successive lectures from the senior members of his extended family, Northumberland, Worcester, and Glendower. Although he thinks he is his own man, these father-figures easily manipulate him into an action that will involve thousands of lives. The private play of power within these families has an enormous public cost. Old certainties about the structure of society under a king whose right to rule was absolute have been shattered by the deposition of Richard II. In the new fractured world under Henry IV, the younger generation has to make its way against an older group of cynical and experienced intriguers.

WHO *IS* PRINCE HAL?

One of the most puzzling aspects of *Henry IV, Part One* for today's critics, directors, and actors is the figure of Prince Hal. Is he a cold-hearted schemer, a misunderstood adolescent, or a genuine hero-in-the-making? Hal is presented as an enigma. His own father completely misreads him, as do most of the other characters in the play. His mission, he tells us, is to create, by means of a dramatic reformation, a dazzling public image. In the meantime it is difficult to judge just who the real prince is.

From Hal's point of view the world offers a range of possibilities. In one direction is the world of Falstaff and Eastcheap, a world offering sensuality, self-indulgence, freedom, comedy, and an escape from responsibility. Here Hal can feel the warmth of friendship, good humor, and instant acceptance, although he can also be lied to, exploited, and drawn into crime. Opposed to Eastcheap is the court, an altogether less appealing environment. Its mood is established by Henry's opening line "So shaken as we are, so wan with care." While it seems a harsh, unforgiving, somber place, where onerous duties beckon, the court too has its other side, offering the support of a real family and a solid base for purposeful action. A third alternative is Hotspur's life of martial action and honor. His perspective also has its attractions, offering the glory of a single-minded commitment to chivalric values without the bother of difficult questions about motives or outcomes.

It is easy to feel sympathetic toward Hal if we view him as a figure trying to make his way through these disparate worlds: a young man with the destiny of the country on his shoulders who has to make difficult choices about the right way to act. But it *is* possible to see him as having already made those choices. His first soliloquy, beginning "I know you all, and will awhile uphold / The unyoked humor of your idleness" (1.2.161, TLN 296), is the problem here. Hal announces a plan to transform himself in the public eye through a dramatic change in behavior. From this speech it appears that he knows where he is going from the very start and that his "loose behavior" is simply part of a stunning bit of image-manipulation. If this is so, it could be argued that Hal is cynically manipulating his friends and family as well. Some critics suggest that this soliloquy is simply a theatrical convention: an announcement about the plot of the play that has nothing to do with personality. Actors still have to deal with the speech, however. It can be presented thoughtfully as if the ideas are only just coming to mind, or, alternatively, delivered with defiance—directed at either Eastcheap or the court.

It is worth noting the similarities between Hal's language in the "I know you all" speech and King Henry's at the beginning of the very next scene. Henry says: "I will from henceforth rather be *myself*, / Mighty and to be feared" (1.3.5–6, TLN 326–27). Hal, comparing himself to the sun breaking through the clouds, says: "That, when he please again to be *himself*, / Being wanted he may be more wondered at" (1.2.166–67, TLN 301–02), and later he promises his father, "I shall hereafter, my thrice-gracious lord, / Be more *myself*" (3.2.92–93, TLN 1911–12). Who is the self that Hal proposes to be? When King Henry talks about being "myself," he seems to mean "myself-as-king," as opposed to his natural disposition or "condition." Perhaps Hal sees himself the same way. Henry and Hal both seem to perceive kingship as involving the assumption of a different but real personality.

Both Falstaff and Hotspur win regard and affection for being themselves, but those selves are obviously flawed. Hotspur is idealistic, forthright, and completely dependable, but he is also a traitor who rashly leads his followers into disaster. Falstaff is considerably wiser than Hotspur—he is inventive, flexible, and witty—but his absolute self-indulgence makes him wholly unreliable and ineffective in the workaday world. Toward the end of the play, Hal has a moment alone on stage with the corpse of Hotspur and the supposed corpse of Falstaff. For both he delivers affectionate but clear-sighted epitaphs. His farewell to Hotspur begins, "Fare thee well, great heart! Ill-weaved ambition, how much art thou shrunk!" (5.4.86–87, TLN 3052–53) and to Falstaff he says, "Poor Jack, Farewell! / I could have better spared a better man" (5.4.102–03, TLN 3069). This is one of Hal's most likeable moments: it shows generosity of spirit, compassion, and honesty. It can also be seen as an emblematic moment of selfhood for Hal. The apparent deaths of his old rival and friend leave space for him to assert his own claims for attention and respect.

FALSTAFF: THE SUBVERSIVE SUBJECT

Hal's finest moment is typically subverted by the figure of Falstaff. When Hal sadly leaves Falstaff's huge corpse on stage the corpse pops up and announces that he had only counterfeited death. It is a breathtaking comic reversal of expectations and a neat counterpoise to the heroics of Hotspur's dying moment. The revival of a character thought to be dead is an old stage tradition used very frequently by Shakespeare, most spectacularly in one of his last plays, *The Winter's Tale*. It is a device that lifts the mood of the audience beyond the fiction of the play, drawing attention to the playwright's sheer audacity.

Falstaff is an audacious creation all round, a figure of comedy and carnival, thrust into the middle of a history play. In the play-scene of 2.4 Hal casts Falstaff in the role of the Vice. He is "that reverend Vice, that grey Iniquity, that father Ruffian, that Vanity in years" (2.4.398–89, TLN 1411) and a "villainous, abominable misleader of youth" (2.4.396, TLN 1420). Hal is referring here to the emblematic figures who would tempt the protagonist of the medieval "morality" play into a life of sin and degradation. The Vice quickly developed into an ambiguous figure who would provide comic relief through energetic clowning, disguise, and wit, enjoying a complex rapport with the audience. Shakespeare draws on these traditions for his portrayal of Falstaff and echoes the morality play in the broad structure of *Henry IV, Part One*. The play can be viewed in terms of antithetical character types and the moral choices placed before Hal, the figure of youth. It is important to remember,

Roger Allam as Falstaff, Shakespeare's Globe, London, 2010. Shakespeare's Globe Picture Library. Photographer John Haynes.

however, that the morality-play casting is partly Hal's construct. In the play-scene he jokingly creates a public image for Falstaff, which complements the rebellious image Hal has created for himself. This self-conscious acknowledgment of theatrical antecedents invites a closer consideration of the role-playing that is so much a part of Hal's story.

Falstaff is reminiscent of many other archetypal comic figures including the braggart soldier, the fool, the trickster, and the rogue. He has also been persuasively linked with the Lord of Misrule: the figure who presides over all the playful pranks and role-reversals of traditional festive holidays (most notably by C.L. Barber in his 1959 study, *Shakespeare's Festive Comedy*). Yet Falstaff is much more interesting and certainly much more fun than any erudite list of dramatic archetypes. Like all rogues, he is an inherently ambiguous figure: a character composed of apparently contradictory elements, who always inspires a mixed response. Falstaff runs away roaring at Gad's Hill, yet falls asleep behind the arras while the sheriff is looking for him; he leads his ragged soldiers to their deaths without compunction, yet delivers compelling speeches about the physical cost of war; he violates Hotspur's corpse and steals the glory of his death, but he makes us laugh and for that we would forgive almost anything.

Falstaff has always inspired a great deal of critical debate. A common theme in discussions of his character is the claim, started by A.C. Bradley, that Falstaff somehow got beyond his author's control. Hal's rejection of Falstaff is the crux of the problem. Hal can only prove his fitness to rule by eventually turning his back on all that Falstaff represents. But for many, Falstaff is simply too full of life to be rejected: he has outstripped his function in the play and drawn all the sympathy we might have for Hal toward himself. Did Falstaff become too large a character for the plays he inhabits? Are the subversions Falstaff represents—his dismissal of honor, his romancing of gluttony, sloth, theft, and anarchy—contained by the wider perspective of the play, or is his outlook too appealing? Whatever we decide, it is important to note that in *Henry IV, Part One* Falstaff is *not* killed off. Despite a few rehearsals for the rejection that occurs at the end of *Part Two*, in *Part One* Falstaff is a comic survivor. Some critics have speculated that Falstaff's absence from *Henry V* can be explained by the sudden departure in 1599 of Will Kempe, the actor in Shakespeare's company who specialized in clown roles (see Wiles 116–17; Aaron 280–85). If this is so, then Falstaff's death can be set down as a solution to a casting problem, and not necessarily something that was planned for his character from the start.

In his "I know you all" soliloquy Hal muses: "If all the year were playing holidays, / To sport would be as tedious as to work" (1.2.170–71, TLN 305–06). It is just such seemingly indisputable assumptions that Falstaff turns upside down. Falstaff is too witty and too changeable for the holiday he represents to ever become as tedious as work. Others in *Henry IV, Part One* consciously play roles, but Falstaff is addicted to theater. He adopts the voice of piety one minute, blasphemy the next; he can contradict himself within the space of a sentence: "I ... swore little, diced not above seven times—a week" (3.3.12–14, TLN 2018). Honor is just a word that should be ignored when necessary and time is something for others to believe in. For Falstaff, identity and language are never fixed or absolute. It is a liberating perspective and, for the length of *Henry IV, Part One* at least, an exhilarating possibility.

DIFFERENT WORLDS

Many voices contribute to the history of *Henry IV, Part One*. It is a play that emphasizes regional difference and the fractured nature of the country Hal will one day rule. Contrasting languages differentiate the court from the tavern; Mortimer speaks a completely different language from his own wife. In *Henry IV*, unlike earlier histories, people on the margins of society are a strong presence. People with no real power—tapsters, carriers, wives, and daughters—have their own stories to tell. An impression of teeming life is conveyed through simple accumulated details such as the carriers' grumbling about fleas and the lack of chamber-pots in a busy inn on the London road.

There are no major roles for women in *Henry IV, Part One*. In Eastcheap, women occupy a marginal space, and despite Hal's roistering reputation, he is never seen with a female companion. Lady Percy (Kate), Lady Mortimer, and Mistress Quickly are memorable characters, but they are not essential to the action, they vanish from the play's conclusion, and they are sometimes cut from the performed text altogether. Obviously this absence reflects Shakespeare's sources and the limited power available to women in the political arena of the fifteenth century, but it reflects the attitudes and assumptions of a patriarchal sixteenth-century culture as well. In Shakespearean tragedy women usually play a pivotal role, but history was constructed as a particularly masculine concern.

Nevertheless, in performance the female characters in *Henry IV* can present a strong alternative point of view to the main business of the action. In the tavern the hostess is the target of a lot of smutty adolescent humor; in Northumberland and Wales, Kate, too, is the object of chauvinist teasing; and Lady Mortimer is a mere pawn in her father's schemes. Yet these women talk back whenever they can. Kate is as fiery as her husband, but much more sensible, and Mortimer's wife can significantly change the mood of the play through the Welsh magic of her song. A basic opposition is established between domestic and public allegiances, and we are made to feel that the men, and Hotspur in particular, would do well to consult their wives more fully. At the end of 3.1, when the rebels depart for war, many productions close with a significant "look" between the women left behind. Their mere presence on stage can provide eloquent expression of an alternative view on the power games that obsess their men. In *Henry IV, Part One* women speak their own separate language.

Diverse speech patterns are a striking feature of *Henry IV, Part One*. Its verse varies from Henry's carefully controlled formality, to Hotspur's impatient forgetfulness—"In Richard's time—what d'ye call the place?/ A plague upon't, it is in Gloucestershire" (1.3.240–41, TLN 570–71)—and its prose contains some of the most spectacular abuse in the language:

> ... thou clay-brained guts, thou knotty-pated fool, thou whoreson, obscene, greasy tallow-catch....
> 'Sblood, you starveling, you eel-skin, you dried neat's tongue, you bull's pizzle, you stock-fish! ... (2.4.197–213, TLN 1184–1203)

Shakespeare greatly extended his use of prose in this history, creating naturalistic voices for a wide range of characters. Common figurative threads link the many dialects of the play, however. Resonant words such as "reckoning" and "time" permeate the discourses of Eastcheap, court, and battlefield, creating subtle connections between ostensibly disparate social groups. Repeated references to the body, to parasites, sickness, and disease, to fat and to famine, function as a constant reminder of the basic physical dimension of political acts.

INTERWEAVING STORIES

The play's linking of different worlds through imagery is extended by its many ironic plot parallels. *Henry IV, Part One* is structured so that the action ranges among several contrasting locations. This not only maintains pace and interest, but also suggests resonant connections between the activities and attitudes of very different people. The first three scenes of the play, for example, move from the court of King Henry to the tavern at Eastcheap and back to the court again. In scene one Henry talks about both his son and Hotspur, setting up expectations that can be assessed in more depth as we meet those characters in the next two scenes. In 1.2 Falstaff and Poins urge Hal to join the Gadshill plot, and at the end of 1.3 Northumberland and Worcester urge Hotspur to join with them in the plot against the king. The juxtaposition of these scenes brings out significant contrasts of character (note Hal's caution as opposed to Hotspur's impetuosity) and, at the same time, makes subtle connection between the rebellion and the robbery. The carriers' scene follows 1.3, with more talk of preying on the commonwealth. Court, rebels, and robbers are thus closely tied, and when Falstaff and his cronies rob the travelers at Gad's Hill, and then are robbed themselves, attentive audience members might even spot an echo of the king's own plight.

The action switches between court, rebels, and revelers through the rest of Acts 2 and 3. Some obvious contrasts emerge, such as that between Hal's mock interview with his father / Falstaff in 2.4 and his real interview in 3.2, and that between Falstaff's embroidered tales in 2.4 and Glendower's Welsh fantasies in 3.1. But many less obvious comparisons can also be made: Hotspur's intimate teasing of his wife, Kate, in 2.3, is immediately followed by Hal's tormenting of the hapless Francis in 2.4. These private moments can convey a lot about Hal and Hotspur and the impact they have on those around them. Both reveal a measure of arrogance in these scenes, but the degrees of affection shown between Kate and Hotspur can vary enormously, while Hal's game with his admirer might reflect tipsy high-spirits, snobbish cruelty, or a more ironic consciousness of the link between apprentice king and apprentice tapster.

In Act 4 the various groups move toward the Shrewsbury battlefield and the pace quickens as scenes change swiftly between rival camps. In Act 5 the battle draws all the main figures of the play together for a climactic confrontation. The battle is not just about Hal and Hotspur, however. Our sense of the human lives and issues at stake is complicated by the additional stories told: stories of vividly realized characters such as the compromised Vernon, earnest Blunt, and fiery Douglas. Momentarily we are reminded, too, of the fate of Falstaff's hundred-and-fifty "peppered" ragamuffins.

For Hal the battle is a rite of passage and his chance to fulfill the promise made to his father to "redeem all this on Percy's head" (3.2.132, TLN 1952). Even before the fighting commences, Hal cuts an impressive figure, prompting his enemy, Vernon, to conclude, "England did never owe so sweet a hope, / So much misconstrued in his wantonness" (5.2.67–68, TLN 2853–54). It seems England is in desperate need of such a hope. Worcester betrays his nephew and his men, Glendower hides in Wales, Northumberland stays home in bed, and Falstaff fakes his own death, while noble lords and ragamuffins are killed on their behalf. Hal rises above all this: he acquits himself bravely on the field, he saves his father's life, and he fights and kills Hotspur. By the end of the play Hal has shown that he can redeem the time he has wasted, whereas Hotspur is proven "time's fool." Hal has become the hero of the hour. Yet that "strangest fellow," Falstaff, survives too, to win applause for making the most of the moment. Despite Hal's heroic achievements, workaday and holiday values still seem evenly, though uneasily, in balance.

At its conclusion, *Henry IV, Part One* remains characteristically open-ended. As Henry divides his powers to march off and meet more rebels, we are left to make our own judgments about what might have been lost and won so far. Shakespeare's dramatization of the reign of Henry IV shows that history is made up of many competing stories. The perspectives of Hal, Hotspur, Falstaff, King Henry, and even of Francis or Kate can each be presented very persuasively. Like all dramatic texts, *Henry IV, Part One* is ultimately a blueprint for performance: it is up to the actors and their audience to decide which history to tell.

HENRY IV, PART ONE IN PERFORMANCE

CONTROVERSIAL BEGINNINGS

While there is clear evidence of the early popularity of *Henry IV, Part One*, the details of its first performances remain shrouded in mystery. It was produced at a time when the affairs of Shakespeare's company, the Lord Chamberlain's Men, were particularly unsettled. By the mid-1590s Shakespeare and the Chamberlain's Men were becoming very successful and prosperous. The famous Globe Theatre was as yet unbuilt, however, and the company lacked a secure base. Their lease on "The Theatre" at Shoreditch expired on 13 April 1597, and, because of disputes with the Puritan owner, they had little hope of renewal. Plans to move into the newly-converted indoor theater in the inner-city precinct of Blackfriars had been scuttled by a petition against them from local residents in November 1596. To make matters worse, between July and October 1597, all the theaters in London were closed by order of the Privy Council in response to the uproar over an allegedly seditious play, *The Isle of Dogs* by Ben Jonson and Thomas Nashe. Shakespeare's company obtained a license to tour at this time, but its future direction was uncertain (Thomson 3–18).

Henry IV, Part One was first staged in the midst of these difficulties. It might have been put on at the Theatre before the company was evicted, or nearby at the Curtain, another venue often used at this time. It would almost certainly have been played at court during the winter of 1597–98 (possibly even earlier) and it was probably in the company's repertoire when they went on tour in 1597. Like other plays of the period, *Henry IV* had to adapt to many different environments and conditions.

What we do know about the play's early history is mostly associated with the fuss created by Shakespeare's original name for Falstaff, Sir John Oldcastle. Shakespeare took up the name from *The Famous Victories of Henry the Fifth* where Oldcastle is one of the prince's roistering companions, but a relatively undeveloped minor character. The prince of *The Famous Victories* is much wilder than Shakespeare's Prince Hal, wholly committed to drinking, swearing, robbing, and wenching. In *Henry IV* these characteristics were transferred to Sir John.

The real Sir John Oldcastle—Lord Cobham by marriage—held Lollard views, which meant that he opposed many of the institutions and practices of the Roman Catholic church. He was eventually executed for heresy and treason. Shakespeare's use of the name apparently offended Oldcastle's descendants and those who thought of the historical figure as a Protestant martyr, even though the real Oldcastle had little in common with Shakespeare's comic creation. One particularly powerful descendant was Sir William Brooke, the seventh Lord Cobham. He was Lord Chamberlain from August 1596 until his death in March 1597 and in this capacity was responsible for Shakespeare's company and for the business of licensing plays. Cobham seems to have been a relatively unsympathetic patron. Known for his puritanical leanings, he was a resident of Blackfriars, responsible for preserving order in the district at the same time that the Lord Chamberlain's Men were looking to open their Blackfriars Theatre (Gildersleeve 184). Some ill-feeling may well have been in the air in 1596 over the Blackfriars issue. We do not know whether Shakespeare intended any offence or what sort of pressure was exerted in response, but we do know that the name Oldcastle was changed to Falstaff (a name previously used in the first part of *Henry VI*) before the play was printed in 1598. Traces of the name Oldcastle can be found in the text of *Henry IV, Part One* and in *Part Two*, and at the end of *Part Two* the epilogue tells us that "Falstaff shall die of a sweat—unless already he be killed with your hard opinions. For Oldcastle died a martyr, and this is not the man."

The disclaimer may have been needed to quench an ongoing scandal: letters show that the plump eighth Lord Cobham, Henry Brooke, was now nicknamed "Falstaff." The Lord Chamberlain's Men were obviously wary of causing further offence. In *The Merry Wives of Windsor*, the name Brooke, assumed by a comically jealous character, was altered to "Broome." Vestiges of the names "Harvey" and "Russell" are also present in the first quarto of *Henry IV, Part One* and these appear to have been altered to "Peto" and "Bardolph" (originally spelt "Bardol" or "Bardoll").[1] Presumably this was done to avoid further offence to prominent families. Interestingly, the Dowager Lady Russell was a leading campaigner against the proposed Blackfriars Theatre in November 1596 (Wells, Taylor, Jowett, and Montgomery 331). Despite all this controversy, however, no documents have as yet turned up to tell us exactly when, where or how *Henry IV, Part One* was presented to its first Elizabethan audience.

THE KING'S MEN AND AFTER

We can safely assume, however, that the play continued to be popular on stage in the decades following its first performance. Shakespeare's company became the "King's Men" after James I came to the throne in 1603, and requests for performances of *Henry IV* at court show that the play was a company staple. Falstaff was a great drawcard: when the play was commissioned for performance on New Year's Night in 1625, it was entitled *The First Part of Sir John Falstaff*, reflecting a common practice of nicknaming plays after their most popular or prominent character. A commendatory verse by Leonard Digges, published with a 1640 edition of Shakespeare's poems, compares Shakespeare with his fellow playwright Ben Jonson and asserts that, while Jonson's comic

---

1   See A Note on the Text, p. 61.

characters might not always cover costs, "let but Falstaff come, Hal, Poins, the rest you scarce shall have a roome / All is so pester'd" (Vickers 1.28). The play was also popular enough to be adapted for private performance. The "Dering manuscript," held by the Folger Shakespeare Library, shows that around 1623 the two Henry IV plays were abridged for private performance in the home of Sir Edward Dering.

Henry IV, Part One was also subjected to substantial alteration after a parliamentary act in 1606 banned the use on stage of profane oaths such as "zounds" (an abbreviation of "by God's wounds") or "sblood" (God's blood). This shift is reflected in the 1623 Folio edition of the play, which lacks many of the oaths present in the 1598 Quarto. Parliament's puritan suspicion of all things theatrical had further, more devastating, impact when the English civil war broke out: in 1642 Parliament banned the performance of stage plays altogether. The theaters were closed and officially Henry IV, Part One was not performed again until after the monarchy was restored and the theaters reopened in 1660. Theatrical activities continued underground during this period, of course, and it is a measure of Falstaff's popularity that some of his scenes from Henry IV were part of the underground repertoire. The actor Robert Cox staged favorite comic scenes from popular plays as "drolls," which were published in a collection called The Wits in 1662 after the anti-playhouse laws were relaxed. The Falstaff piece, "The Bouncing Knight, or the Robbers Robbed," was placed first in the volume.

Falstaff helped keep Henry IV, Part One in fairly regular performance on the English stage over the next three centuries, but as British theater came to be more and more dominated by powerful actor-managers, his popularity did not always work to the play's advantage. It did not offer a strong enough starring role for actor-managers unsuited to the part of Falstaff, and there was little scope, too, for a company's leading lady. In 1774 Francis Gentleman, the editor of Bell's acting editions of Shakespeare, wrote of Henry IV, Part One:

> the play as it now stands, is free from superfluities, and possesses much strength of character and sentiment; yet we are sorry to say, that the want of ladies, and matter to interest female auditors, lies so heavy on it, that through an excellent Falstaff only, can it enjoy occasional life. (Odell 2:41)

Though excellent Falstaffs such as James Quin (1693–1766), the American actor James Hackett (1800–71), and Samuel Phelps (1804–78) brought *Henry IV, Part One* some stage success, it was not until the twentieth century that the play's status was secured as one of the great ensemble pieces of Western theater. From the Restoration period to the beginning of the twentieth century, performances of *Henry IV, Part One* were mostly about famous Falstaffs, Hotspurs, and elaborate scenery. In the early twentieth century, however, thinking about the staging of Shakespeare's plays underwent radical change. Directors began to recognize the advantages of the simplicity of the Elizabethan stage in terms of immediacy and fluidity of action, and to experiment with new ways of staging the plays. For *Henry IV, Part One* this meant that its multiple locations and contrasting scenes could come to the fore, and so too its capacity to showcase the talents of a whole company.

TWENTIETH-CENTURY HISTORY "CYCLES"

One of the many new possibilities that emerged in the twentieth century was the idea of grouping the history plays together, with the staging of history "cycles" instead of individual plays. The notion of performing *Henry IV, Part One* in the context of Shakespeare's other history plays entails a significant shift in perspective. The two parts of *Henry IV* tell the story of Prince Hal's apprenticeship for the crown and lead on, in *Henry V*, to the culmination of all this in Hal's triumph as king against the French at Agincourt. Viewed in the context of the later plays, *Henry IV, Part One* becomes more the story of Prince Hal than a play about Falstaff or Hotspur. In his study of *Henry IV, Part One* in the Shakespeare in Performance Series, Scott McMillin calls this the "one decisive change" to mark the stage history of the play. McMillin notes (1–4) that although Hal's prominence is only apparent when the plays are viewed together, across all three plays Shakespeare actually wrote more lines for the prince than for any other character.

In England the tradition of staging the play as part of a larger history cycle effectively began in 1951, when four history plays—*Richard II*, *1 Henry IV*, *2 Henry IV*, and *Henry V*—were staged at the Shakespeare Memorial Theatre in Stratford-upon-Avon as part of the Festival of Britain. Over the course of the season the plays were performed on a single permanent set with actors keeping their roles from one play to the next. Anthony Quayle directed the series, with assistance from John Kidd for *Henry IV, Part One* and from Michael Redgrave for *Henry IV, Part Two*. Quayle had assembled a large highly-skilled cast. He played Falstaff himself, Michael Redgrave played both Richard II and Hotspur, Harry Andrews was Henry IV, and Richard Burton—at the time a relatively unknown young Welsh actor—was cast as Hal.

Quayle's production emphasized the connectedness of Shakespeare's history plays. Each play fed into the next, presenting the interwoven stories of Richard II's deposition and Prince Hal's gradual transformation into Henry V. The casting was integral to the over-all conception of the tetralogy and created an important shift of emphasis in *Henry IV, Part One*. Although Redgrave as Hotspur and Quayle as Falstaff were the acknowledged stars, both were prepared to rein in their performances to give more space to the roles of Henry IV and Prince Hal. Redgrave's Hotspur was a rough, impetuous Northumbrian, attractive in many respects, but less thoughtful, modest, and ultimately less interesting than Hal. Quayle's Falstaff was also designed to be less attractive than was usual. He seemed less genial, less in tune with Hal, more grotesque and more self-conscious in his role as the prince's jester than before.

The producers chose Richard Burton for Hal because it was thought that he might just have the stage presence and personal magnetism needed to maintain interest in the character across three separate plays. In the event the choice paid off. Burton, an actor whose eyes had "the far-away look of a young man whose inner life may be much more important than his outer," (Wilson and Worsley 47) presented a new prince whose consciousness of his destiny informed every moment. From the beginning his prince was aloof, reserved and never fully part of the Eastcheap world. His "I know you all" speech at the end of 1.2 was delivered with serious intent, and an enduring stage tradition was established in the play-scene of 2.4 where Falstaff's plea "banish not him thy Harry's company—banish plump Jack, and banish all the world" was followed by a momentous pause, before Burton delivered "I do, I will" as a chilling rehearsal for Falstaff's rejection at the end of *Part Two*.

The experience of performing history cycles unleashed a huge range of possibilities for *Henry IV, Part One* at a time when audiences might have suspected the play had nowhere new to go. Just six years before Quayle's production, John Burrell's production for the Old Vic company in London had appeared to set an enduring standard. Although presented by a particularly strong cast in repertory with *Part Two*, this production followed the traditional practice of casting its major stars, Ralph Richardson and Laurence Olivier, as Falstaff and Hotspur respectively. By all accounts they completely dominated the play. Richardson's Falstaff was quick-witted, jovial, and endearing, while Olivier's Hotspur was a dashing hero in tights. Hotspur had frequently been played with a stammer. Olivier hit upon the inspired notion of stammering only on the letter "w," allowing him to end on the gloriously pathetic line: "and food for w—." Ironically this dramatic death was also the last gasp of a long stage tradition. Subsequent Hotspurs were caught up in a wider story.

SHIFTING INTERPRETATIONS

Since 1951 *Henry IV, Part One* has been produced on its own and in combination with *Part Two* by companies all over the world. History cycles, however, require large casts and companies with the resources to commit to a long-term project, so most of these have originated in England. Some spectacular cycles have been staged outside Britain, and in translation, including Leopold Lindtberg's productions of the first and second tetralogies in Vienna in the early 1960s and Ariane Mnouchkine's Kabuki-inspired productions of *Richard II* and *Henry IV, Part One* for Théâtre du Soleil in Paris in the 1980s. The most frequently discussed and well-documented cycles, nevertheless, have been from British institutions such as the RSC and the BBC. The cycle-thinking of these companies has inevitably led to a strong focus on the story of Prince Hal, but there has been very little consistency in the way that story is told. In fact *Henry IV* is remarkable for the diversity of interpretations its history has attracted on stage and in film. Successive directors have been able to offer contradictory yet plausible re-readings of the politics and relationships explored within the story of the rebellious prince.

Two particularly influential history cycles in Britain were both mounted under the title, *The Wars of the Roses*. The first of these was directed by Peter Hall, John Barton, and Clifford Williams for the Royal Shakespeare Company (RSC) in Stratford-upon-Avon as part of the 1964 quadricentennial celebration of Shakespeare's birth. The second, directed by Michael Bogdanov for the English Shakespeare Company, was staged in Britain between 1986 and 1989, and subsequently toured extensively around the world. Both cycles embraced the *Henry VI* plays and *Richard III* as well as the plays of the second tetralogy, so *Henry IV* was seen not just in the context of events dramatized in *Richard II* and *Henry V*, but also as a preliminary to all the violence of the Wars of the Roses culminating in the horrors of *Richard III*. Staged together, these histories engendered a dark sense of how political opportunism and the struggle for power is repeated from one generation to the next. Bogdanov's production was staged in eclectic modern dress (in *Henry IV, Part One* Prince Hal wore blue jeans and Gadshill sported a spectacular mohawk while the king and court wore Victorian dress-coats) and consistently pointed to contemporary connections: connections between dysfunctional families and destructive political decisions, connections between theater and the image-making of politics, connections between the world on stage and Margaret Thatcher's Britain after the Falklands War.

Film and television versions of the *Henry IV* plays have also been strongly influenced by cycle thinking. When the BBC produced *Henry IV, Part One* in 1979, as part of a project to film the entire Shakespeare canon, David Giles directed the second tetralogy as one series. His *Henry IV, Part One* is geared toward telling the story of the future Henry V, a hero who, whatever his faults, did become a great king. David Gwillim accordingly presents a fairly likeable Prince Hal throughout the tetralogy: a prince who is sick of play-acting, disillusioned with his companions, and keen to test his skills in the real world.

While the emphasis is on Hal in the BBC version, Orson Welles's 1965 cult classic, *Chimes at Midnight*, is all about Falstaff. It is based on the two parts of *Henry IV* but also draws on *Richard II, Henry V,* and *The Merry Wives of Windsor*. Welles himself played Falstaff in the film, and obviously identified strongly with the role. The film begins with some dialogue between Falstaff and Justice Shallow from *Henry IV, Part Two*. The two old men come inside to sit beside a fire and reminisce. At Falstaff's "We have heard the chimes at midnight, Master Robert Shallow" and Shallow's reply, "That we have, that we have ..." the scene fades out and the history begins. Shakespeare's history is thus framed by Falstaffian nostalgia and the story, shaped from Falstaff's perspective, becomes one of betrayal, the passing of time, and the imposition of a new world order. *Chimes at Midnight* has been hugely influential and is extensively referenced in Gus Van Sant's 1991 film, *My Own Private Idaho*. Van Sant provides a modern reworking of the story in which the Hal figure, played by Keanu Reeves, is a streetwise rent boy rebelling against his father, the mayor of Portland. Van Sant disconnects *Henry IV* from British history, and adds a nineties twist to the prodigal son story.

INTO A NEW MILLENNIUM

The final decade of the twentieth century, and the first decade of the twenty-first, proved a golden age for Shakespeare's English histories on stage, particularly in England, North America, and Australia. In England, Adrian Noble began his directorship of the RSC with a well-received and impressively designed production of both parts of *Henry IV* at Stratford-upon-Avon in 1991. Peter Holland has labeled these "the triumphant histories," noting Noble's "exciting stage pictures," innovative use of vertical space, and creative use of visual devices that echoed and resonated across the two plays. The battle of Shrewsbury, for example, made striking use of the throne:

> ... through the stage floor there came, rising further and further, a seething, writhing tableau, figures struggling in slow motion for the throne with a woman screaming silently at the horror of war to one side. (Holland 106)

As in many late twentieth-century productions, father-son relationships were central: Michael Billington's glowing review of the production's transfer to London describes Julian Glover's king as "a harsh head of state whose peremptoriness provokes the rebels and whose steadfast denial of emotion alienates his son," and Robert Stevenson's "deeply moving" Falstaff as "a solitary hedonist yearning for a son." Michael Maloney's Prince Hal yearned for affection too, but from a father who was unable to respond.

The 1990s also saw several interesting productions of the Henry IV plays outside Britain. Ron Daniels directed both parts for the American Repertory Theatre in 1993, using images of the American Civil War for the depiction of the court while setting the world of the tavern in the 1990s with a punk Prince Hal (Tropea 40). Barbara Gaines presented a more traditional staging of the two plays in 1999 for Chicago's Shakespeare Repertory that could be seen individually or in a single evening. The production was acclaimed for its strong lead performances (Gaines and the Chicago Shakespeare Theatre revisited the plays again in 2006 and presented them at the RSC's Swan Theatre as part of the Complete Works season). In Australia, John Bell directed a conflated four-hour version of both parts of *Henry IV* for the Bell Shakespeare Company in 1998 and followed this with a linked production of *Henry V* in 1999. Bell had performed in the play himself as Prince Hal in Richard Wherret's landmark, Breugel-inspired *Henry IV* in Sydney in 1978. His own production was set in contemporary Britain, reflecting Bell's belief that "the historical references are so specific, it would have seemed folly to try and 'Australianise' it" (Bell 258–59). Instead, the production created space for its audience to draw analogies with the late twentieth century through the evocation of a corrupt modern world. The cast wore grungy thrift-shop clothes, the music was aggressive heavy rock, and the focus of the set was a steep ramp flanked by wire-mesh fencing suggesting a bleak and dangerously out-of-control society. Joel Edgerton's Hal had to make his way through a Britain marked by division and inequality.

The 2000s were ushered in by another RSC history play cycle at Stratford-upon-Avon, "This England," encompassing eight plays but with varying venues, design concepts, and directors. The two parts of *Henry IV* were directed by Michael Attenborough and staged at the Swan Theatre in traditional costume, in sharp contrast to *Richard II* in modern dress at The Other Place. According to Russell Jackson, William Houston presented a "thrillingly unnerving" prince (120) and Desmond Barrit's Falstaff was "surprisingly gentle: quick-witted but never domineering" (118). Nevertheless, for many critics it was David Troughton's careworn king who impressed the most: the physical discomfort he endured from the crown spoke volumes about his uneasy head. At the end of 5.1 in *Part One*, when Falstaff drew Hal aside as the others left the stage, Troughton's Henry paused momentarily to look at his son and Falstaff together. His sense of exclusion from their intimacy was palpable.

Interestingly, many stage productions of *Henry IV, Part One* from the first decade of the twenty-first century reflected a return to the days when the figure of Falstaff dominated the play. Reviews of Scott Wentworth's 2001 Henriad production in Stratford Ontario single out Douglas Campbell's Falstaff as the highlight, and of course the

Matthew Macfadyen as Hal and Michael Gambon as Falstaff, National Theatre, London, 2005. National Theatre Archive. Photo © Catherine Ashmore.

casting of Kevin Kline as Falstaff for the first Broadway production of the twenty-first century at New York's Lincoln Center in 2003–04 sent a clear signal that he would be the center of the show. As Diana E. Henderson has pointed out, the Lincoln Center production had several other recognizable cast members—including Ethan Hawke as Hotspur and Richard Easton as Henry IV—but it was Kline who featured in publicity and reviews (378). Directed by Jack O'Brien, and using an adaptation of the two parts of *Henry IV* by Dakin Matthews, the production has been described as "a conservative, boiled-down version of Shakespeare's history" which relegated the king and his heir to the background and served instead as "a generous vehicle for Kevin Kline and Ethan Hawke" (Magelssen 99).

Other acclaimed Falstaffs of the decade included Michael Gambon in 2005, David Warner in 2007–08, and Roger Allam in 2010. Nicholas Hytner directed Gambon in tandem productions of the two parts of *Henry IV* at London's National Theatre, having first talked to him about the possibility five years earlier:

> ... it all started off with Michael. Though I suspect that every produc-
> tion of *Henry IV* should start there, because if you don't know who's

going to play Falstaff there's no point in doing them. (Hytner qtd. in Merlin 2)

In the event, reviews of Gambon's performance were glowing. He presented a complex Falstaff who was "mischievous, cowardly, garrulous, twinkly, sly, bibulous" (Evans 74), but also "money-grubbing, crude and deeply, darkly afraid of death" (Wolf). Gambon's star-power was balanced by strong performances from the rest of the cast: Matthew Macfadyen's conflicted prince convincingly shifted from slouching petulance in his early scenes to serious princely commitment later on, David Harewood presented a credibly martial, but thoughtful and humorous Hotspur, and David Bradley conveyed the king's anguish and anger at his son's apparent betrayal. Hytner's direction drew attention to the wider implications of the history with simple aural and visual images of a war-devastated land, and a specially commissioned sound-scape (performed live) established a moody, unsettling atmosphere.

At the RSC's Courtyard Theatre in Stratford-upon-Avon and later at the Roundhouse in London, David Warner also presented a highly regarded Falstaff in 2007–08 ("fit to rank with the finest—an unsmiling but fabulous, insouciant amuser" [de Jongh] and "a subtle but sly and heartbreaking Falstaff" [Gelber]). This performance was part of a major history cycle that relied heavily on ensemble playing. Michael Boyd directed the cycle and started with the Henry VI plays, first staged in 2006, then in 2007–08 moved on to Shakespeare's "prequel." When all eight plays were finally running, 34 actors were playing about 264 parts (Hewison). The cycle was praised for the depth and strength of its acting, its stylized representations of an England at war, and its striking visual imagery. Some reviewers felt nevertheless that there was a downside to the cycle format: the individuality of a play such as Henry IV, Part One tended to be subsumed by the overall concept of the cycle and its sense of the sweep of history. More than one review reported that it was hard to respond to the humor of Henry IV, Part One after the emotive demands of Richard II.

This consequence of the history cycle format was even more evident with Benedict Andrews's highly compressed (eight plays over eight hours) adaptation of the English histories as "The War of the Roses Part 1 and Part 2" for the Sydney Theatre Company in 2009. The cycle was visually stunning and bookended by impressive performances by

Cate Blanchett as Richard II and Pamela Rabe as Richard III, but the two parts of *Henry IV* got lost somewhere in the middle, reduced to the bare bones of Henry IV's guilt and regret, and a mutually exploitative sexual relationship between Ewen Leslie's prince and John Gaden's Falstaff. In effect Shakespeare's play became a radically new text, contributing to a grueling nightmare vision of the workings of power.

Shakespeare's Globe in London provided a much jollier and more traditional production of the play in 2010. The two parts of *Henry IV* were directed by Dominic Dromgoole with cast members retaining their roles from one play to the next. Jamie Parker played a high-spirited prince and Roger Allam won the Olivier best actor award for his charismatic Falstaff. While Allam's performance was richly comic, it was also seen as a popularizing move that distorted the balance of the plays. Peter J. Smith complained that "the Globe's tendency toward populism demanded and got, in the shape of Roger Allam's Falstaff, an abiding comic presence which seemed quite to outweigh the plays' more serious questions to do with the nature of political power" (Shurgot and Smith 83). Globe Theatre On Screen has released DVDs of the two plays, which vividly illustrate how well they work on an Elizabethan thrust stage. Allam develops an intimate relationship with the audience as *Part One* progresses, and his performance, along with the additional songs, jigs, and comic stage business creates an interesting tension between the play's momentum as the telling of a historical story and its impact as pure entertainment for the present moment.

Comparison of this record of the 2010 Globe stage production with the most recent film of the play, a BBC2 television version screened in 2012 (also released on DVD), shows just how different *Henry IV, Part One* can be in tone and emphasis. The BBC2 film was the second installment in a four-part adaptation of Shakespeare's second tetralogy produced under the title *The Hollow Crown*. Richard Eyre directed the two parts of *Henry IV* and created a viscerally real medieval world for the two plays. Unlike the colorful stage environment of the Globe production, the *mise en scène* of Eyre's *Henry IV* adaptations is overwhelmingly grey. Eastcheap comes across as a place of filth, rags, and desperation, and Henry IV's court likewise seems unrelievedly grim and cold. The battle of Shrewsbury is set in a winter landscape of snow and mud. Jeremy Irons as Henry IV presents a sympathetic king who could plausibly "pluck allegiance from men's hearts" (3.2.52, TLN 1871), but he does not preside over a merry old England. In *Part One* he is already showing signs of the illness that will kill him in *Part Two*, and this, combined with the realistic squalor of Mistress Quickly's tavern, makes it difficult to see why Tom Hiddleston's handsome, heroic prince wants to spend so much time in Falstaff's world.

It is clear from the 2010 Globe DVD that audiences in the theater had occasion to experience the seductiveness of Falstaff's company through the course of the production. The prince's reasons for lingering in Eastcheap are self-evident for an audience sharing the laughter engendered by a comic, self-aware live performance. On film, it is harder for Falstaff to establish that rapport. In *The Hollow Crown*, Simon Russell Beale delivers a nuanced performance as Falstaff, but the realist mode of the film changes the balance of the play and inevitably reduces Falstaff's stature. Unlike Allam's commanding figure, Beale's Falstaff has to look up to Hal, and his clowning is always tinged by a hint of underlying panic. Eyre's *Part One* also exploits the potential of film to tell much of the story through visual imagery. The dialogue is heavily cut (even Henry's opening speech) and scenes are rearranged to allow the story to unfold more rapidly. Characters from *Part Two*, including Doll Tearsheet and the young princes Humphrey and Thomas, play silent but important roles in *Part One*. In this version the drive of the historical narrative takes precedence over Falstaffian indulgence.

The performance history of *Henry IV, Part One* provides vivid illustration of the multiple and often contradictory possibilities the playscript offers. Different voices have been privileged in different times and places. The play has been staged as both pro and anti-war, as celebrating the establishment of strong, effective central government, and as showing the cynicism and heartlessness of a Machiavellian power machine. It has been presented as an affirmation of the importance of order in society and as a radical expression of anarchic impulses. Some productions have exploited the play's potential for rich comedy and pageantry; others have conjured up a darker, more somber mood. In the face of such evidence it is absurd to posit any definitive, "correct" way of doing *Henry IV, Part One*. The text will defy us at every turn.

SHAKESPEARE'S LIFE

BY DAVID BEVINGTON

The website of the Internet Shakespeare Editions (http://internetshakespeare. uvic.ca), in the section "Life & Times," has further information on many topics mentioned here: Shakespeare's education, his religion, the lives and work of his contemporaries, and the rival acting companies in London.

William Shakespeare was baptized on 26 April 1564, in Holy Trinity Church, Stratford-upon-Avon. He is traditionally assumed to have been born three days earlier, on 23 April, the feast day of St. George, England's patron saint. His father, John Shakespeare, prospering for years as a tanner, glover, and dealer in commodities such as wool and grain, rose to become city chamberlain or treasurer, alderman, and high bailiff, the town's highest municipal position. Beginning in 1577, John Shakespeare encountered financial difficulties, with the result that he was obliged to mortgage his wife's property and miss council meetings. Although some scholars argue that he was secretly a Catholic, absenting himself also from Anglican church services for that reason, the greater likelihood is that he stayed at home for fear of being processed for debt. His wife, Mary, did come from a family with ongoing Catholic connections, but most of the evidence suggests that Shakespeare's parents were respected members of the Established Church. John's civic duties involved him in carrying out practices of the Protestant Reformation. John and Mary baptized all their children at the Anglican Holy Trinity Church, and were buried there.

As civic official, John must have sent his son William to the King Edward VI grammar school close by their house on Henley Street. Student records from the period have perished, but information about the program of education is plentifully available. William would have studied Latin grammar and authors, including Ovid, Virgil, Plautus, Seneca, and others that left an indelible print on the plays he wrote in his early years.

Shakespeare did not, however, go to university. The reasons are presumably two: his father's financial difficulties, and, perhaps even more crucially, Shakespeare's own marriage at the age of eighteen to Anne Hathaway. Neither Oxford or Cambridge would ordinarily admit married students. Anne was eight years older than William. She was also three months pregnant when they were married in November 1582. A special license had to be obtained from the Bishop of Worcester to allow them to marry quickly, without the customary readings on three successive Sundays in church of the banns, or announcements of intent to marry. The couple's first child, Susanna, was born in late May 1583. Twins, named Hamnet and Judith, the last of their children, followed in February 1585. Thereafter, evidence is scarce as to Shakespeare's whereabouts or occupation for about seven years. Perhaps he taught school, or was apprenticed to his father, or joined some company of traveling actors. At any event, he turns up in London in 1592. In that year, he was subjected to a vitriolic printed attack by a fellow dramatist, Robert Greene, who seems to have been driven by professional envy to accuse Shakespeare of being an "upstart crow" who had beautified himself with the feathers of other writers for the stage, including Christopher Marlowe, George Peele, Thomas Nashe, and Greene himself.

Shakespeare was indeed well established as a playwright in London by the time of this incident in 1592. In that same year Thomas Nashe paid tribute to the huge success of the tragic death of Lord Talbot in a play, and the only play we know that includes Talbot is Shakespeare's *1 Henry vi*. We do not know for what acting company or companies Shakespeare wrote in the years before 1594, or just how he got started, but he seems to have been an actor as well as dramatist. Two other plays about the reign of Henry vi also belong to those early years, along with his triumphantly successful *Richard iii*. These four English history plays, forming his first historical tetralogy, were instrumental in defining the genre of the English history play. Following shortly after the great defeat of the Spanish Armada in 1588, these plays celebrated England's ascent from a century of devastating civil wars to the accession in 1485 of the Tudor Henry vii, grandfather of Queen Elizabeth I. Shakespeare's early work also includes some fine ventures into comedy, including *A Comedy of Errors*, *The Two Gentlemen of Verona*, *Love's Labor's Lost*, and *The Taming of the Shrew*. He wrote only one tragedy at this time, *Titus Andronicus*, a revenge tragedy based on fictional early Roman history. Shakespeare also turned his hand to narrative poetry in these early years. *Venus and Adonis* in 1593 and *The Rape of Lucrece* in 1594, dedicated to the Earl of Southampton, seem to show Shakespeare's interest in becoming a published poet, though ultimately he chose drama as more fulfilling and lucrative. He probably wrote some of his sonnets in these years, perhaps to the Earl of Southampton, though they were not published until 1609 and then without Shakespeare's authorization.

Shakespeare joined the newly-formed Lord Chamberlain's Men, as an actor-sharer and playwright, in 1594, along with Richard Burbage, his leading man. This group quickly became the premier acting company in London, in stiff competition with Edward Alleyn and the Lord Admiral's Men. For the Lord Chamberlain's group, Shakespeare wrote his second and more artistically mature four-play series of English histories, including *Richard II*, the two *Henry IV* plays centered on the Prince who then becomes the monarch and victor at Agincourt in *Henry V* (1599). He also wrote another history play, *King John*, in these years. Concurrently Shakespeare achieved great success in romantic comedy, with *A Midsummer Night's Dream*, *The Merchant of Venice*, and *The Merry Wives of Windsor*. He hit the top of his form in romantic comedy in three plays of 1598–1600 with similar throw-away titles: *Much Ado About Nothing*, *As You Like It*, and *Twelfth Night, or What You Will*. Having fulfilled that amazing task, he set comedy aside until years later.

During these years Shakespeare lived in London, apart from his family in Stratford. He saw to it that they were handsomely housed and provided for; he bought New Place, one of the two finest houses in town. Presumably he went home to Stratford when he could. He was comfortably well off, owning as he did one share among ten in an acting company that enjoyed remarkable success artistically and financially. He suffered a terrible tragedy in 1596 when his only son and heir, Hamnet, died at the age of eleven. In that year, Shakespeare applied successfully for a coat of arms for his father, so that John, and William too, could each style himself as gentleman. John died in 1601, Shakespeare's mother in 1608.

Having set aside romantic comedy and the patriotic English history at the end of the 1590s, Shakespeare turned instead to problematic plays such as *All's Well That Ends Well*, *Measure for Measure*, and *Troilus and Cressida*, the last of which is ambivalently a tragedy (with the death of Hector), a history play about the Trojan War, and a bleak existential drama about a failed love relationship. He also took up writing tragedies in earnest. *Romeo and Juliet*, in 1594–96, is a justly famous play, but in its early acts it is more a comedy than a tragedy, and its central figures are not tragic protagonists of the stature of those he created in

1599 and afterwards: *Julius Caesar, Hamlet, Othello, King Lear, Macbeth, Timon of Athens, Antony and Cleopatra,* and *Coriolanus,* this last play written in about 1608. Whether Shakespeare was moved to write these great tragedies by sad personal experiences, or by a shifting of the national mood in 1603 with the death of Queen Elizabeth and the accession to the throne of James VI of Scotland to become James I of England (when the Lord Chamberlain's Men became the King's Men), or by a growing skepticism and philosophical pessimism on his part, is impossible to say; perhaps he felt invigorated artistically by the challenge of excelling in the relatively new (for him) genre of tragedy.

Equally hard to answer with any certainty is the question of why he then turned, in his late years as a dramatist, to a form of comedy usually called romance, or tragicomedy. The genre was made popular by his contemporaries Beaumont and Fletcher, and it is worth noting that the long indigenous tradition of English drama, comprising the cycles of mystery plays and the morality plays, was essentially tragicomic in form. The plays of this phase, from *Pericles* (c. 1606–08) to *Cymbeline, The Winter's Tale,* and *The Tempest* in about 1608–11, would seem to overlap somewhat the late tragedies in dates of composition. These romances are like the early romantic comedies in many ways: young heroines in disguise, plots of adventure and separation leading to tearfully joyful reunions, comic high-jinks, and so on. Yet these late romances are also as tinged with the tragic vision that the dramatist had portrayed so vividly: death threatens or actually occurs in these plays, the emotional struggles of the male protagonists are nearly tragic in their psychic dimensions, and the restored happiness of the endings is apt to seem miraculous.

Shakespeare seems to have retired from London to Stratford-upon-Avon some time around 1611; *The Tempest* may have been designed as his farewell to the theater and his career as dramatist, after which he appears to have collaborated with John Fletcher, his successor at the King's Men, in *Henry VIII* and *The Two Noble Kinsmen* (1613–14). His elder daughter, Susanna, had married the successful physician John Hall in 1607. In his last will and testament Shakespeare left various bequests to friends and colleagues, but to Anne, his wife, nothing other than his "second-best bed." Whether this betokens any estrangement between him and the wife, whom he had married under the necessity of her pregnancy and from whom he then lived apart during the two decades or so when he resided and worked in London, is a matter of hot debate. Divorce was impossible, whether contemplated or not. He did take good care of her and his family, and he did retire to Stratford. Anne lived on with Susanna and John Hall until she died in 1623. Shakespeare was buried on 25 April 1616, having died perhaps on 23 April, fifty-two years to the day after his birth if we accept the tradition that he was born on the Feast of St. George. He lies buried under the altar of Holy Trinity, next to his wife and other family members. A memorial bust, erected some time before 1623, is mounted on the chancel wall.

SHAKESPEARE'S THEATER

BY DAVID BEVINGTON

The website of the Internet Shakespeare Editions (http://internetshakespeare. uvic.ca) includes an extensive discussion of the theaters of Shakespeare's time, and the audiences that attended them: click on "Life & Times" and choose the menu item "Stage."

Where Shakespeare's plays of the early 1590s were performed we do not know. When he joined the newly-formed Lord Chamberlain's Men in 1594, with Richard Burbage as his leading man, most public performances of Shakespeare's plays would have been put on in a building called The Theatre, since, when it was erected in 1576 by Richard Burbage's father James Burbage, it was the only structure in London designed specifically for the performance of plays, and indeed the first such building in the history of English theater. Earlier, plays were staged by itinerant companies in inns and innyards, great houses, churchyards, public squares, and any other place that could be commandeered for dramatic presentation. In Shakespeare's time the professional companies still toured, but to a lesser extent, and several of them also derived part of their income from private performances at court.

The Theatre had been erected in Shoreditch (also called Moorfields), a short walking distance north of London's walls, in order to evade the too-often censorious regulations of the city's governing council. There, spectators might have chosen to see *Romeo and Juliet, A Midsummer Night's Dream, The Merchant of Venice, King John*, or *Richard II*. They would also have seen some earlier Shakespeare plays that he had brought with him (perhaps as the price needed to pay for a share in the company) when he joined the Lord Chamberlain's Men: plays such as *Richard III* and *The Taming of the Shrew*. When in the late 1590s the Puritan-leaning owner of the land on which the building stood, Giles Allen, refused to renew their lease because he wished "to pull down the same, and to convert the wood and timber thereof to some better use," the Lord Chamberlain's Men performed for a while in the nearby Curtain Theatre. Eventually, in 1599, they solved their problem with the landlord by moving lock, stock, and barrel across the River Thames to the shore opposite from London, just to the west of London Bridge, where audiences could reach the new theater—the Globe—by bridge or by water taxi, and where the players were still outside the authority of the city of London. At the time of this move, the River Thames was frozen over solid in an especially harsh winter, so that possibly they slid the timbers of their theater across on the ice.

At any event, the Globe Theatre that they erected in Southwark, not far from the location of today's reconstructed Globe, was in the main the same building they had acted in before. Because timbers were all hand-hewn and fitted, the best plan was to reassemble them as much as was feasible. No doubt the company decided on some modifications, especially in the acting area, based on their theatrical experience, but the house remained essentially as before.

No pictures exist today of the interiors of the Theatre, the Curtain, or the Globe. We do have Visscher's View of London (1616) and other representations showing the exteriors of some theatrical buildings, but for the important matter of the interior design we have only a drawing of the Swan Theatre, copied by a Dutchman, Arend van Buchell, from a lost original by the Dutch Johannes de Witt when he visited London in about 1596–98. In many respects, the Swan seems to have been typical of such buildings. As seen in the accompanying illustration, the building appears to be circular or polygonal, with a thatched roof (called *tectum* in the illustration's labels) over the galleries containing seats and another roof over the stage, but leaving the space for standing spectators open to the heavens. (In the modern Globe, similarly constructed, spectators intending to stand in the yard for a performance can purchase a plastic rain poncho to ward off England's frequent rain showers.) From other kinds of information about Elizabethan playhouses, we can estimate a diameter of about 70 feet for the interior space. A large rectangular stage labeled the *proscaenium* (literally, "that which stands before the scene"), approximately 43 feet wide and 27 feet deep, juts out from one portion of the wall into the yard or *planities siue arena* ("the plain place or arena"). The stage stands about 5½ feet above the surface of the yard. Two pillars support the roof over the stage, which in turn is surmounted by a hut. A flag is flying at the top, while a trumpeter at a door in the hut is presumably announcing the performance of a play. The spectators' seats are arrayed in three tiers of galleries. Stairway entrances (*ingressus*) are provided for spectators to gain access from the yard to the seats, labeled *orchestra* on the first level and nearest the stage, and *porticus* above.

ABOVE, LEFT: This sketch of the Swan is the most complete we have of any theater of the time. The Swan was built in 1596; Shakespeare's company, The Chamberlain's Men, played there in the same year. RIGHT: This view of the first Globe by the Dutch engraver J.C. Visscher was printed in 1625, but must be taken from an earlier drawing, since the first Globe was burnt to the ground in 1613 at the first performance of Shakespeare's *Henry VIII*. There is substantial evidence that Visscher simplified the appearance of the theater by portraying it as octagonal: most scholars now believe that it had twenty sides, thus making it seem more circular than in this engraving.

The stage area is of greatest concern, and here the Swan drawing evidently does not show everything needed for performance in a theater such as the Globe. No trapdoor is provided, though one is needed in a number of Renaissance plays for appearances by ghostly or diabolical visitations from the infernal regions imagined to lie beneath the earth. The underside of the stage roof is not visible in this drawing, but from the plays themselves and other sources of information we gather that this underside above the actors' heads, known as the "heavens," displayed representations of the sun, moon, planets, and stars (as in today's London Globe). The back wall of the stage in the drawing, labeled *mimorum ades* or "housing for the actors," provides a visual barrier between the stage itself and what was commonly known as the "tiring house" or place where the actors could attire themselves and be ready for their entrances. The two doors shown in this wall confirm an arrangement evidently found in other theaters like the Globe, but the absence of any other means of access to the tiring house raises important questions. Many plays, by Shakespeare and others, seem to require some kind of "discovery space," located perhaps between the two doors, to accommodate a London shop, or a place where in *The Tempest* Prospero can pull back a curtain to "discover" Miranda and Ferdinand playing chess, or a place to which Falstaff, in the great tavern scene of *1 Henry IV*, can retire to avoid the Sheriff's visit and then be heard snoring offstage before he exits at scene's end into the tiring house. The modern Globe has such a discovery space.

Above the stage in the Swan drawing is what appears to be a gallery of six bays in which we can see seated figures watching the actors on the main stage, thereby surrounding those actors with spectators on all sides. But did theaters like the Swan or the Globe regularly seat spectators above the stage like this? Were such seats reserved for dignitaries and persons of wealth? Other documents refer to a "lords' room" in such theaters. The problem is complicated by the fact that many Elizabethan plays require some upper acting area for the play itself, as when Juliet, in Act II of *Romeo and Juliet*, appears "*above*" at her "*window*" to be heard by Romeo and then converses with him, or later, when Romeo and Juliet are seen together "*aloft*" at her "window" before Romeo descends, presumably by means of a rope ladder in full view of the audience, to go to banishment (3.5). Richard II appears "*on the walls*" of Flint Castle when he is surrounded by his enemies and is obliged to descend (behind the scenes) and then enter on the main stage to Bolingbroke (*Richard II*, 3.3). Instances are numerous. The gallery above the stage, shown in the Swan drawing, must have provided the necessary acting area "*above*." On those many occasions when the space was needed for action of this sort, seemingly the acting company would not seat spectators there. It is unclear how spectators sitting above would have seen action in the "discovery space" since it may have been beneath them.

On stage, in the drawing, a well-dressed lady, seated on a bench and accompanied perhaps by her lady-in-waiting, receives the addresses of a courtier or soldier with a long-handled weapon or staff of office. Even though the sketch is rough and imperfect, it does suggest the extent to which the plays of Shakespeare and his contemporaries were acted on this broad, open stage with a minimum of scenic effects. The actors would identify their fictional roles and their location by their dialogue, their costumes, and their gestures. On other occasions, when, for example, a throne was needed for a throne scene, extras could bring on such large objects and then remove them when they were no longer needed. Beds, as in the final scene of *Othello*, were apparently thrust on stage from the tiring house. The building itself was handsomely decorated and picturesque, so that the stage picture was by no means unimpressive, yet the visual effects were not designed to inform the audience about setting or time of the action. The play texts and the actors took care of that.

We have a verbal description of the Globe Theatre by Thomas Platter, a visitor to London in 1599, on the occasion of a performance of *Julius Caesar*. The description unfortunately says little about the stage, but it is otherwise very informative about the London playhouses:

> The playhouses are so constructed that they play on a raised platform, so that everyone has a good view. There are different galleries and places, however, where the seating is better and more comfortable and therefore more expensive. For whoever cares to stand below pays only one English penny, but if he wishes to sit, he enters by another door and pays another penny, while if he desires to sit in the most comfortable seats, which are cushioned, where he not only sees everything well but can also be seen, then he pays yet another English penny at another door. And during the performance food and drink are carried around the audience, so that for what one cares to pay one may also have refreshment.

Shakespeare's company may have included ten or so actor/sharers, who owned the company jointly and distributed important roles among themselves. Richard Burbage was Shakespeare's leading man from 1594 until Shakespeare's retirement from the theater. Other actor/sharers, such as John Heminges and Henry Condell, who would edit the First Folio collection of Shakespeare's plays in 1623, were his longtime professional associates. The quality of performance appears to have been high. Hired men generally took minor roles of messengers, soldiers, and servants. The women's parts were played by boys, who were trained by the major actors in a kind of apprenticeship and remained as actors of women's parts until their voices changed. Many went on in later years to be adult actors.

WILLIAM SHAKESPEARE AND *HENRY IV, PART ONE*:
A BRIEF CHRONOLOGY

(Some dates are approximate, notably those of the plays.)

1367	Births of Richard and Henry, male heirs to the first and third sons of Edward III.
1377	Death of Edward III; his grandson, Richard II, becomes king at age 10.
1386	Birth of Henry of Monmouth, later Henry V.
1391	Birth of Edmund Mortimer, 5th Earl of March, great-grandson to the second son of Edward III, via the female line.
1398	Richard II banishes his cousin, Henry Bolingbroke, from England for 10 years; Edmund, Earl of March, declared Richard II's heir.
1399	Death of Henry Bolingbroke's father, Duke of Lancaster, 3 February; Richard II seizes Lancastrian estates and banishes Henry for life. By October Richard is deposed and Henry is crowned Henry IV.
1400	Death of Richard II at Pontefract Castle. Henry IV leads unsuccessful campaign against Scotland. Owen Glendower raises rebellion in Wales.
1402	Owen Glendower defeats and captures Sir Edmund Mortimer (uncle to Edmund, Earl of March). Henry Percy (Hotspur) defeats Scots at Battle of Holmedon.
1403	The Percy family joins forces with Glendower and Sir Edmund Mortimer against Henry IV. Hotspur's army defeated at battle of Shrewsbury, 21 July.
1405	"Yorkshire Rising," led by Earl of Northumberland, defeated.
1413	Death of Henry IV and accession of Henry V.
1414	Lollard rebellion, led by Sir John Oldcastle, suppressed.
1415	Henry V defeats French at Agincourt.
1417	Sir John Oldcastle captured and executed by hanging and burning.
1419	Treaty of Troyes. Henry V marries French princess, Katherine.

1422	Death of Henry v. Accession of Henry vi at eight months old.
1455–85	"Wars of the Roses": intermittent civil war between houses of Lancaster and York.
1485	Henry Tudor defeats Richard iii at battle of Bosworth and is crowned Henry vii.
1485–1509	Reign of Henry vii.
1509–47	Reign of Henry viii.
1534	Act of Supremacy, declaring Henry viii head of the Church of England.
1547–53	Reign of Edward vi.
1548	Edward Hall's *The Union of the Two Noble and Illustrious Families of Lancaster and York*.
1553–58	Reign of Mary i; England returns to Catholicism.
1558–1603	Reign of Elizabeth i; England returns to Protestantism.
1559	*The Mirror for Magistrates*.
1563	Adoption of the Thirty-Nine Articles of the English Church.
1564	William Shakespeare born, c. 23 April.
1569	Northern Catholic rebellion suppressed.
1576	James Burbage builds The Theatre.
1577	Raphael Holinshed's *Chronicles of England, Scotland, and Ireland* (revised ed. 1587).
1580	John Stow's *Chronicles of England*.
1582	Shakespeare marries Anne Hathaway.
1583	Birth of Susanna, 26 May.
1583–84	Plots against Elizabeth on behalf of Mary Queen of Scots.
1585	Births of Shakespeare's son Hamnet and his twin sister Judith, 2 February. Earl of Leicester sent to aid the Dutch against the Spanish.
1587	Execution of Mary Queen of Scots, 8 February.
1588	At some point, Shakespeare moves to London; family remains in Stratford. War with Spain; the Spanish Armada fleet destroyed in July.
1588–94	Shakespeare writes the early comedies and histories and the early tragedy *Titus Andronicus*.
1592	Shakespeare attacked in print by Robert Greene. Christopher Marlowe's *Edward ii*. John Stow's *Annals*.

1593	Poem, *Venus and Adonis*. Death of Marlowe, 30 May.
1593–1603	*The Sonnets*.
1594	Shakespeare joins the Lord Chamberlain's Men. Poem, *The Rape of Lucrece*.
1594–95	*A Midsummer Night's Dream, Richard II, Romeo and Juliet*.
1595	Samuel Daniel, *The First Four Bookes of the Civil Wars between the Two Houses of Lancaster and Yorke*.
1596	Death of Shakespeare's son, Hamnet, in August. Campaign against Lord Chamberlain's Men's planned Blackfriars theater (November).
1596–98	*The Merchant of Venice, Henry IV Parts One and Two*.
1597	Earl of Essex sent to Ireland to put down a rebellion led by the Earl of Tyrone.
1598	Publication of anonymous play, *The Famous Victories of Henry the Fifth*.
1598–99	*Much Ado About Nothing, The Merry Wives of Windsor*.
1599	Shakespeare's company moves to the Globe. *As You Like It, Henry V, Julius Caesar*.
1600–02	*Twelfth Night, Troilus and Cressida, Hamlet, All's Well That Ends Well*.
1601	Shakespeare's father dies. Essex's abortive rebellion and his execution.
1603	Death of Elizabeth I; coronation of James I, 24 March. Shakespeare's company, the Lord Chamberlain's Men, becomes the King's Men.
1603–04	*Measure for Measure, Othello*.
1604	James's confrontation of the Puritans at the Hampton Court Conference. Peace with Spain.
1605	The Gunpowder Plot foiled, 5 November.
1605–06	*King Lear*.
1606–07	*Macbeth, Timon of Athens, Antony and Cleopatra, Pericles*.
1608	*Coriolanus*.
1609–11	*Cymbeline, The Winter's Tale, The Tempest*.
1613–14	*Henry VIII, The Two Noble Kinsmen*. Shakespeare in retirement, living in Stratford. Globe Theatre burns down and is soon rebuilt.
1616	Death of Shakespeare, c. 23 April.
1623	Publication of the First Folio.

A NOTE ON THE TEXT

Henry IV, Part One was printed in 1598, within two years of its first performance. It was unusual for Shakespeare's company to sell such a popular play so quickly; the acting companies generally kept box-office successes to themselves for as long as possible. The publication probably had something to do with the Oldcastle controversy (see Introduction, p. 32–33), confirming as it does that the names Oldcastle, Harvey, and Russell had been permanently changed to Falstaff, Peto, and Bardolph. Early single-play editions of Shakespeare's works were printed in "quarto" form—small, relatively economical publications. The earliest surviving complete copy of *Henry IV, Part One*, the 1598 quarto, is referred to by most editors as Q1.

The title page of Q1 tells us that it was printed by Peter Short for Andrew Wise in 1598. Wise had established his rights to the play by listing it in the Stationer's Register on February 25 the same year. Surprisingly, however, it appears that Q1 was not the first printed version of *Henry IV, Part One* and that two editions were printed within a very short space of time. In the 1860s a single sheet containing eight pages of the play was found in the binding of another book. This sheet, now held in the Folger Library and known as Q0, contains part of the dialogue between Northumberland, Hotspur, and Worcester in 1.3, and all of 2.1 and 2.2 (the Carriers' scene and the Gad's Hill robbery). It is generally agreed that Q0 was the earlier text and that Q1 was printed directly from Q0.

In Elizabethan and Jacobean times, each new press run of a book required that the individual pieces of type be set up all over again. This was tedious and often pressured work and obviously there was a great deal of room for error. Printers preferred, whenever possible, to work from an already printed copy. *Henry IV, Part One* was printed several times: including Q2 in 1599, Q3 in 1604, Q4 in 1608, Q5 in 1613, Q6 in 1622, and the First Folio (F) in 1623. Since each of the quartos was based upon the previous edition, and F shows evidence that it was set from a copy of Q5, each takes us further away from the play first handed over to Andrew Wise. Q2's title page claims that it is "Newly corrected by W. Shake-speare"; but since it overlooks several obvious errors and introduces a few new ones, scholars generally agree that its changes were produced by the printing house, not the author.

The First Folio (F) is a slightly different case. F removes some of the play's profanities, reflecting changes in what was allowed to be said on stage since the "Act to Restrain Abuses of Players" of 1606, and introduces act and scene divisions to the play. These changes may reflect the understanding that the folio editors—Shakespeare's theatre colleagues John Heminge and Henry Condell—had of how the play had been produced on the Jacobean stage. F also adds some colloquial elision, rewrites some stage directions, substitutes the spelling "Bardolph" for Bardol(l), and provides a few convincing corrections for words that do not make sense in Q1.

One other early version of the play has survived and is held in the Folger Library: the Dering manuscript of 1622. This manuscript, a conflation of *Henry IV, Part One* and *Henry IV, Part Two* for private performance, provides interesting evidence of how the play could be adapted to different playing circumstances. While not an authoritative text, it does contain a fortuitous reading that is adopted by most editors: Falstaff's line in 2.4, "convey my trustful queen," is changed to "convey my tristful queen." "Tristful" means "sorrowful" and continues Falstaff's joke about the laughing hostess's "trickling tears."

The copy-text for this Broadview/ISE edition is Q1, supplemented by the eight pages that have survived from Q0. Readings from F have been adopted in cases where they clearly make more sense than what has been printed in Q0–1. The spelling, punctuation, and formatting of the original text have been modernized in this edition and act-scene-line numbering follows conventional practice (e.g., 2.4.5–10 for act 2, scene 4, lines 5–10). TLNs (Through Line Numbers), originally created by Charlton Hinman for *The Norton Facsimile: The First Folio of Shakespeare* (New York: Norton, 1968), have also been supplied at the top of each page to integrate with the system used by the Internet Shakespeare Editions (http://internetshakespeare.uvic.ca).

This text uses the act and scene divisions provided in F, but follows the established practice in modern editions of adding a scene division (5.3) at TLN 2889. Stage directions from Q0–1 are reproduced in italics with added material placed in square brackets. Speech prefixes have been regularized throughout and preference has been given to familiar forms of names for people and places.

ABBREVIATIONS

BEVINGTON	David Bevington, ed. *Henry IV, Part 1* in *The Oxford Shakespeare*. Oxford: Clarendon, 1987.
DANIEL	Samuel Daniel. *The First Four Books of the Civil Wars between the Two Houses of Lancaster and York*, 1595.
DENT	R.W. Dent. *Shakespeare's Proverbial Language: An Index*. Berkeley: U of California P, 1981.
DNB	*Oxford Dictionary of National Biography*. Web.
FAMOUS VICTORIES	*The Famous Victories of Henry the Fifth*, 1598.
HALL	Edward Hall. *Union of the Two Noble and Illustrious Families of Lancaster and York*, 1548.
HOLINSHED	Raphael Holinshed. *Chronicles of England, Scotland, and Ireland*, rev. ed., 1587.
HUMPHREYS	A.R. Humphreys, ed. *The First Part of King Henry IV*. The Arden Shakespeare. 1960. London and New York: Routledge, 1989.
KASTAN	David Scott Kastan, ed. *King Henry IV Part 1*. The Arden Shakespeare. London: Thomson Learning, 2002.
OED	*Oxford English Dictionary*. Web.
PARTRIDGE	Eric Partridge. *Shakespeare's Bawdy: A Literary & Psychological Essay and a Comprehensive Glossary*. London: Routledge, 1947.
RSC	Royal Shakespeare Company.
STOW	John Stow. *Chronicles of England*, 1580.
TLN	"Through line number(s)," the system of continuous line numbering used in the Internet Shakespeare Editions online texts; see A Note on the Text, p. 62.

THE HISTORY OF HENRY THE FOURTH,
PART ONE

[1.1]¹

Enter the king, Lord John of Lancaster, Earl of Westmorland, with others.
KING. So shaken as we are, so wan with care,
    Find we° a time for frighted peace to pant   *Let us now find*
    And breathe short-winded accents of new broils²
    To be commenced in strands° afar remote.   *shores*
    No more the thirsty entrance³ of this soil   5
    Shall daub° her lips with her own children's blood,   *paint, smear*
    No more shall trenching⁴ war channel her fields,
    Nor bruise her flow'rets with the armèd hoofs
    Of hostile paces.° Those opposèd eyes,   *the tread of horses*
    Which, like the meteors of a troubled heaven,   10
    All of one nature, of one substance bred,
    Did lately meet in the intestine° shock   *internal*
    And furious close⁵ of civil butchery,
    Shall now in mutual well-beseeming ranks
    March all one way, and be no more opposed   15
    Against acquaintance, kindred, and allies.
    The edge of war, like an ill-sheathèd knife,
    No more shall cut his master. Therefore, friends,
    As far as to the sepulcher⁶ of Christ—
    Whose soldier now, under whose blessèd cross   20
    We are impressèd° and engaged to fight—   *conscripted*
    Forthwith a power⁷ of English shall we levy,⁸
    Whose arms were molded in their mother's womb

---

1 The location of this first scene is unspecified, but Henry's speech quickly establishes that this is a formal meeting somewhere at court.
2 Talk of new conflicts.
3 The earth's thirsty mouth.
4 Ploughing or cutting.
5 Confrontation, clash.
6 Tomb. Henry is referring here to Jerusalem, the burial place of Christ and the focus of the Crusades.
7 Army.
8 Enlist, muster (OED).

To chase these pagans in those holy fields
25   Over whose acres walked those blessèd feet
Which fourteen hundred years ago were nailed,
For our advantage, on the bitter cross.
But this our purpose now is twelve month old,
And bootless° 'tis to tell you we will go.   *useless*
30   Therefor° we meet not now. Then let me hear   *For that purpose*
Of you, my gentle cousin° Westmorland,   *kinsman*
What yesternight our Council did decree
In forwarding this dear expedience.°   *urgent enterprise*
WESTMORLAND. My liege, this haste was hot in question,[1]
35   And many limits of the charge[2] set down
But yesternight, when all athwart° there came   *perversely, awry*
A post° from Wales, loaden with heavy news,   *messenger*
Whose worst was that the noble Mortimer,
Leading the men of Herefordshire to fight
40   Against the irregular and wild Glendower,
Was by the rude hands of that Welshman taken,
A thousand of his people butcherèd,
Upon whose dead corpse° there was such misuse,   *corpses*
Such beastly shameless transformation
45   By those Welshwomen done as may not be
Without much shame retold or spoken of.
KING. It seems then that the tidings of this broil
Brake off our business for the holy land.
WESTMORLAND. This matched with other did, my gracious lord,
50   For more uneven and unwelcome news
Came from the north, and thus it did import:
On Holy-rood day[3] the gallant Hotspur there—
Young Harry Percy—and brave Archibald,
That ever valiant and approvèd[4] Scot,
55   At Holmedon[5] met, where they did spend
A sad and bloody hour,

---

1   Being hotly debated.
2   Specifications of military duties and resources.
3   The festival of the Exaltation of the Cross, September 14 (OED).
4   Proven; tested or tried (OED).
5   Humbleton, in Northumberland.

As by discharge of their artillery,
And shape of likelihood[1] the news was told;

---

1 Going by what was likely.

1.1.45:   WELSHWOMEN (TLN 49)

Westmorland's allusion to the atrocities committed by Welsh women is
a direct echo of Holinshed's initial evasiveness (see Appendix A1, p.185).
Holinshed does, however, describe the "the shameful villainy" in vivid
detail later, noting that "the women of Wales cut off their privities, and
put one part thereof into the mouths of every dead man, in such sort
that the cullions hung down to their chins; and not so contented, they
did cut off their noses and thrust them into their tails ..." (see Appendix
A1, p.196). The Welsh women's gruesome castration of dead English
soldiers can be seen as emblematic of a general Welsh threat to English
masculinity. Perhaps the Welsh women were exacting revenge for the
brutality of Henry iv's campaigns in Wales, or perhaps the story was
simply English propaganda.

Westmorland's speech is the first of many references to the Welsh in
the play, most of which voice English stereotypes of the Welsh character
and language as alien, subversive, and barbaric. Shakespeare undercuts
and complicates these stereotypes, however, through his depiction of
Welsh characters. Lady Mortimer presents another, contrasting, view of
Welsh womanhood in 3.1 (albeit the difficulty of finding an actor to speak
and sing in Welsh has meant that this role has frequently been cut from
the play in performance). Ironically, Lady Mortimer's presence can also
be seen as emasculating: Glendower chides Mortimer for being reluc-
tant to leave her, "you are as slow / As hot Lord Percy is on fire to go"
(3.1.259–60, TLN 1809-10). Terence Hawkes has described her singing
as expressive of a feminine, "narcotic" aspect of the Welsh that reflects
the culture's "larger, subversive, and in a complex sense 'effeminate' role
in early modern Britain" ("Bryn Glas" 124).

Glendower defeated Sir Edmund Mortimer's English force at the
battle of Bryn Glas, near the village of Pilleth in the county of Powys, on
22 June 1402.

For he that brought them° in the very heat   *the news*
60   And pride of their contention[1] did take horse
    Uncertain of the issue any way.
  KING. Here is a dear, a true industrious friend,[2]
    Sir Walter Blunt, new lighted from his horse,
    Stained with the variation of each soil
65   Betwixt that Holmedon and this seat of ours,
    And he hath brought us smooth and welcome news:
    The Earl of Douglas is discomfited;[3]
    Ten thousand bold Scots, two-and-twenty knights,
    Balked[4] in their own blood did Sir Walter see
70   On Holmedon's plains. Of prisoners Hotspur took
    Mordake, Earl of Fife and eldest son
    To beaten Douglas, and the Earl of Athol,
    Of Murray, Angus, and Menteith.
    And is not this an honorable spoil?
75   A gallant prize? Ha, cousin, is it not?
  WESTMORLAND. In faith it is—a conquest for a prince to boast of.
  KING. Yea, there thou mak'st me sad, and mak'st me sin
    In envy, that my lord Northumberland
    Should be the father to so blest a son—
80   A son who is the theme of honor's tongue,
    Amongst a grove the very straightest plant,
    Who is sweet fortune's minion° and her pride—   *favorite*
    Whilst I by looking on the praise of him
    See riot and dishonor stain the brow
85   Of my young Harry. Oh, that it could be proved
    That some night-tripping fairy had exchanged
    In cradle clothes our children where they lay,
    And called mine Percy, his Plantagenet![5]
    Then would I have his Harry, and he mine.

---

1 At the height of the battle.
2 No entrance is specified for Blunt in this scene and he is given no lines. Some editors argue that "Here" means simply "at court," but from Henry's colorful description Blunt would make a striking on-stage figure.
3 Overthrown in battle, see also 3.2.114, TLN 1934.
4 (1) heaped up (OED) (2) thwarted.
5 The royal family name.

But let him from my thoughts. What think you, coz,   90
Of this young Percy's pride? The prisoners
Which he in this adventure hath surprised
To his own use he keeps, and sends me word
I shall have none but Mordake Earl of Fife.
WESTMORLAND. This is his uncle's teaching. This is Worcester,   95
Malevolent to you in all aspects,
Which makes him prune[1] himself, and bristle up
The crest of youth against your dignity.
KING. But I have sent for him to answer this;
And for this cause awhile we must neglect   100
Our holy purpose to Jerusalem.
Cousin, on Wednesday next our council we
Will hold at Windsor. So inform the lords.
But come yourself with speed to us again,
For more is to be said and to be done,   105
Than out of anger can be utterèd.
WESTMORLAND. I will my liege.   *Exeunt.*

[1.2][2]

Enter Prince of Wales, and Sir John Falstaff.
FALSTAFF. Now Hal, what time of day is it lad?
PRINCE. Thou art so fat-witted with drinking of old sack,[3] and
    unbuttoning thee after supper, and sleeping upon benches
    after noon, that thou hast forgotten to demand that truly which
    thou wouldst truly know. What a devil hast thou to do with the   5
    time of the day? Unless hours were cups of sack, and minutes
    capons,[4] and clocks the tongues of bawds,[5] and dials[6] the signs
    of leaping-houses,[7] and the blessed sun himself a fair hot wench

---

1 Preen (as a bird tends its feathers).
2 Although often assumed to be the tavern, the location is unspecified.
3 White wine (often sweetened with sugar).
4 Castrated roosters, fattened for the table.
5 Pimps or procurers.
6 Sundials.
7 Brothels.

in flame-colored taffeta,[1] I see no reason why thou shouldst be
10   so superfluous[2] to demand the time of the day.

FALSTAFF. Indeed you come near me now, Hal, for we that take
purses go by[3] the moon and the seven stars,[4] and not by Phoebus,[5]
"he, that wand'ring knight so fair."[6] And I prithee, sweet wag,
when thou art a king, as God save thy grace—"majesty" I should
15   say, for grace thou wilt have none—

PRINCE. What, none?

FALSTAFF. No, by my troth, not so much as will serve to be prologue
to an egg and butter.[7]

PRINCE. Well, how then? Come, roundly,[8] roundly.

20   FALSTAFF. Marry[9] then, sweet wag, when thou art king let not us
that are squires of the night's body be called thieves of the day's
beauty: let us be Diana's foresters,[10] gentlemen of the shade, min-
ions of the moon, and let men say we be men of good government,
being governed as the sea is, by our noble and chaste mistress the
25   moon, under whose countenance we steal.

PRINCE. Thou sayst well, and it holds well too, for the fortune of
us that are the moon's men doth ebb and flow like the sea, being
governed as the sea is by the moon. As for proof now: a purse of
gold most resolutely snatched on Monday night and most dis-
30   solutely spent on Tuesday morning; got with swearing "lay by!",[11]
and spent with crying "bring in!";[12] now in as low an ebb as the
foot of the ladder,[13] and by and by in as high a flow as the ridge[14]
of the gallows.

---

1 Thin silk; in red, the kind of fabric worn by prostitutes.
2 Excessive; doing more than is necessary.
3 (1) tell the time by (2) travel by.
4 The Pleiades, part of the constellation Taurus.
5 The sun.
6 Falstaff seems to be quoting from a ballad.
7 A light meal, presumably not worthy of "grace."
8 Plainly and frankly (OED).
9 A mild oath; here adding emphasis, like "indeed."
10 Followers of Diana, goddess of the moon and the hunt.
11 Stand and deliver!
12 Bring in food and drink.
13 Used to climb to the gallows.
14 Crossbar at the top of the gallows.

FALSTAFF. By the Lord, thou sayst true, lad; and is not my hostess
of the tavern a most sweet wench? 35

PRINCE. As the honey of Hybla,[1] my old lad of the castle.[2] And is
not a buff jerkin[3] a most sweet robe of durance?

FALSTAFF. How now, how now, mad wag? What, in thy quips and
thy quiddities?[4] What a plague have I to do with a buff jerkin?

PRINCE. Why, what a pox have I to do with my hostess of the tavern? 40

FALSTAFF. Well, thou hast called her to a reckoning[5] many a time
and oft.

PRINCE. Did I ever call for thee to pay thy part?

FALSTAFF. No, I'll give thee thy due, thou hast paid all there.

PRINCE. Yea and elsewhere, so far as my coin would stretch, and 45
where it would not I have used my credit.

FALSTAFF. Yea, and so used it that were it not here apparent that
thou art heir apparent—but I prithee, sweet wag, shall there be
gallows standing in England when thou art king, and resolution
thus fubbed[6] as it is with the rusty curb of old Father Antic[7] the 50
law? Do not thou when thou art king hang a thief.

PRINCE. No, thou shalt.

FALSTAFF. Shall I? Oh, rare! By the Lord, I'll be a brave judge.

PRINCE. Thou judgest false already. I mean thou shalt have the
hanging of the thieves, and so become a rare hangman. 55

FALSTAFF. Well, Hal, well; and in some sort it jumps with my humor
as well as waiting in the court, I can tell you.

PRINCE. For obtaining of suits?[8]

---

1 A town in Sicily, famous for its honey.
2 (1) a pun on Falstaff's original name, Sir John Oldcastle (2) a lad about town
(The Castle was a well-known brothel).
3 Leather jacket: a garment often worn by an officer of the law, hence "durance"
meaning (1) hard-wearing and (2) imprisonment.
4 Quibbles.
5 Tavern bill.
6 Cheated.
7 A grotesque or ludicrous figure; in earlier drama, a performer playing a bizarre
clownish role.
8 (1) petitions (2) clothes.

References to hanging are common in *Henry IV, Part One*, especially from Falstaff who mentions hanging around fifteen times. Execution by hanging was the ultimate punishment for theft in Tudor England; other common punishments included branding and whipping. A letter to the Lord Treasurer from Edward Hext, a justice of the peace in Somersetshire, reports 40 prisoners executed in the district in 1596 (a further 35 were "burnt in the hand," 37 were whipped for felony, and 112 were acquitted). Hext was concerned about the number of thieves and robbers abroad in the county because of failures in the legal system. He complains of "infinite numbers of the idle and wandering people, and robbers of the land ... [who] live idly in the alehouses, day and night eating and drinking excessively" (Strype 407). Hanging was a topical subject for the play's first audience: failed harvests between 1594 and 1597 contributed to a general rise in crimes involving theft, and a concomitant increase in the frequency of public executions.

Falstaff's line "Do not thou when thou art king hang a thief" and Prince Hal's ambiguous reply are used in Kenneth Branagh's 1989 film adaptation of *Henry V*. The line is given to Bardolph as Henry V recalls happier times in a flashback just before Bardolph is hanged for theft.

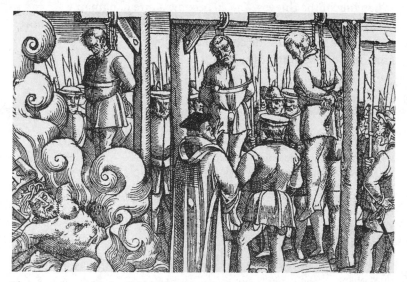

Three men hanged at the gibbet, John Foxe's *Book of Martyrs*, 1563.

FALSTAFF. Yea, for obtaining of suits, whereof the hangman hath
no lean wardrobe. 'Sblood,[1] I am as melancholy as a gib cat,[2] or   60
a lugged[3] bear.

PRINCE. Or an old lion, or a lover's lute.

FALSTAFF. Yea, or the drone of a Lincolnshire bagpipe.

PRINCE. What sayst thou to a hare, or the melancholy of Moorditch?[4]

FALSTAFF. Thou hast the most unsavory similes, and art indeed the   65
most comparative,[5] rascalliest sweet young prince. But Hal, I
prithee trouble me no more with vanity. I would to God thou and
I knew where a commodity[6] of good names were to be bought. An
old lord of the Council rated[7] me the other day in the street about
you, sir, but I marked him not; and yet he talked very wisely, but   70
I regarded him not; and yet he talked wisely, and in the street too.

PRINCE. Thou didst well, for wisdom cries out in the streets[8] and
no man regards it.

FALSTAFF. Oh, thou hast damnable iteration,[9] and art indeed able to
corrupt a saint. Thou hast done much harm upon me, Hal, God   75
forgive thee for it. Before I knew thee, Hal, I knew nothing; and
now am I, if a man should speak truly, little better than one of
the wicked. I must give over this life, and I will give it over. By
the Lord, an[10] I do not, I am a villain. I'll be damned for never a
king's son in Christendom.   80

PRINCE. Where shall we take a purse tomorrow, Jack?

FALSTAFF. Zounds,[11] where thou wilt, lad, I'll make one; an I do not,
call me villain and baffle[12] me.

---

1 By Christ's blood (an oath).
2 Tomcat.
3 Baited.
4 A foul-smelling ditch, associated with melancholy.
5 Adept at (abusive) comparisons (Kastan); see also 3.2.67, TLN 1886.
6 Supply.
7 Berated, scolded.
8 A paraphrase of Proverbs 1.20, "Wisdom cryeth without: she uttereth her voice
in the streets."
9 Repetition. Falstaff implies that Hal is twisting the Scriptures.
10 If (a form often used by Falstaff; see also 1.2.82, TLN 208; 2.2.18, TLN 757;
2.2.37, TLN 778).
11 An oath derived from "by God's wounds" (OED).
12 Publicly disgrace.

PRINCE. I see a good amendment of life[1] in thee, from praying to
85   purse-taking.
FALSTAFF. Why, Hal, 'tis my vocation, Hal. 'Tis no sin for a man to
labor in his vocation.

Enter Poins

POINS! Now shall we know if Gadshill[2] have set a match.[3] O, if men
were to be saved by merit, what hole in hell were hot enough for
90   him? This is the most omnipotent villain that ever cried "Stand!"
to a true man.
PRINCE. Good morrow Ned.
POINS. Good morrow, sweet Hal. [*To Falstaff*] What says Monsieur
Remorse? What says Sir John Sack and Sugar: Jack? How agrees
95   the devil and thee about thy soul, that thou soldest him on Good
Friday[4] last, for a cup of Madeira and a cold capon's leg?
PRINCE. Sir John stands to his word, the devil shall have his bargain,
for he was never yet a breaker of proverbs: he will give the devil
his due.
100   POINS. [*To Falstaff*] Then art thou damned for keeping thy word with
the devil.
PRINCE. Else he had been damned for cozening[5] the devil.
POINS. But my lads, my lads, tomorrow morning by four o'clock
early at Gad's Hill, there are pilgrims going to Canterbury[6] with
105   rich offerings, and traders riding to London with fat purses. I
have vizards[7] for you all; you have horses for yourselves. Gadshill
lies tonight in Rochester.[8] I have bespoke supper tomorrow night
in Eastcheap.[9] We may do it as secure as sleep. If you will go, I

---

1 An echo of the Geneva Bible (Matthew 3.8, Luke 15.7, Acts 3.19).
2 The thief's nickname comes from the hill where he does much of his work.
3 Set up the robbery.
4 I.e., a time of strict fasting.
5 Cheating.
6 Canterbury became one of the most popular pilgrimage sites in Britain following the murder of Archbishop Thomas Becket at Canterbury Cathedral in 1170.
7 Masks.
8 A cathedral town on the road from London to Canterbury, close to Gad's Hill.
9 A major market street in London.

will stuff your purses full of crowns;[1] if you will not, tarry at home
and be hanged.   110

FALSTAFF. Hear ye Yedward,[2] if I tarry at home and go not I'll hang
you for going.

POINS. You will, chops?[3]

FALSTAFF. Hal, wilt thou make one?

PRINCE. Who, I rob? I a thief? Not I, by my faith.   115

FALSTAFF. There's neither honesty, manhood, nor good fellowship
in thee, nor thou camest not of the blood royal, if thou darest not
stand for ten shillings.

PRINCE. Well then, once in my days I'll be a madcap.[4]

FALSTAFF. Why that's well said.   120

PRINCE. Well, come what will, I'll tarry at home.

FALSTAFF. By the Lord, I'll be a traitor then, when thou art king.

PRINCE. I care not.

POINS. Sir John, I prithee leave the prince and me alone. I will lay
him down such reasons for this adventure that he shall go.   125

FALSTAFF. Well, God give thee the spirit of persuasion and him the
ears of profiting, that what thou speakest may move and what he
hears may be believed, that the true prince may—for recreation
sake—prove a false thief; for the poor abuses of the time want
countenance.[5] Farewell, you shall find me in Eastcheap.   130

PRINCE. Farewell, the latter spring; farewell, All-Hallown sum-
mer.[6]   [*Exit Falstaff.*]

POINS. Now, my good sweet honey lord, ride with us tomorrow. I
have a jest to execute that I cannot manage alone. Falstaff, Peto,
Bardolph, and Gadshill shall rob those men that we have already 135
waylaid—yourself and I will not be there—and when they have
the booty, if you and I do not rob them, cut this head off from
my shoulders.

PRINCE. How shall we part with them in setting forth?

---

1 Coins (worth around 5 shillings each).
2 A countrified version of Poins's first name, Edward.
3 "Chubby cheeks."
4 A reckless person.
5 Lack patronage.
6 A spell of warm weather in the late autumn.

140 POINS. Why, we will set forth before or after them and appoint them a place of meeting, wherein it is at our pleasure to fail. And then will they adventure upon the exploit themselves, which they shall have no sooner achieved but we'll set upon them.

PRINCE. Yea, but 'tis like that they will know us by our horses, by our
145 habits, and by every other appointment to be ourselves.

POINS. Tut, our horses they shall not see—I'll tie them in the wood; our vizards we will change after we leave them; and, sirrah, I have cases of buckram[1] for the nonce,[2] to immask our noted outward garments.

150 PRINCE. Yea, but I doubt[3] they will be too hard for us.

POINS. Well, for two of them, I know them to be as true-bred cowards as ever turned back; and for the third, if he fight longer than he sees reason, I'll forswear arms. The virtue of this jest will be the incomprehensible lies that this same fat rogue will
155 tell us when we meet at supper: how thirty at least he fought with, what wards,[4] what blows, what extremities he endured; and in the reproof[5] of this lives the jest.

PRINCE. Well, I'll go with thee. Provide us all things necessary, and meet me tomorrow night in Eastcheap; there I'll sup. Farewell.

160 POINS. Farewell, my lord.   *Exit Poins.*

PRINCE. I know you all, and will a while uphold[6]
The unyoked humor[7] of your idleness.
Yet herein will I imitate the sun,[8]
Who doth permit the base contagious clouds
165 To smother up his beauty from the world,
That when he please again to be himself,
Being wanted° he may be more wondered at   *missed*
By breaking through the foul and ugly mists
Of vapors that did seem to strangle him.

---

1 Suits of coarse cloth.
2 Purpose; occasion.
3 Fear.
4 Defensive movements.
5 Disproof, discrediting.
6 Support and go along with.
7 Unrestrained nature or inclination.
8 An image traditionally associated with royalty.

Elizabethans saw correspondence between various orders of being, hence the sun is commonly equated with kingship. In *Troilus and Cressida* Ulysses asserts that the planets observe degree, and "therefore is the glorious planet Sol / In noble eminence enthroned" (1.3.89-90, TLN 548-49). In *Richard II* the deposed king obsessively meditates on his loss of sun-like majesty with lines such as: "Oh, that I were a mockery king of snow / Standing before the sun of Bolingbroke" (4.1.261-62, TLN 2182-83) and "Was this the face / That, like the sun, did make beholders wink?" (4.1.284-85, TLN 2206-07).

Prince Hal's reformation is linked to the sun later in *Henry IV, Part One* when Vernon describes the prince and his followers:

> Glittering in golden coats like images,
> As full of spirit as the month of May,
> And gorgeous as the sun at midsummer;
> > (4.1.100-02, TLN 2329-31)

and in *Henry V* the Chorus asserts that, as king, his countenance will illuminate his soldiers' night:

> A largess universal like the sun
> His liberal eye doth give to everyone, ...
> A little touch of Harry in the night.
> > (4.0.43-47, TLN 1832-36)

In an open-air theater, Prince Hal's references to the sun and clouds can also gain immediate topicality depending on the weather that day.

ABOVE: Sebald Beham, "Sol," from The Seven Planets with the Signs of the Zodiac (1539). From Wikimedia Commons, http://www.commons.wikimedia.org.

170 If all the year were playing holidays,
To sport would be as tedious as to work;
But when they seldom come, they wished-for come,
And nothing pleaseth but rare accidents.
So when this loose behavior I throw off
175 And pay the debt I never promisèd,
By how much better than my word I am,
By so much shall I falsify men's hopes;
And like bright metal on a sullen ground, .
My reformation, glitt'ring o'er my fault,
180 Shall show more goodly and attract more eyes
Than that which hath no foil[1] to set it off.
I'll so offend to make offense a skill,
Redeeming time[2] when men think least I will.   *Exit.*

[1.3]

Enter the king, Northumberland, Worcester, Hotspur, Sir Walter Blunt,
with others.

KING. My blood hath been too cold and temperate,
Unapt to stir at these indignities,
And you have found me,° for accordingly   *found me so*
You tread upon my patience. But be sure
5 I will from henceforth rather be myself,
Mighty and to be feared, than my condition,°   *natural disposition*
Which hath been smooth as oil, soft as young down,
And therefore lost that title of respect
Which the proud soul ne'er pays but to the proud.
10 WORCESTER. Our house, my sovereign liege, little deserves
The scourge of greatness to be used on it,
And that same greatness too, which our own hands
Have holp° to make so portly.°   *helped; grand*
NORTHUMBERLAND. My lord—
15 KING. Worcester, get thee gone, for I do see
Danger and disobedience in thine eye.

---

1 A thin leaf of metal placed under a precious stone to increase its brilliancy (OED
*n.*1, 5a).
2 I.e., through payment of the "debt" referred to eight lines earlier (TLN 310).

O sir, your presence is too bold and peremptory,
And majesty might never yet endure
The moody frontier[1] of a servant brow.
You have good leave to leave us. When we need   20
Your use and counsel we shall send for you.   *Exit Worcester.*
[*To Northumberland*] You were about to speak.
NORTHUMBERLAND.   Yea my good lord.
Those prisoners in your highness' name demanded,
Which Harry Percy here at Holmedon took,
Were, as he says, not with such strength denied   25
As is delivered° to your majesty.   reported
Either envy, therefore, or misprision[2]
Is guilty of this fault, and not my son.
HOTSPUR. My liege, I did deny no prisoners.
But I remember when the fight was done,   30
When I was dry with rage and extreme toil,
Breathless and faint, leaning upon my sword,
Came there a certain lord, neat and trimly dressed,
Fresh as a bridegroom, and his chin, new-reaped,
Showed like a stubble-land at harvest-home.[3]   35
He was perfumèd like a milliner,[4]
And 'twixt his finger and his thumb he held
A pouncet-box,[5] which ever and anon
He gave his nose and took't away again,
Who° therewith angry, when it next came there   *i.e., the nose*   40
Took it in snuff,[6] and still he smiled and talked;
And as the soldiers bore dead bodies by,
He called them untaught knaves, unmannerly,
To bring a slovenly unhandsome corpse
Betwixt the wind and his nobility.   45
With many holiday[7] and lady terms

1   (1) threatening forehead (2) enemy fortress or rampart.
2   (1) mistake (2) failure to appreciate or recognize the value of something (OED).
3   The time when the last of the harvest is brought in.
4   A seller of fancy wares, accessories, and articles of (female) apparel (OED n.2).
5   Perfume box with perforated lid.
6   (1) snuffed it up (2) took offense.
7   I.e., not down to earth, workaday terms.

He questioned me, amongst the rest demanded
My prisoners in your majesty's behalf.
I then, all smarting with my wounds being cold,
50   To be so pestered with a popinjay,°   *parrot, dandy*
Out of my grief and my impatience
Answered neglectingly, I know not what,
He should, or he should not, for he made me mad
To see him shine so brisk, and smell so sweet,
55   And talk so like a waiting gentlewoman
Of guns, and drums, and wounds, God save the mark!
And telling me the sovereign'st° thing on earth   *best*
Was parmacity,[1] for an inward bruise,
And that it was great pity, so it was,
60   This villainous saltpetre[2] should be digged
Out of the bowels of the harmless earth,
Which many a good tall fellow had destroyed
So cowardly, and but for these vile guns
He would himself have been a soldier.
65   This bald unjointed[3] chat of his, my lord,
I answered indirectly, as I said,
And I beseech you, let not his report
Come current° for an accusation   *be accepted*
Betwixt my love and your high majesty.
70 BLUNT. The circumstance considered, good my lord,
Whate'er Lord Harry Percy then had said
To such a person, and in such a place,
At such a time, with all the rest retold,
May reasonably die, and never rise
75   To do him wrong, or any way impeach°   *call in question*
What then he said, so he unsay it now.
KING. Why, yet he doth deny his prisoners,
But with proviso and exception
That we at our own charge shall ransom straight

---

1 Spermaceti, a remedy made from whale oil.
2 The chief constituent of gunpowder, also used medicinally (OED).
3 Barren, meaningless, and disjointed.

His brother-in-law,[1] the foolish Mortimer,   80
Who, on my soul, hath wilfully betrayed
The lives of those that he did lead to fight
Against that great magician, damned Glendower,
Whose daughter, as we hear, that Earl of March°   *i.e., Mortimer*
Hath lately married. Shall our coffers then   85
Be emptied to redeem a traitor home?
Shall we buy treason, and indent[2] with fears[3]
When they have lost and forfeited themselves?
No, on the barren mountains let him starve,
For I shall never hold that man my friend   90
Whose tongue shall ask me for one penny cost
To ransom home revolted Mortimer.
HOTSPUR. Revolted Mortimer!
He never did fall off,[4] my sovereign liege,
But by the chance of war. To prove that true   95
Needs no more but one tongue for all those wounds,
Those mouthèd wounds, which valiantly he took
When on the gentle Severn's[5] sedgy° bank   *reedy*
In single opposition, hand to hand,
He did confound the best part of an hour   100
In changing hardiment[6] with great Glendower.
Three times they breathed, and three times did they drink,
Upon agreement, of swift Severn's flood,
Who then, affrighted with their bloody looks,
Ran fearfully among the trembling reeds   105
And hid his crisp head in the hollow bank,
Bloodstainèd with these valiant combatants.
Never did bare and rotten policy°   *cunning*
Color[7] her working with such deadly wounds,

---

1 Kate, Hotspur's wife (historically named Elizabeth), is sister to Sir Edmund
Mortimer, captive and son-in-law to Glendower.
2 Enter into an agreement.
3 (1) cowards (2) threats.
4 Shift his allegiance.
5 The river Severn, the longest river in Britain, passing through English counties
as well as Wales.
6 Exchanging boldness.
7 Paint or disguise (with a covering of blood).

110   Nor never could the noble Mortimer
      Receive so many, and all willingly.
      Then let not him be slandered with revolt.[1]
      KING. Thou dost belie[2] him, Percy, thou dost belie him.
      He never did encounter with Glendower.
115   I tell thee, he durst as well have met the devil alone
      As Owen Glendower for an enemy.
      Art thou not ashamed? But, sirrah, henceforth
      Let me not hear you speak of Mortimer.
      Send me your prisoners with the speediest means,
120   Or you shall hear in such a kind from me
      As will displease you. My Lord Northumberland
      We license your departure with your son.
      Send us your prisoners, or you will hear of it.
               Exit King [with all but Hotspur and Northumberland].
      HOTSPUR. An if° the devil come and roar for them   *Even if*
125   I will not send them. I will after straight
      And tell him so, for I will ease my heart,
      Albeit° I make a hazard of my head.   *Even though*
      NORTHUMBERLAND. What, drunk with choler?° Stay   *anger*
          and pause awhile.
      Here comes your uncle.

      Enter Worcester.
      HOTSPUR.   Speak of Mortimer?
130   Zounds, I will speak of him, and let my soul
      Want° mercy if I do not join with him.   *Lack*
      Yea, on his part I'll empty all these veins,
      And shed my dear blood drop by drop in the dust,
      But I will lift the downtrod Mortimer
135   As high in the air as this unthankful king,
      As this ingrate and cankered[3] Bolingbroke.[4]
      NORTHUMBERLAND. Brother, the king hath made your nephew
          mad.

---

1   Slandered by an accusation of revolt against the king.
2   Misrepresent.
3   Ungrateful and diseased (see also 1.3.175, TLN 499).
4   I.e., Henry IV.

WORCESTER. Who struck this heat up after I was gone?

HOTSPUR. He will forsooth have all my prisoners,
  And when I urged the ransom once again   140
  Of my wife's brother, then his cheek looked pale,
  And on my face he turned an eye of death,
  Trembling even at the name of Mortimer.

WORCESTER. I cannot blame him: was not he proclaimed
  By Richard, that dead is, the next of blood?[1]   145

NORTHUMBERLAND. He was; I heard the proclamation.
  And then it was when the unhappy king—
  Whose wrongs in us[2] God pardon!—did set forth
  Upon his Irish expedition,
  From whence he, intercepted, did return   150
  To be deposed, and shortly murderèd.

WORCESTER. And for whose death we in the world's wide mouth
  Live scandalized and foully spoken of.

HOTSPUR. But soft,° I pray you, did King Richard then   *hold on*
  Proclaim my brother° Edmund Mortimer   *i.e., brother-in-law* 155
  Heir to the crown?

NORTHUMBERLAND. He did, myself did hear it.

HOTSPUR. Nay then, I cannot blame his cousin king
  That wished him on the barren mountains starve.
  But shall it be that you that set the crown
  Upon the head of this forgetful man,   160
  And for his sake wear the detested blot
  Of murderous subornation,[3] shall it be
  That you a world of curses undergo,
  Being the agents or base second means,
  The cords, the ladder, or the hangman rather?   165
  Oh, pardon me that I descend so low
  To show the line° and the predicament   *degree*
  Wherein you range° under this subtle king!   *move*
  Shall it for shame be spoken in these days,
  Or fill up chronicles in time to come,   170
  That men of your nobility and power

---

1 Next in line for the throne.
2 Wrongs done by us (against King Richard).
3 Bribing or corrupting someone into an evil action, in this case, murder.

Did gage° them both in an unjust behalf—   engage, pledge
As both of you, God pardon it, have done—
To put down Richard, that sweet lovely rose,
And plant this thorn, this canker,[1] Bolingbroke?
175 And shall it in more shame be further spoken
That you are fooled, discarded, and shook off
By him for whom these shames ye underwent?
No, yet time serves wherein you may redeem
Your banished honors, and restore yourselves
180 Into the good thoughts of the world again,
Revenge the jeering and disdained° contempt   disdainful
Of this proud king, who studies day and night
To answer° all the debt he owes to you   repay
Even with the bloody payment of your deaths.
185 Therefore, I say—
WORCESTER.   Peace, cousin, say no more.
And now I will unclasp a secret book,
And to your quick-conceiving discontents
I'll read you matter deep and dangerous,
190 As full of peril and adventurous spirit
As to o'erwalk a current roaring loud
On the unsteadfast footing of a spear.[2]
HOTSPUR. If he fall in, good night, or sink or swim.[3]
Send danger from the east unto the west,
195 So[4] honor cross it from the north to south,
And let them grapple. Oh, the blood more stirs
To rouse a lion than to start° a hare!   startle
NORTHUMBERLAND. Imagination of some great exploit
Drives him beyond the bounds of patience.
200 [HOTSPUR]. By heaven, methinks it were an easy leap
To pluck bright honor from the pale-faced moon,
Or dive into the bottom of the deep,
Where fathom-line could never touch the ground,
And pluck up drownèd honor by the locks,

---

1 A wild rose, but also suggesting the canker-worm, a plant disease.
2 A reference to the perilous sword bridges of medieval romances.
3 If he falls he's done for, whether he sinks or swims.
4 As long as. Hotspur doesn't mind danger, as long as honor is part of it.

So he that doth redeem her thence might wear,   205
Without co-rival,[1] all her dignities.
But out upon° this half-faced fellowship!   *enough of*
WORCESTER. He apprehends a world of figures[2] here,
  But not the form of what he should attend.
  Good cousin, give me audience for a while.   210
HOTSPUR. I cry you mercy.
WORCESTER.   Those same noble Scots
  That are your prisoners—
HOTSPUR.   I'll keep them all;
  By God, he shall not have a Scot[3] of them,
  No, if a Scot would save his soul he shall not.
  I'll keep them, by this hand.
WORCESTER.   You start away,   215
  And lend no ear unto my purposes.
  Those prisoners you shall keep.
HOTSPUR.   Nay, I will; that's flat.
  He said he would not ransom Mortimer,
  Forbade my tongue to speak of Mortimer;
  But I will find him when he lies asleep,   220
  And in his ear I'll holla "Mortimer!"
  Nay, I'll have a starling shall be taught to speak
  Nothing but "Mortimer," and give it him
  To keep his anger still in motion.
WORCESTER. Hear you, cousin, a word.   225
HOTSPUR. All studies here I solemnly defy,
  Save how to gall and pinch this Bolingbroke.
  And that same sword-and-buckler[4] Prince of Wales.
  But that I think his father loves him not
  And would be glad he met with some mischance,   230
  I would have him poisoned with a pot of ale.
WORCESTER. Farewell, kinsman. I'll talk to you
  When you are better tempered to attend.
NORTHUMBERLAND. Why, what a wasp-stung and impatient fool

---

1 One of two or more rivals ranked as equals (OED).
2 (1) images (2) figures of speech.
3 (1) Scotsman (2) small payment or tax (cf. 5.4.113, TLN 3079–80).
4 Swashbuckling.

235   Art thou to break into this woman's mood
      Tying thine ear to no tongue but thine own!
    HOTSPUR. Why, look you, I am whipped and scourged with rods,
      Nettled and stung with pismires,° when I hear   *ants*
      Of this vile politician[1] Bolingbroke.
240   In Richard's time—what d'ye call the place?
      A plague upon't, it is in Gloucestershire.
      'Twas where the madcap duke his uncle kept,
      His uncle York—where I first bowed my knee
      Unto this king of smiles, this Bolingbroke—
245   'Sblood, when you and he came back from Ravenspurgh.[2]
    NORTHUMBERLAND. At Berkeley castle.[3]
    HOTSPUR. You say true.
      Why, what a candy deal of courtesy
      This fawning greyhound then did proffer me!
250   "Look when[4] his infant fortune came to age,"
      And "gentle Harry Percy," and "kind cousin."
      Oh, the devil take such cozeners!° God forgive me,   *cheats*
      Good uncle, tell your tale; I have done.
    WORCESTER. Nay, if you have not, to it again.
      We will stay your leisure.
255 HOTSPUR.   I have done, i'faith.
    WORCESTER. Then once more to your Scottish prisoners.
      Deliver them up[5] without their ransom straight;
      And make the Douglas' son[6] your only mean°   *means*
      For powers in Scotland, which for divers° reasons   *various*
260   Which I shall send you written, be assured
      Will easily be granted. [*To Northumberland*] You, my lord,
      Your son in Scotland being thus employed,
      Shall secretly into the bosom creep
      Of that same noble prelate[7] well-beloved,

---

1 Generally used in a derogatory sense in Shakespeare's day: a schemer.
2 Where Bolingbroke landed on his return from exile in 1399.
3 In Gloucestershire.
4 Look to the time when.
5 Release them.
6 See 1.1.71, TLN 75.
7 Church dignitary of high rank.

The archbishop. 265

HOTSPUR. Of York, is't not?

WORCESTER. True, who bears hard
His brother's death at Bristol, the Lord Scrope.
I speak not this in estimation,
As what I think might be, but what I know 270
Is ruminated, plotted, and set down,
And only stays° but to behold the face   *waits*
Of that occasion° that shall bring it on.   *opportunity*

HOTSPUR. I smell it; upon my life, it will do well!

NORTHUMBERLAND. Before the game is afoot thou still let'st slip.[1] 275

HOTSPUR. Why, it cannot choose but be a noble plot—
And then the power of Scotland and of York
To join with Mortimer, ha?

WORCESTER.   And so they shall.

HOTSPUR. In faith, it is exceedingly well aimed.

WORCESTER. And 'tis no little reason bids us speed 280

---

1 A hunting analogy: the action of setting the dogs loose.

1.3.250:   HENRY'S PROMISES (TLN 580)

Hotspur is recalling promises of future favor delivered by Henry
Bolingbroke on his return to England. Shakespeare dramatizes the
Gloucestershire meeting in *Richard II*, 2.3. The young Harry Percy
offers his service and Henry replies:

> I thank thee, gentle Percy, and be sure
> I count myself in nothing else so happy
> As in a soul rememb'ring my good friends;
> And as my fortune ripens with thy love,
> It shall be still thy true love's recompense.
> (2.3.45-49, TLN 1154-58)

It is understandable that Hotspur now remembers this as "a candy
deal of courtesy." However, his father Northumberland also
addressed Bolingbroke in sugary terms in the scene:

(continued)

To save our heads by raising of a head;°   *forming an army*
For, bear ourselves as even° as we can,   *steadily*
The king will always think him in our debt,
And think we think ourselves unsatisfied
285   Till he hath found a time to pay us home.°   *fully repay us*
And see already how he doth begin
To make us strangers to his looks of love.
HOTSPUR. He does, he does. We'll be revenged on him.

I am a stranger here in Gloucestershire.
These high wild hills and rough uneven ways
Draws out our miles and makes them wearisome.
And yet your fair discourse hath been as sugar,
Making the hard way sweet and delectable.

(2.3.3-7, TLN 1108-12)

CAPTION: Bolingbroke and Northumberland (*R2*, 2.3). From *The Plays of William Shakespeare*. The Historical Plays. Eds. Charles and Mary Cowden Clarke. Ill. H.C. Selous. London: Cassell, Petter, Galpin, and Company, c. 1830. (http://internetshakespeare.uvic.ca/Theater/collection/27511/27519/)

WORCESTER. Cousin, farewell. No further go in this
    Than I by letters shall direct your course.   290
    When time is ripe, which will be suddenly,°   *very soon*
    I'll steal to Glendower and Lord Mortimer,
    Where you and Douglas and our powers at once,[1]
    As I will fashion it, shall happily meet,
    To bear our fortunes in our own strong arms,   295
    Which now we hold at much uncertainty.
NORTHUMBERLAND. Farewell, good brother. We shall thrive, I
        trust.
HOTSPUR. Uncle, adieu. Oh, let the hours be short
    Till fields and blows and groans applaud our sport!   *Exeunt.*

[2.1][2]

Enter a Carrier[3] with a lantern in his hand.

FIRST CARRIER. Heigh-ho! An it be not four by the day,[4] I'll be
    hanged. Charles's Wain[5] is over the new chimney, and yet our
    horse not packed. What, ostler![6]
OSTLER. [*Within*] Anon, anon![7]
FIRST CARRIER. I prithee, Tom,[8] beat Cut's[9] saddle, put a few   5
    flocks[10] in the point.[11] Poor jade is wrung in the withers,[12] out of
    all cess.[13]

---

1 All together.
2 Location: An inn yard, somewhere on the London-Canterbury road.
3 Someone who transports goods, in this case the turkeys mentioned at 2.1.24,
TLN 662.
4 Four in the morning. The carrier is probably exaggerating the lateness of the
hour.
5 The constellation of the Great Bear or the Plough.
6 Stableman or groom.
7 Just a minute!
8 Probably the name of the second carrier.
9 Common name for a workhorse.
10 Tufts of wool.
11 Pommel.
12 Strained between the shoulder-blades.
13 Measure.

Enter another Carrier.

SECOND CARRIER. Peas and beans are as dank here as a dog, and
that is the next way to give poor jades the bots.[1] This house is
turned upside down since Robin Ostler[2] died.

FIRST CARRIER. Poor fellow never joyed since the price of oats rose;
it was the death of him.

SECOND CARRIER. I think this be the most villainous house in all
London road for fleas. I am stung like a tench.[3]

FIRST CARRIER. Like a tench? By the mass, there is ne'er a king
Christian could be better bit than I have been since the first cock.

SECOND CARRIER. Why, they will allow us ne'er a jordan,[4] and then
we leak in your chimney, and your chamber-lye[5] breeds fleas like
a loach.[6]

FIRST CARRIER. What, ostler! Come away and be hanged, come
away!

SECOND CARRIER. I have a gammon[7] of bacon and two races[8] of
ginger to be delivered as far as Charing Cross.[9]

FIRST CARRIER. God's body, the turkeys in my pannier[10] are quite
starved! What, ostler! A plague on thee, hast thou never an eye in
thy head? Canst not hear? An 'twere not as good deed as drink[11] to
break the pate[12] on thee, I am a very villain. Come, and be hanged!
Hast no faith in thee?

Enter Gadshill.

GADSHILL. Good morrow, carriers. What's o'clock?

FIRST CARRIER. I think it be two o'clock.

---

1 Worms.
2 An ostler could be an innkeeper as well as a groom (OED 1.b). In this instance
the surname indicates his profession.
3 A fish with spotted markings.
4 Chamber-pot.
5 Urine.
6 Another fish with markings like flea-bites.
7 The bottom piece of a flitch of bacon, including the hind leg (OED).
8 Roots of ginger.
9 To the west of London, hence on the opposite side to Rochester.
10 Basket.
11 A common saying; see also 2.2.19, TLN 757.
12 Head.

GADSHILL. I prithee lend me thy lantern to see my gelding in the stable.

FIRST CARRIER. Nay, by God, soft. I know a trick worth two of that, i'faith.

GADSHILL. [To Second Carrier] I pray thee, lend me thine.   35

SECOND CARRIER. Ay, when? Canst tell? "Lend me thy lantern," quoth he. Marry, I'll see thee hanged first.

GADSHILL. Sirrah carrier, what time do you mean to come to London?

SECOND CARRIER. Time enough to go to bed with a candle, I war-   40
rant thee. Come, neighbor Mugs, we'll call up the gentlemen. They will along with company, for they have great charge.[1]

Exeunt [Carriers].

Enter Chamberlain.

GADSHILL. What ho, chamberlain![2]

CHAMBERLAIN. "At hand, quoth pickpurse."[3]

GADSHILL. That's even as fair as[4] "at hand, quoth the chamberlain,"   45
for thou variest no more from picking of purses than giving direction doth from laboring: thou layest the plot how.

CHAMBERLAIN. Good morrow, Master Gadshill. It holds current
that I told you yesternight. There's a franklin[5] in the Weald of
Kent[6] hath brought three hundred marks[7] with him in gold. I   50
heard him tell it to one of his company last night at supper, a kind
of auditor, one that hath abundance of charge too, God knows
what. They are up already, and call for eggs and butter; they will
away presently.

---

1 A lot to be responsible for.
2 Servant responsible for looking after the bed-chambers of the inn.
3 A common saying, like "ready and waiting."
4 That's no different from saying.
5 Land-holder.
6 The name of the tract of country, formerly wooded, including the portions of
Sussex, Kent, and Surrey which lie between the North and South Downs (see OED
weald 1, quoting this passage).
7 Around 200 pounds in gold. The mark was not a coin but rather a monetary
unit equivalent in value to two-thirds of a pound sterling (OED).

55 GADSHILL. Sirrah, if they meet not with Saint Nicholas's clerks,[1] I'll give thee this neck.

CHAMBERLAIN. No, I'll none of it: I pray thee keep that for the hangman, for I know thou worshippest Saint Nicholas as truly as a man of falsehood may.

60 GADSHILL. What talkest thou to me of the hangman? If I hang, I'll make a fat pair of gallows, for if I hang, old Sir John hangs with me, and thou knowest he is no starveling. Tut, there are other Trojans[2] that thou dreamest not of, the which for sport's sake are content to do the profession some grace, that would, if

65 matters should be looked into, for their own credit's sake make all whole. I am joined with no foot-landrakers,[3] no long-staff sixpenny strikers,[4] none of these mad mustachio purple-hued maltworms,[5] but with nobility and tranquility, burgomasters[6] and great oneyers;[7] such as can hold in,[8] such as will strike sooner

70 than speak, and speak sooner than drink, and drink sooner than pray. And yet, zounds, I lie, for they pray continually to their saint the commonwealth; or rather, not pray to her, but prey on her; for they ride up and down on her and make her their boots.[9]

CHAMBERLAIN. What, the commonwealth their boots? Will she

75 hold out water in foul way?

GADSHILL. She will, she will, justice hath liquored her.[10] We steal as in a castle, cocksure; we have the recipe of fernseed,[11] we walk invisible.

CHAMBERLAIN. Nay, by my faith, I think you are more beholding to

80 the night than to fernseed for your walking invisible.

---

1 Highwaymen.

2 Companions, good mates.

3 Thieves who robbed on foot.

4 Desperate thieves who would use a long staff or pike to attack their victims.

5 Moustached, florid-faced beer drinkers.

6 Town councillors.

7 Possibly "great ones" or "great owners."

8 (1) keep a secret (2) hold their ground.

9 Booty as well as boots.

10 Those in authority have (1) "greased" her to make her watertight (suggesting bribery) or (2) got her drunk.

11 Ferns were thought to produce invisible seeds and popular myth suggested they might be used to produce an invisibility potion.

GADSHILL. Give me thy hand; thou shalt have a share in our purchase, as I am a true man.

CHAMBERLAIN. Nay, rather let me have it as you are a false thief.

GADSHILL. Go to, "homo"[1] is a common name to all men. Bid the
ostler bring my gelding out of the stable. Farewell, you muddy 85
knave.   [*Exeunt.*]

[2.2][2]

Enter Prince, Poins, and Peto.[3]

POINS. Come, shelter, shelter! I have removed Falstaff's horse, and
he frets like a gummed velvet.[4]

PRINCE. Stand close.

                                              [*Poins and Peto hide.*]

Enter Falstaff.

FALSTAFF. Poins! Poins, and be hanged! Poins!

PRINCE. Peace, ye fat-kidneyed rascal! What a brawling dost thou 5
keep!

FALSTAFF. Where's Poins, Hal?

PRINCE. He is walked up to the top of the hill. I'll go seek him.

                                          [*He joins Poins and Peto.*]

FALSTAFF. I am accursed to rob in that thief's company. The rascal hath removed my horse and tied him I know not where. If 10
I travel but four foot by the square[5] further afoot, I shall break
my wind. Well, I doubt not but to die a fair death, for all this
if I scape[6] hanging for killing that rogue.[7] I have forsworn his
company hourly any time this two-and-twenty years, and yet I

---

1 Latin for man.
2 The scene takes place somewhere on the road at Gad's Hill, later on the same
night.
3 Editors disagree about the stage directions in this scene, especially with regard
to whether Bardolph should enter here or later with Gadshill. The difficulties created by the directions in Q0 and Q1 are discussed in the ISE online edition.
4 Stiffened velvet which would "fret" or wear easily.
5 A measuring tool.
6 Escape.
7 I.e., Poins, who has "removed" Falstaff's horse.

15   am bewitched with the rogue's company. If the rascal have not
given me medicines[1] to make me love him, I'll be hanged. It could
not be else—I have drunk medicines. Poins! Hal! A plague upon
you both! Bardolph! Peto! I'll starve ere I'll rob a foot further. An
'twere not as good a deed as drink to turn true man and to leave
20   these rogues, I am the veriest varlet that ever chewed with a tooth.
Eight yards of uneven ground is threescore and ten miles afoot
with me, and the stony-hearted villains know it well enough. A
plague upon it when thieves cannot be true one to another!

They whistle.

Whew! A plague upon you all!

[Prince, Poins and Peto come forward.]

25   Give me my horse, you rogues; give me my horse, and be hanged!

PRINCE. Peace, ye fat-guts. Lie down, lay thine ear close to the
ground, and list if thou canst hear the tread of travelers.

FALSTAFF. Have you any levers to lift me up again, being down?
'Sblood, I'll not bear my own flesh so far afoot again for all the
30   coin in thy father's exchequer. What a plague mean ye to colt[2]
me thus?

PRINCE. Thou liest: thou art not colted, thou art uncolted.

FALSTAFF. I prithee, good Prince Hal, help me to my horse, good
king's son.

35   PRINCE. Out, ye rogue, shall I be your ostler?

FALSTAFF. Hang thyself in thine own heir-apparent garters![3] If I be
ta'en, I'll peach[4] for this. An I have not ballads made on you all
and sung to filthy tunes, let a cup of sack be my poison. When a
jest is so forward—and afoot too—I hate it.

Enter Gadshill [and Bardolph].

40   GADSHILL. Stand!

FALSTAFF. So I do, against my will.

---

1 Potions.
2 (1) befool, cheat (2) horse.
3 Falstaff plays with a common saying about hanging in one's own garters: as
heir-apparent, Hal is a member of the Order of the Garter.
4 Impeach, inform against.

POINS. Oh, 'tis our setter,[1] I know his voice. Bardolph, what news?

BARDOLPH. Case ye,[2] case ye, on with your vizards! There's money of the king's coming down the hill; 'tis going to the king's exchequer.

FALSTAFF. You lie, ye rogue, 'tis going to the king's tavern.   45

GADSHILL. There's enough to make us all.

FALSTAFF. To be hanged.

PRINCE. Sirs, you four shall front them in the narrow lane. Ned Poins and I will walk lower. If they scape from your encounter, then they light on us.   50

PETO. How many be there of them?

GADSHILL. Some eight or ten.

FALSTAFF. Zounds, will they not rob us?

PRINCE. What, a coward, Sir John Paunch?

FALSTAFF. Indeed I am not John of Gaunt[3] your grandfather, but   55 yet no coward, Hal.

PRINCE. Well, we leave that to the proof.

POINS. Sirrah Jack, thy horse stands behind the hedge. When thou need'st him, there thou shalt find him. Farewell, and stand fast.

FALSTAFF. Now cannot I strike him if I should be hanged.   60

PRINCE. [*Aside to Poins*] Ned, where are our disguises?

POINS. [*Aside to the prince*] Here, hard by, stand close.

[*Exeunt Prince and Poins.*]

FALSTAFF. Now, my masters, happy man be his dole,[4] say I; every man to his business.

Enter the travelers.[5]

[FIRST TRAVELER]. Come, neighbor, the boy shall lead our horses   65 down the hill. We'll walk afoot a while, and ease their legs.

THIEVES. Stand!

TRAVELER. Jesus bless us!

---

1 Thieves' slang for the person who sets up the crime.
2 Disguise yourselves.
3 A familiar pun on "gaunt" meaning "thin."
4 A common saying: "may happiness be each man's lot."
5 According to Hal in 2.4, there are four travelers. Q0 and Q1 do not specify how their speeches should be divided.

FALSTAFF. Strike, down with them, cut the villains' throats. Ah,
70   whoreson caterpillars,[1] bacon-fed knaves! They hate us youth.
Down with them, fleece them!

TRAVELER. Oh, we are undone, both we and ours forever!

FALSTAFF. Hang, ye gorbellied[2] knaves, are ye undone? No, ye fat
chuffs,[3] I would your store were here. On, bacons, on! What, ye
75   knaves, young men must live. You are grand-jurors,[4] are ye? We'll
jure[5] ye, faith.

Here they rob them and bind them. Exeunt.

Enter the prince and Poins.

PRINCE. The thieves have bound the true men. Now could thou and
I rob the thieves and go merrily to London, it would be argument[6] for a week, laughter for a month, and a good jest forever.
80 POINS. Stand close, I hear them coming.

[They hide.]

Enter the thieves again.

FALSTAFF. Come, my masters, let us share, and then to horse before
day. An the prince and Poins be not two arrant[7] cowards, there's
no equity stirring. There's no more valor in that Poins than in a
wild duck.

As they are sharing the prince and Poins set upon them.

85 PRINCE. Your money.

POINS. Villains!

They all run away, and Falstaff after a blow or two
runs away too, leaving the booty behind them.

PRINCE. Got with much ease. Now merrily to horse. The thieves are
all scattered and possessed with fear so strongly that they dare

---

1 I.e., parasites.
2 Pot-bellied.
3 Misers.
4 Members of a grand jury as opposed to a petty jury.
5 Make jurors of you (OED).
6 A hot topic.
7 Downright.

not meet each other. Each takes his fellow for an officer. Away,
good Ned. Falstaff sweats to death, and lards the lean earth as he
walks along. Were't not for laughing, I should pity him.

POINS. How the fat rogue roared! _Exeunt._

[2.3]¹

_Enter Hotspur [alone] reading a letter._²
[HOTSPUR]. "But for mine own part, my lord, I could be well contented to be there, in respect of the love I bear your house."³ He
 could be contented; why is he not then? In respect of the love he
 bears our house! He shows in this he loves his own barn better
 than he loves our house. Let me see some more. "The purpose   5
 you undertake is dangerous,"—Why, that's certain: 'tis dangerous to take a cold, to sleep, to drink; but I tell you, my lord fool,
 out of this nettle danger we pluck this flower safety. "The purpose
 you undertake is dangerous, the friends you have named uncertain, the time itself unsorted,⁴ and your whole plot too light for   10
 the counterpoise of⁵ so great an opposition." Say you so, say you
 so? I say unto you again, you are a shallow, cowardly hind,⁶ and
 you lie. What a lack-brain is this! By the Lord, our plot is a good
 plot as ever was laid, our friends true and constant; a good plot,
 good friends, and full of expectation;⁷ an excellent plot, very   15
 good friends. What a frosty-spirited rogue is this! Why, my lord
 of York commends the plot and the general course of the action.
 Zounds, an I were now by this rascal, I could brain him with his
 lady's fan! Is there not my father, my uncle, and myself? Lord
 Edmund Mortimer, my lord of York, and Owen Glendower? Is   20
 there not besides the Douglas? Have I not all their letters, to meet
 me in arms by the ninth of the next month? And are they not
 some of them set forward already? What a pagan rascal is this, an
 infidel! Ha, you shall see now, in very sincerity of fear and cold

---

1 Although no location is mentioned, Hotspur is clearly at home in this scene. It
has been traditionally located at Warkworth Castle in Northumberland.
2 The identity of the letter-writer is not revealed and clearly does not matter.
3 Family.
4 Unfitted, unsuitable.
5 To counteract.
6 Peasant.
7 Promise.

Hal's joke here is that Falstaff sweats fat, but his comment is also prophetic. See *Henry IV, Part Two*: "for anything I know, Falstaff shall die of a sweat" (Epilogue 27-28, TLN 3346-47); and *Henry V*: "he is so shaked of a burning quotidian tertian, that it is most lamentable to behold" (2.1.118-20, TLN 616-17).

The sweating sickness, or "English sweat," was a rapidly fatal disease that was epidemic in the fifteenth and sixteenth centuries. The physician John Caius published a detailed description in 1552 in which he noted that the disease tended to afflict those who over-indulged in food and drink: "they which had this sweat ... were either men of wealth, ease and welfare, or of the poorer sort such as were idle persons, good ale drinkers, and tavern haunters." The disease did not afflict laborers, "thin dieted" people, or people from countries of "moderate and good diet" (Caius 334). The sweating sickness was not known until the reign of Henry VII, and its last outbreak was in 1551, so Shakespeare's references to it in the history plays about Henry V are anachronistic.

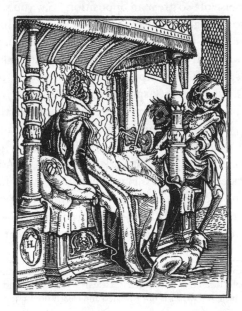

Hans Holbein the Younger (1498-1543), "The Dance of Death: The Duchess." From Wikimedia Commons, http://www.commons.wikimedia.org.

heart will he to the king, and lay open all our proceedings! Oh, I   25
could divide myself and go to buffets[1] for moving such a dish of
skim-milk with so honorable an action! Hang him! Let him tell
the king; we are prepared. I will set forward tonight.

Enter his lady.

How now, Kate? I must leave you within these two hours.

LADY PERCY. O my good lord, why are you thus alone?   30
For what offense have I this fortnight been
A banished woman from my Harry's bed?
Tell me, sweet lord, what is't that takes from thee
Thy stomach, pleasure, and thy golden sleep?
Why dost thou bend thine eyes upon the earth?   35
And start° so often when thou sit'st alone?   *jump*
Why hast thou lost the fresh blood in thy cheeks,
And given my treasures and my rights of thee
To thick-eyed musing and curst melancholy?
In thy faint slumbers I by thee have watched,[2]   40
And heard thee murmur tales of iron wars,
Speak terms of manage° to thy bounding steed,   *horsemanship*
Cry courage to the field. And thou hast talked
Of sallies and retires,[3] of trenches, tents,
Of palisadoes,[4] frontiers,° parapets,   *fortresses* 45
Of basilisks,[5] of cannon, culverin,[6]
Of prisoners' ransom, and of soldiers slain,
And all the currents of a heady fight.
Thy spirit within thee hath been so at war,
And thus hath so bestirred thee in thy sleep,   50
That beads of sweat have stood upon thy brow
Like bubbles in a late-disturbèd stream;
And in thy face strange motions° have appeared,   *expressions*

---

1 Fight with myself.
2 Remained awake, kept vigil.
3 Sudden attacks and retreats.
4 Defenses constructed out of stakes.
5 Large cannon.
6 Small cannon.

Such as we see when men restrain their breath
55 On some great sudden heft.¹ Oh, what portents are these?
Some heavy business hath my lord in hand,
And I must know it, else he loves me not.
HOTSPUR. What ho!

[*Enter Servant.*]
                              Is Gilliams with the packet gone?
SERVANT. He is, my lord, an hour ago.
60 HOTSPUR. Hath Butler brought those horses from the sheriff?
SERVANT. One horse, my lord, he brought even now.
HOTSPUR. What horse? Roan?² A crop-ear, is it not?
SERVANT. It is, my lord.
HOTSPUR.   That roan shall be my throne.
    Well, I will back him straight.³ O *Esperance!*⁴
65 Bid Butler lead him forth into the park.   [*Exit servant.*]
LADY PERCY. But hear you, my lord.
HOTSPUR. What sayst thou, my lady?
LADY PERCY. What is it carries you away?
HOTSPUR. Why, my horse, my love, my horse.
70 LADY PERCY. Out, you mad-headed ape!
    A weasel hath not such a deal of spleen
    As you are tossed with. In faith,
    I'll know your business, Harry, that I will.
    I fear my brother Mortimer⁵ doth stir
75 About his title, and hath sent for you
    To line° his enterprise; but if you go—   *strengthen*
HOTSPUR. So far afoot? I shall be weary, love.
LADY PERCY. Come, come, you paraquito,° answer me   *parrot*
    Directly unto this question that I ask.
80 In faith, I'll break thy little finger, Harry,

---

1 Heaving; the effort made when attempting to lift a weight.
2 A dull red or reddish-grey horse.
3 I will mount him straight away.
4 Hope: "Esperance ma comforte" (in hope is my strength) is a Percy family motto.
5 Lady Percy's brother, Edmund Mortimer, was not Richard's proclaimed heir, but is here conflated with his nephew, Edmund Mortimer the Earl of March. (Later in the play Mortimer calls Lady Percy his aunt: see 3.1.193, TLN 1730.)

THE SPLEEN (TLN 927)

Elizabethan thinking about the relationship between the body and the personality centered around the idea of the four humors: bodily fluids which were supposed to govern the temperament. The four humors were black bile, yellow bile, phlegm, and blood, and an excess of any one of these could create a personality imbalance. Hotspur exemplifies a choleric personality, believed to be caused by an excess of yellow bile. The spleen was often associated with black bile and a melancholic disposition, but as a source of a range of emotions, and especially anger, it could also be linked to a choleric disposition. Choleric people were quarrelsome, bold, violent, and impulsive, and also likely to be red-haired and thin. Northumberland accuses Hotspur of being "drunk with choler" (1.3.128, TLN 450) and Worcester describes him as "hare-brained [and] governed by a spleen" (5.2.19, TLN 2901). Prince Hal, Falstaff, Kate, Mortimer, and Hotspur all make reference to humors in this play.

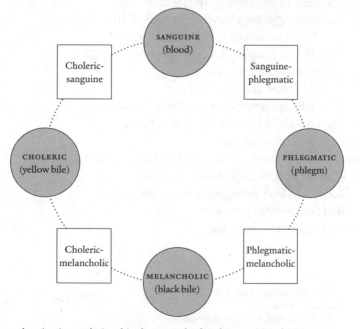

Chart showing interrelationships between the four humors. See the Internet Shakepeare Editions website page on humors (http://internetshakespeare.uvic.ca/ Library/SLT/ideas/order/humours.html).

An if thou wilt not tell me all things true.
HOTSPUR. Away, away, you trifler! Love? I love thee not,
I care not for thee, Kate. This is no world
To play with mammets[1] and to tilt[2] with lips.
85 We must have bloody noses and cracked crowns,[3]
And pass them current,[4] too. God's me,[5] my horse!
What sayst thou, Kate? What wouldst thou have with me?
LADY PERCY. Do you not love me? Do you not indeed?
Well, do not then, for since you love me not
90 I will not love myself. Do you not love me?
Nay, tell me if you speak in jest or no.
HOTSPUR. Come, wilt thou see me ride?
And when I am a-horseback, I will swear
I love thee infinitely. But hark you, Kate.
95 I must not have you henceforth question me
Whither I go, nor reason whereabout.[6]
Whither I must, I must; and, to conclude,
This evening must I leave you, gentle Kate.
I know you wise, but yet no farther wise
100 Than Harry Percy's wife; constant you are,
But yet a woman; and for secrecy
No lady closer, for I well believe
Thou wilt not utter what thou dost not know.
And so far will I trust thee, gentle Kate.
105 LADY PERCY. How, so far?
HOTSPUR. Not an inch further. But hark you Kate,
Whither I go, thither shall you go too.
Today will I set forth, tomorrow you.
Will this content you, Kate?
110 LADY PERCY. It must of force.[7]   *Exeunt.*

---

1 (1) dolls, puppets (2) female breasts (Partridge).
2 Joust or contend.
3 (1) heads and (2) coins (worth around 5 shillings).
4 Keep in circulation (as currency).
5 An oath, derived from "God save me."
6 Ask me what I'm doing.
7 Of necessity.

[2.4]¹

Enter Prince and Poins.

PRINCE. Ned, prithee come out of that fat² room, and lend me thy
hand to laugh a little.

POINS. Where hast been, Hal?

PRINCE. With three or four loggerheads,³ amongst three or four-
score hogsheads.⁴ I have sounded the very bass-string of humili- 5
ty.⁵ Sirrah, I am sworn brother to a leash of drawers,⁶ and can
call them all by their Christian names, as Tom, Dick, and Francis.
They take it already upon their salvation that though I be but
Prince of Wales, yet I am the king of courtesy, and tell me flatly I
am no proud Jack like Falstaff, but a Corinthian,⁷ a lad of mettle, 10
a good boy (by the Lord, so they call me) and when I am king of
England I shall command all the good lads in Eastcheap. They
call drinking deep "dyeing scarlet,"⁸ and when you breathe in your
watering⁹ they cry "hem!" and bid you "play it off!" To conclude, I
am so good a proficient in one quarter of an hour that I can drink 15
with any tinker in his own language during my life. I tell thee Ned,
thou hast lost much honor that thou wert not with me in this
action. But, sweet Ned—to sweeten which name of Ned I give
thee this pennyworth of sugar, clapped even now into my hand by
an underskinker,¹⁰ one that never spake other English in his life 20
than "Eight shillings and sixpence," and "You are welcome," with
this shrill addition, "Anon, anon, sir! Score¹¹ a pint of bastard¹²

---

1 The tavern location is swiftly established through the dialogue here.
2 Stuffy.
3 Blockheads.
4 Casks.
5 (1) humbled myself to the lowest level of social interaction (2) listened to the
lowest of humanity.
6 A set of tapsters or barmen.
7 A good drinking companion (from the proverbial wealth, luxury, and licen-
tiousness of ancient Corinth, OED).
8 A reference to (1) the heavy drinker's red complexion, or (2) the fact that the
inevitable product of drinking, urine, was used to fix scarlet dye (Wilson).
9 Pause in your drinking.
10 Junior barman.
11 Chalk up.
12 Sweet Spanish wine.

in the Half-moon!"[1] or so. But, Ned, to drive away the time till
Falstaff come, I prithee do thou stand in some by-room, while I
25   question my puny drawer to what end he gave me the sugar, and
do thou never leave calling "Francis!" that his tale to me may be
nothing but "Anon!" Step aside, and I'll show thee a precedent.[2]

                                                          [*Exit Poins.*]

POINS. [*Within*] Francis!

PRINCE. Thou art perfect.

30 POINS. [*Within*] Francis!

Enter Drawer.

FRANCIS. Anon, anon, sir! [*Calling*] Look down into the Pomgarnet,[3]
    Ralph!

PRINCE. Come hither, Francis.

FRANCIS. My lord.

35 PRINCE. How long hast thou to serve,[4] Francis?

FRANCIS. Forsooth, five years, and as much as to—

POINS. [*Within*] Francis!

FRANCIS. Anon, anon, sir.

PRINCE. Five year! By'r Lady,[5] a long lease for the clinking of pewter.

40   But Francis, darest thou be so valiant as to play the coward with
thy indenture,[6] and show it a fair pair of heels, and run from it?

FRANCIS. O Lord, sir, I'll be sworn upon all the books[7] in England,
    I could find in my heart—

POINS. [*Within*] Francis!

45 FRANCIS. Anon sir.

PRINCE. How old art thou Francis?

FRANCIS. Let me see, about Michaelmas[8] next I shall be—

POINS. [*Within*] Francis!

FRANCIS. Anon sir. Pray stay a little my lord.

---

1   The name of one of the rooms in the tavern.
2   Example.
3   A variant on "pomegranate," referring here to another room in the tavern.
4   How much longer is your apprenticeship? (normally seven years).
5   By our Lady (a mild oath).
6   Contract.
7   Bibles.
8   The feast of St. Michael, 29 September.

"ANON, ANON, SIR":
THE PRINCE AND POINS (TLN 988)

Shakespeare echoes the "anon, anon" joke in *Henry IV, Part Two*, when the prince and Poins disguise themselves as drawers to trick Falstaff. They finally reveal themselves, saying "Anon, anon, sir" in answer to Falstaff's order for sack (2.4.282, TLN 1308).

Poins's role in *Henry IV, Part One* is puzzling. In the first half of the play he appears to be closer to the prince than any of the other tavern characters apart from Falstaff. He and the prince work together in tricking the others at Gadshill and in jesting at Francis's and Falstaff's expense. At the end of 2.4 however, it is Peto who stays behind with the prince to meet the sheriff, whereas it would seem more logical for Poins to remain and for Peto to hide from the carrier. It has been suggested that the actor playing Poins had to be withdrawn from 2.4 in order to double the part of another character in the next scene (Bowers 189-98). Poins disappears from *Part One* after 2.4, but reappears as Hal's companion in *Henry IV, Part Two*. He seems to be of higher social status than Bardolph or Peto and, according to Falstaff in *Part Two*, is loved by the prince because he "plays at quoits well ... and swears with a good grace, and wears his boots very smooth" (*2H4* 2.4.244-48, TLN 1269-73). In the 2012 BBC *Hollow Crown* series the script is altered so that Poins (David Dawson) shares in picking Falstaff's pockets at the end of 2.4 and enters with the prince in 3.3. This Poins is young, handsome, and dresses similarly to Hal; he clearly resents Falstaff as a rival for Hal's favor.

Prince Henry and Poins (2.4). From *The Plays of William Shakespeare. The Historical Plays*. Eds. Charles and Mary Cowden Clarke. Ill. H.C. Selous. London: Cassell, Petter, Galpin, and Company, c.1830. (http://internetshakespeare.uvic.ca/Theater/collection/12171/12160/)

50 PRINCE. Nay, but hark you, Francis. For the sugar thou gavest me,
    'twas a pennyworth, was't not?

FRANCIS. O Lord, I would it had been two!

PRINCE. I will give thee for it a thousand pound. Ask me when thou
    wilt, and thou shalt have it.

55 POINS. [*Within*] Francis!

FRANCIS. Anon, anon.

PRINCE. Anon, Francis? No, Francis, but tomorrow, Francis; or,
    Francis, a-Thursday; or, indeed, Francis, when thou wilt. But
    Francis—

60 FRANCIS. My lord?

PRINCE. Wilt thou rob this[1] leathern-jerkin, crystal-button, not-
    pated,[2] agate-ring, puke-stocking, caddis-garter,[3] smooth-tongue
    Spanish pouch?[4]

FRANCIS. O Lord, sir, who do you mean?

65 PRINCE. Why, then, your brown bastard[5] is your only drink! For
    look you, Francis, your white canvas doublet will sully. In Barbary,
    sir, it cannot come to so much.[6]

FRANCIS. What sir?

POINS. [*Within*] Francis!

70 PRINCE. Away, you rogue! Dost thou not hear them call?

Here they both call him. The Drawer stands
amazed, not knowing which way to go.

Enter Vintner.

VINTNER. What, standest thou still, and hearest such a calling? Look
    to the guests within.   [*Exit Francis.*]
    My lord, old Sir John with half a dozen more are at the door. Shall
    I let them in?

75 PRINCE. Let them alone a while, and then open the door.

[*Exit Vintner.*]

---

1 I.e., the innkeeper, who "owns" his apprentice and will therefore be robbed if
Francis runs away.

2 Short haired; a cropped hairstyle associated with puritans.

3 Wearing dark woolen stockings and worsted tape garters.

4 Wallet made of Spanish leather.

5 Sweet Spanish wine, in this case "brown" as opposed to white.

6 Hal seems to imply that Francis is better off staying where he is (it = the sugar,
grown in Barbary, North Africa).

Poins!

POINS. Anon, anon sir!

Enter Poins.

PRINCE. Sirrah, Falstaff and the rest of the thieves are at the door.
Shall we be merry?

POINS. As merry as crickets, my lad. But hark ye, what cunning   80
match[1] have you made with this jest of the drawer? Come, what's
the issue?[2]

PRINCE. I am now of all humors[3] that have showed themselves
humors since the old days of goodman Adam[4] to the pupil[5] age
of this present twelve o'clock at midnight.   85

[Enter Francis.]

What's o'clock Francis?

FRANCIS. Anon, anon, sir.   *[Exit Francis.]*

PRINCE. That ever this fellow should have fewer words than a parrot,
and yet the son of a woman! His industry is upstairs and down-
stairs, his eloquence the parcel of a reckoning.[6] I am not yet of   90
Percy's mind, the Hotspur of the North, he that kills me[7] some
six or seven dozen of Scots at a breakfast, washes his hands, and
says to his wife, "Fie upon this quiet life! I want work." "O my
sweet Harry," says she, "how many hast thou killed today?" "Give
my roan horse a drench,"[8] says he, and answers, "Some fourteen," 95
an hour after; "a trifle, a trifle." I prithee call in Falstaff. I'll play
Percy, and that damned brawn[9] shall play Dame Mortimer his
wife. "Rivo!"[10] says the drunkard. Call in Ribs, call in Tallow.[11]

---

1 Game.
2 What's the point?
3 Moods.
4 I.e., since the time of Adam and Eve.
5 Infant.
6 The details of a tavern bill.
7 Kills.
8 Drink.
9 The flesh of the boar (OED).
10 Cheers!
11 Lard, dripping.

Enter Falstaff [with Gadshill, Peto, and Bardolph. Francis follows with wine.]

POINS. Welcome, Jack. Where hast thou been?

100 FALSTAFF. A plague of[1] all cowards, I say, and a vengeance too, marry and amen! Give me a cup of sack, boy. Ere I lead this life long, I'll sew netherstocks,[2] and mend them and foot them[3] too. A plague of all cowards! Give me a cup of sack, rogue. Is there no virtue extant?[4]

He drinketh.

105 PRINCE. Didst thou never see Titan[5] kiss a dish of butter (pitiful hearted Titan!) that melted at the sweet tale of the sun's? If thou didst, then behold that compound.[6]

FALSTAFF. You rogue, here's lime[7] in this sack too. There is nothing but roguery to be found in villainous man, yet a coward is worse 110 than a cup of sack with lime in it. A villainous coward! Go thy ways, old Jack, die when thou wilt. If manhood, good manhood, be not forgot upon the face of the earth, then am I a shotten her-ring.[8] There lives not three good men unhanged in England, and one of them is fat and grows old, God help the while. A bad world, 115 I say. I would I were a weaver, I could sing psalms,[9] or anything. A plague of all cowards, I say still.

PRINCE. How now, woolsack, what mutter you?

FALSTAFF. A king's son! If I do not beat thee out of thy kingdom with a dagger of lath,[10] and drive all thy subjects afore thee like 120 a flock of wild geese, I'll never wear hair on my face more. You, Prince of Wales!

_____

1 On.

2 Stockings.

3 Make the feet for them.

4 Valor still in existence.

5 The sun.

6 See that mixture of elements. Hal seems to be describing Falstaff's glowing round face as it meets his cup of sack.

7 Added to wine to make it dry and sparkling.

8 A herring that has shot its roe and is therefore particularly lean.

9 Many weavers were protestant refugees from the Netherlands, known for their psalm singing.

10 A wooden dagger used as a comic stage property by the Vice figure in morality plays.

PRINCE. Why, you whoreson round man, what's the matter?

FALSTAFF. Are not you a coward? Answer me to that. And Poins there?

POINS. Zounds, ye fat paunch, an ye call me coward, by the Lord   125
I'll stab thee.

FALSTAFF. I call thee coward? I'll see thee damned ere I call thee
coward, but I would give a thousand pound I could run as fast
as thou canst. You are straight enough in the shoulders; you care
not who sees your back. Call you that backing of your friends? A   130
plague upon such backing! Give me them that will face me. Give
me a cup of sack. I am a rogue if I drunk today.

PRINCE. O villain, thy lips are scarce wiped since thou drunkest last.

FALSTAFF. All is one for that.

He drinketh.

A plague of all cowards, still say I.   135

PRINCE. What's the matter?

FALSTAFF. What's the matter? There be four of us here have ta'en a
thousand pound this day morning.

PRINCE. Where is it, Jack, where is it?

FALSTAFF. Where is it? Taken from us it is. A hundred upon poor   140
four of us.

PRINCE. What, a hundred, man?

FALSTAFF. I am a rogue if I were not at half-sword[1] with a dozen
of them, two hours together. I have scaped by miracle. I am
eight times thrust through the doublet, four through the hose,   145
my buckler[2] cut through and through, my sword hacked like a
handsaw. *Ecce signum.*[3] I never dealt better since I was a man. All
would not do. A plague of all cowards! Let them speak. [*Indicates
Gadshill, Peto, and Bardolph.*] If they speak more or less than truth,
they are villains and the sons of darkness.   150

[PRINCE]. Speak sirs, how was it?

[GADSHILL]. We four set upon some dozen—

FALSTAFF. Sixteen at least, my lord.

[GADSHILL]. And bound them.

PETO. No, no, they were not bound.   155

---

1 In close combat.
2 Shield.
3 Behold the proof (Latin).

FALSTAFF. You rogue, they were bound every man of them, or I am a Jew else, an Hebrew Jew.

[GADSHILL]. As we were sharing, some six or seven fresh men set upon us.

160 FALSTAFF. And unbound the rest; and then come in the other.

PRINCE. What, fought you with them all?

FALSTAFF. All? I know not what you call all, but if I fought not with fifty of them, I am a bunch of radish. If there were not two- or three-and-fifty upon poor old Jack, then am I no two-legged

165 creature.

PRINCE. Pray God you have not murdered some of them.

FALSTAFF. Nay, that's past praying for. I have peppered[1] two of them. Two I am sure I have paid[2]—two rogues in buckram[3] suits. I tell thee what, Hal, if I tell thee a lie, spit in my face, call me horse.

170 Thou knowest my old ward[4]—here I lay,[5] and thus I bore my point.[6] Four rogues in buckram let drive at me.

PRINCE. What, four? Thou saidst but two even now.

FALSTAFF. Four, Hal, I told thee four.

POINS. Ay, ay, he said four.

175 FALSTAFF. These four came all afront, and mainly[7] thrust at me. I made me no more ado, but took all their seven points in my target,[8] thus.

PRINCE. Seven? Why, there were but four even now.

FALSTAFF. In buckram?

180 POINS. Ay, four in buckram suits.

FALSTAFF. Seven, by these hilts,[9] or I am a villain else.

PRINCE. Prithee, let him alone. We shall have more anon.

FALSTAFF. Dost thou hear me, Hal?

PRINCE. Ay, and mark thee too, Jack.

---

1 Hit repeatedly, beat severely (see OED pepper v. 3, quoting this passage; also 5.3.35, TLN 2929).
2 Put paid to, killed.
3 A coarse linen or cotton fabric.
4 A defensive posture in swordplay.
5 This is how I set myself up.
6 Sword.
7 Forcefully.
8 Shield.
9 I.e., this hilt.

FALSTAFF. Do so, for it is worth the listening to. These nine in buck- 185
ram that I told thee of—

PRINCE. So, two more already.

FALSTAFF. Their points being broken—

POINS. Down fell their hose.[1]

FALSTAFF. Began to give me ground. But I followed me close, came 190
in foot and hand, and, with a thought, seven of the eleven I paid.

PRINCE. Oh, monstrous! Eleven buckram men grown out of two!

FALSTAFF. But, as the devil would have it, three misbegotten knaves
in Kendal green[2] came at my back and let drive at me; for it was
so dark, Hal, that thou couldst not see thy hand. 195

PRINCE. These lies are like their father that begets them,[3] gross as
a mountain, open, palpable. Why, thou clay-brained guts, thou
knotty-pated[4] fool, thou whoreson obscene greasy tallow-catch[5]—

FALSTAFF. What, art thou mad? Art thou mad? Is not the truth the
truth? 200

PRINCE. Why, how couldst thou know these men in Kendal green
when it was so dark thou couldst not see thy hand? Come, tell us
your reason. What sayst thou to this?

POINS. Come, your reason, Jack, your reason.

FALSTAFF. What, upon compulsion? Zounds, an I were at the 205
strappado,[6] or all the racks in the world, I would not tell you on
compulsion. Give you a reason on compulsion? If reasons[7] were
as plentiful as blackberries, I would give no man a reason upon
compulsion, I.

PRINCE. I'll be no longer guilty of this sin. This sanguine[8] coward, 210
this bed-presser, this horse-back-breaker, this huge hill of flesh—

---

1 Poins uses a pun on *points* referring to the laces which attached doublet to hose.
2 A coarse cloth, produced in the town of Kendal.
3 Hal links Falstaff with the devil, described in the Bible as "a liar, and the father
thereof" (John 8.44).
4 Thick-headed.
5 (1) a pan to catch dripping, or, possibly, (2) a variant spelling of "tallow-keech":
a lump of fat.
6 An instrument of torture.
7 Possibly a pun on *raisins* as in *As You Like It* 2.7.100, TLN 1076.
8 Red-faced.

FALSTAFF. 'Sblood, you starveling, you eel-skin, you dried neat's[1] tongue, you bull's pizzle,[2] you stock-fish.[3] Oh, for breath to utter what is like thee! You tailor's yard,[4] you sheath,[5] you bow-case,
215   you vile standing tuck![6]

PRINCE. Well, breathe awhile, and then to it again, and when thou hast tired thyself in base comparisons, hear me speak but this.

POINS. Mark, Jack.

PRINCE. We two saw you four set on four, and bound them, and
220   were masters of their wealth. Mark now how a plain tale shall put you down. Then did we two set on you four, and, with a word,[7] outfaced you from your prize, and have it; yea, and can show it you here in the house. And Falstaff, you carried your guts away as nimbly, with as quick dexterity, and roared for mercy, and still
225   run and roared, as ever I heard bull-calf. What a slave art thou, to hack thy sword as thou hast done, and then say it was in fight! What trick, what device, what starting-hole[8] canst thou now find out to hide thee from this open and apparent shame?

POINS. Come, let's hear, Jack; what trick hast thou now?

230 FALSTAFF. By the Lord, I knew ye as well as he that made ye. Why, hear you, my masters. Was it for me to kill the heir-apparent? Should I turn upon the true prince? Why, thou knowest I am as valiant as Hercules; but beware instinct. The lion will not touch the true prince[9]—instinct is a great matter. I was now a coward
235   on instinct. I shall think the better of myself and thee during my life: I for a valiant lion, and thou for a true prince. But by the Lord, lads, I am glad you have the money. Hostess, clap to the doors. Watch tonight, pray tomorrow. Gallants, lads, boys, hearts

---

1 Ox's.
2 Bull's penis, sometimes dried and used as a whip.
3 Dried cod.
4 Measuring stick, but also a pun on yard = penis.
5 Scabbard.
6 A short sword, arming sword, or truncheon.
7 With a brief shout (Humphreys).
8 Bolt-hole.
9 A folkloric belief traceable to Pliny that, as king of the beasts, the lion will recognize and respect royalty (Humphreys).

of gold, all the titles of good fellowship come to you! What, shall
we be merry, shall we have a play extempore?[1]   240
PRINCE. Content, and the argument shall be thy running away.
FALSTAFF. Ah, no more of that, Hal, an thou lovest me.

Enter Hostess.
HOSTESS. O Jesu, my lord the prince!
PRINCE. How now, my lady the hostess, what sayst thou to me?
HOSTESS. Marry, my lord, there is a nobleman of the court at door   245
would speak with you. He says he comes from your father.
PRINCE. Give him as much as will make him a royal[2] man, and send
him back again to my mother.
FALSTAFF. What manner of man is he?
HOSTESS. An old man.   250
FALSTAFF. What doth gravity out of his bed at midnight? Shall I give
him his answer?
PRINCE. Prithee do, Jack.
FALSTAFF. Faith, and I'll send him packing.   *Exit.*
PRINCE. Now sirs, by'r Lady, you fought fair; so did you, Peto; so   255
did you, Bardolph. You are lions, too, you ran away upon instinct,
you will not touch the true prince, no fie!
BARDOLPH. Faith, I ran when I saw others run.
PRINCE. Faith, tell me now in earnest, how came Falstaff's sword
so hacked?   260
PETO. Why, he hacked it with his dagger, and said he would swear
truth out of England but he would make you believe it was done
in fight, and persuaded us to do the like.
BARDOLPH. Yea, and to tickle our noses with speargrass,[3] to make
them bleed; and then to beslubber our garments with it, and   265
swear it was the blood of true men. I did that I did not this seven
year before—I blushed to hear his monstrous devices.
PRINCE. O villain, thou stolest a cup of sack eighteen years ago, and
wert taken with the manner,[4] and ever since thou hast blushed

---

1 Improvised.
2 A *royal* was a coin worth 10 shillings whereas a "noble" was only worth 6 shillings and 8 pence.
3 Possibly couch-grass, or spearwort, a plant used by beggars to raise blisters.
4 Caught in the act.

270   extempore.[1] Thou hadst fire and sword on thy side, and yet thou
       rannest away. What instinct hadst thou for it?

BARDOLPH. My lord, do you see these meteors? Do you behold these
       exhalations?[2]

PRINCE. I do.

275 BARDOLPH. What think you they portend?

PRINCE. Hot livers, and cold purses.

BARDOLPH. Choler,[3] my lord, if rightly taken.

Enter Falstaff.

PRINCE. No, if rightly taken, halter.[4] Here comes lean Jack; here
       comes bare-bone. How now, my sweet creature of bombast?[5]

280   How long is't ago, Jack, since thou sawest thine own knee?

FALSTAFF. My own knee? When I was about thy years, Hal, I was
       not an eagle's talon in the waist; I could have crept into any alder-
       man's thumb-ring. A plague of sighing and grief, it blows a man
       up like a bladder. There's villainous news abroad. Here was Sir

285   John Bracy from your father; you must to the court in the morn-
       ing. That same mad fellow of the North, Percy, and he of Wales
       that gave Amamon[6] the bastinado,[7] and made Lucifer cuckold,[8]
       and swore the devil his true liegeman[9] upon the cross of a Welsh
       hook[10]—what a plague call you him?

290 POINS. Owen Glendower.

FALSTAFF. Owen, Owen, the same; and his son-in-law Mortimer,
       and old Northumberland, and that sprightly Scot of Scots,
       Douglas, that runs a-horseback up a hill perpendicular—

---

1 I.e., because of Bardolph's red, alcohol-induced complexion.
2 Bardolph's skin eruptions, which he suggests are indicative of turmoil underneath.
3 A fiery temperament.
4 As in the hangman's noose.
5 Padding; inflated, empty language.
6 A principal devil (Humphreys).
7 Beating on the soles of the feet.
8 Man whose wife has committed adultery, traditionally marked by the wearing of horns on the head.
9 Made the devil swear allegiance.
10 A weapon which, unlike the sword, could not be used to represent the holy cross.

PRINCE. He that rides at high speed and with his pistol kills a sparrow flying. 295

FALSTAFF. You have hit it.

PRINCE. So did he never the sparrow.

FALSTAFF. Well, that rascal hath good mettle[1] in him, he will not run.

PRINCE. Why, what a rascal art thou, then, to praise him so for
running! 300

FALSTAFF. A-horseback, ye cuckoo, but afoot he will not budge a
foot.

PRINCE. Yes, Jack, upon instinct.

FALSTAFF. I grant ye, upon instinct. Well, he is there too, and one
Mordake, and a thousand blue-caps[2] more. Worcester is stolen 305
away tonight. Thy father's beard is turned white with the news.
You may buy land now as cheap as stinking mackerel.

PRINCE. Why then, it is like, if there come a hot June and this civil
buffeting hold, we shall buy maidenheads[3] as they buy hobnails:
by the hundreds. 310

FALSTAFF. By the mass, lad, thou sayst true; it is like we shall have
good trading that way. But tell me, Hal, art not thou horrible
afeard? Thou being heir-apparent, could the world pick thee out
three such enemies again as that fiend Douglas, that spirit Percy,
and that devil Glendower? Art thou not horribly afraid? Doth not 315
thy blood thrill at it?

PRINCE. Not a whit, i'faith. I lack some of thy instinct.

FALSTAFF. Well, thou wilt be horribly chid tomorrow when thou
comest to thy father. If thou love me, practice an answer.

PRINCE. Do thou stand for my father, and examine me upon the 320
particulars of my life.

FALSTAFF. Shall I? Content. This chair shall be my state,[4] this dagger
my scepter, and this cushion my crown.

PRINCE. Thy state is taken for a joint-stool, thy golden scepter for
a leaden dagger, and thy precious rich crown for a pitiful bald 325
crown.[5]

---

1 (1) courage (2) metal: good metal would not run or melt.
2 Scots.
3 Virginities.
4 Throne.
5 Head.

2.4.322: "THIS CHAIR SHALL BE MY STATE"
(TLN 1334)

Clear stage directions are conveyed within the dialogue for this rehearsal of Hal's interview with his father. Falstaff mobilizes a joint-stool, leaden dagger, and cushion to represent throne, scepter and crown; and lines like "here is my leg" and "here I stand" direct the positioning of bodies on stage. The staging of this scene seems to have changed very little over the centuries (though, strangely, it was omitted from many nineteenth-century productions). Both Falstaff and Hal sit in state to portray King Henry; both apparently stand up to play the prince. On an Elizabethan stage with pillars, Falstaff would have to position his "throne" a fair way downstage to ensure good sight-lines for his long speeches in "King Cambyses' vein." His listeners would have to be arranged so as not to block the view of his seated figure for an audience on three sides of the stage. They might sit or kneel on the stage floor, or the stool might be raised in some way (in modern productions his stool is often placed on a table). Throughout the inner play Falstaff and Hal play to two audiences. For an Elizabethan audience surrounding the action, and able to see the crowd enjoying the mirth beyond the stage and in galleries above, onstage and offstage audiences would easily merge. The audience becomes part of the rowdy tavern scene and an intimate link is established between actor and spectators. The scene conveys the added fun of seeing an accomplished actor *over*act in an outmoded style: this adds a metatheatrical edge to Falstaff's performance, reminding the audience of the layers of performance being presented on stage.

ABOVE: Michael Gambon as Falstaff in *Henry IV, Part One*, directed by Nicholas Hytner, National Theatre, London, 2005. National Theatre Archive. Photo © Catherine Ashmore.

FALSTAFF. Well, an the fire of grace be not quite out of thee, now
shalt thou be moved. Give me a cup of sack to make my eyes look
red, that it may be thought I have wept; for I must speak in pas-
sion, and I will do it in King Cambyses' vein.[1]   330

PRINCE. Well, here is my leg.[2]

FALSTAFF. And here is my speech. Stand aside, nobility.

HOSTESS. O Jesu, this is excellent sport, i'faith.

FALSTAFF. Weep not, sweet Queen, for trickling tears are vain.

HOSTESS. O the Father, how he holds his countenance!   335

FALSTAFF. For God's sake, lords, convey[3] my tristful[4] Queen,
For tears do stop the floodgates of her eyes.

HOSTESS. O Jesu, he doth it as like one of these harlotry[5] players
as ever I see!

FALSTAFF. Peace, good pint-pot; peace, good tickle-brain—Harry, I   340
do not only marvel where thou spendest thy time, but also how
thou art accompanied. For though the camomile, the more it is
trodden on, the faster it grows,[6] so youth, the more it is wasted,
the sooner it wears. That thou art my son I have partly thy mother's word, partly my own opinion, but chiefly a villainous trick[7]   345
of thine eye, and a foolish hanging of thy nether[8] lip, that doth
warrant me. If then thou be son to me, here lies the point. Why,
being son to me, art thou so pointed at? Shall the blessed sun of
heaven prove a micher,[9] and eat blackberries? A question not to
be asked. Shall the son of England prove a thief, and take purses?   350
A question to be asked. There is a thing, Harry, which thou hast
often heard of, and it is known to many in our land by the name
of pitch.[10] This pitch, as ancient writers do report, doth defile. So

---

1 In the overblown style of the play *Cambyses, King of Persia* (1569) by Thomas
Preston.

2 My bow.

3 Escort.

4 Sorrowful; see A Note on the Text, p. 62.

5 Trashy.

6 Proverbial (Dent C34).

7 Trait.

8 Lower.

9 Truant.

10 A dark resinous substance derived from tar. Falstaff echoes Ecclesiasticus 13.1,
"He that toucheth pitch, shall be defiled with it."

doth the company thou keepest. For, Harry, now I do not speak
355   to thee in drink, but in tears; not in pleasure, but in passion; not
in words only, but in woes also. And yet there is a virtuous man
whom I have often noted in thy company, but I know not his
name.

PRINCE. What manner of man, an it like your majesty?

360   FALSTAFF. A goodly, portly man, i'faith, and a corpulent; of a cheerful look, a pleasing eye, and a most noble carriage; and, as I think,
his age some fifty, or, by'r Lady, inclining to threescore. And now
I remember me, his name is Falstaff. If that man should be lewdly
given, he deceiveth me; for, Harry, I see virtue in his looks. If,
365   then, the tree may be known by the fruit, as the fruit by the tree,
then peremptorily[1] I speak it: there is virtue in that Falstaff. Him
keep with, the rest banish. And tell me now, thou naughty varlet,
tell me, where hast thou been this month?

PRINCE. Dost thou speak like a king? Do thou stand for me, and
370   I'll play my father.

FALSTAFF. Depose me. If thou dost it half so gravely, so majestically,
both in word and matter, hang me up by the heels for a rabbit
sucker,[2] or a poulter's[3] hare.

PRINCE. Well, here I am set.

375   FALSTAFF. And here I stand. Judge, my masters.

PRINCE. Now, Harry, whence come you?

FALSTAFF. My noble lord, from Eastcheap.

PRINCE. The complaints I hear of thee are grievous.

FALSTAFF. 'Sblood, my lord, they are false. [*Aside*] Nay, I'll tickle ye[4]
380   for a young prince i'faith.

PRINCE. Swearest thou, ungracious boy? Henceforth ne'er look on
me. Thou art violently carried away from grace. There is a devil
haunts thee in the likeness of an old fat man; a tun[5] of man is
thy companion. Why dost thou converse with that trunk[6] of

---

1 Conclusively.
2 Baby rabbit.
3 Poultry dealer's.
4 I'll amuse you (Falstaff drops out of character for a moment).
5 (1) a large barrel, or (2) ton.
6 (1) a large chest or container (2) torso.

humors,[1] that bolting-hutch[2] of beastliness, that swollen parcel   385
of dropsies,[3] that huge bombard[4] of sack, that stuffed cloak-bag
of guts, that roasted Manningtree ox[5] with the pudding[6] in his
belly, that reverend Vice, that gray Iniquity, that father Ruffian,
that Vanity[7] in years? Wherein is he good, but to taste sack and
drink it? Wherein neat and cleanly, but to carve a capon and eat   390
it? Wherein cunning, but in craft? Wherein crafty, but in villainy?
Wherein villainous, but in all things? Wherein worthy, but in
nothing?

FALSTAFF. I would your grace would take me with you. Whom
means your grace?   395

PRINCE. That villainous, abominable misleader of youth, Falstaff;
that old white-bearded Satan.

FALSTAFF. My lord, the man I know.

PRINCE. I know thou dost.

FALSTAFF. But to say I know more harm in him than in myself were   400
to say more than I know. That he is old, the more the pity, his
white hairs do witness it. But that he is, saving your reverence,[8] a
whoremaster, that I utterly deny. If sack and sugar be a fault, God
help the wicked. If to be old and merry be a sin, then many an
old host that I know is damned. If to be fat be to be hated, then   405
Pharaoh's lean kine[9] are to be loved. No, my good lord, banish
Peto, banish Bardolph, banish Poins, but for sweet Jack Falstaff,
kind Jack Falstaff, true Jack Falstaff, valiant Jack Falstaff, and
therefore more valiant being, as he is, old Jack Falstaff, banish
not him thy Harry's company, banish not him thy Harry's com-   410
pany. Banish plump Jack, and banish all the world.

PRINCE. I do, I will.

---

1 Moods, or the excess bodily fluids which were thought to cause them.
2 Sifting bin.
3 Watery fluids creating the disease known as "dropsy."
4 Leather wine-cask.
5 Roasted ox from the fair at Manningtree.
6 Stuffing.
7 Hal lists a series of characters from morality plays: Vice, Iniquity, Ruffian, and
Vanity.
8 An apologetic saying: "with all due respect."
9 Cattle. In Genesis 41, the seven lean kine of Pharaoh's dream presage seven
years of famine.

[Knocking within. Exeunt Hostess, Francis, and Bardolph.]

Enter Bardolph running.

BARDOLPH. O my lord, my lord, the sheriff with a most monstrous watch[1] is at the door.

415 FALSTAFF. Out, ye rogue! Play out the play! I have much to say in the behalf of that Falstaff.

Enter the Hostess.

HOSTESS. O Jesu! My lord, my lord!

PRINCE. Heigh, heigh, the devil rides upon a fiddlestick![2] What's the matter?

420 HOSTESS. The sheriff and all the watch are at the door. They are come to search the house. Shall I let them in?

FALSTAFF. Dost thou hear, Hal? Never call a true piece of gold a counterfeit. Thou art essentially made, without seeming so.[3]

PRINCE. And thou a natural coward without instinct.

425 FALSTAFF. I deny your major.[4] If you will deny the sheriff, so. If not, let him enter. If I become not a cart[5] as well as another man, a plague on my bringing up.[6] I hope I shall as soon be strangled with a halter as another.

PRINCE. Go, hide thee behind the arras.[7] The rest walk up above.

430 Now, my masters, for a true face and good conscience.

FALSTAFF. Both which I have had, but their date is out;[8] and therefore I'll hide me.

[Falstaff hides.]

PRINCE. Call in the sheriff.

[Exeunt all but the prince and Peto.]

---

1 Watchmen, officers responsible for keeping order in the streets.
2 I.e., here's a fine commotion (OED).
3 Made of genuine stuff, despite appearances.
4 (1) premise, but also a quibble on (2) officer, or possibly (3) mayor (like the sheriff, a high-ranking official of London).
5 I.e., gallows cart.
6 (1) upbringing, but also (2) bringing up to the gallows.
7 Heavy tapestry wall-hanging.
8 Lease has expired.

Enter Sheriff and the Carrier.

PRINCE. Now Master Sheriff, what is your will with me?

SHERIFF. First pardon me my lord. A hue and cry[1]   435
   Hath followed certain men unto this house.

PRINCE. What men?

SHERIFF. One of them is well known, my gracious lord,
   A gross fat man.

CARRIER. As fat as butter.   440

PRINCE. The man, I do assure you, is not here,
   For I myself at this time have employed him.
   And, Sheriff, I will engage° my word to thee   *pledge*
   That I will by tomorrow dinner-time[2]
   Send him to answer thee, or any man,   445
   For anything he shall be charged withal.
   And so let me entreat you leave the house.

SHERIFF. I will, my lord. There are two gentlemen
   Have in this robbery lost three hundred marks.

PRINCE. It may be so. If he have robbed these men,   450
   He shall be answerable.[3] And so, farewell.

SHERIFF. Good night, my noble lord.

PRINCE. I think it is good morrow,° is it not?   *morning*

SHERIFF. Indeed, my lord, I think it be two o'clock.

                              Exit [*with Carrier*].

PRINCE. This oily rascal is known as well as Paul's.[4] Go call him   455
   forth.

PETO. Falstaff!

                           [*He draws back the arras.*]
Fast asleep behind the arras, and snorting like a horse.

PRINCE. Hark how hard he fetches breath. Search his pockets.

            [*Peto*] *searches his pocket, and finds certain papers.*

PRINCE. What hast thou found?   460

---

1 Outcry calling for the pursuit of a felon (OED), or the pursuit itself.

2 I.e., around noon.

3 Liable to be called to account.

4 St. Paul's Cathedral, a well-known meeting place and a notorious haunt for
thieves and pickpockets.

PETO. Nothing but papers, my lord.

PRINCE. Let's see what they be, read them.

[PETO]. [*reading*] Item: a capon. 2s. 2d.[1]

ITEM: sauce. 4d.

465 ITEM: sack, two gallons. 5s. 8d.

ITEM: anchovies and sack after supper. 2s. 6d.

ITEM: bread. ob.[2]

[PRINCE]. Oh, monstrous! But one halfpennyworth of bread to this
intolerable deal of sack! What there is else, keep close;[3] we'll read

470 it at more advantage. There let him sleep till day. I'll to the court
in the morning. We must all to the wars, and thy place shall be
honorable. I'll procure this fat rogue a charge of foot,[4] and I know
his death will be a march of twelve score.[5] The money shall be
paid back again, with advantage.[6] Be with me betimes[7] in the

475 morning; and so good morrow, Peto.

PETO. Good morrow, good my lord.   *Exeunt.*

[3.1][8]

Enter Hotspur, Worcester, Lord Mortimer, Owen Glendower.

MORTIMER. These promises are fair, the parties sure,
    And our induction[9] full of prosperous hope.

HOTSPUR. Lord Mortimer and cousin[10] Glendower, will you sit
    down? And uncle Worcester—a plague upon it, I have forgot

5   the map!

GLENDOWER. No here it is;
    Sit, cousin Percy, sit, good cousin Hotspur;
    For by that name as oft as Lancaster[11] doth speak of you,

---

1 Two shillings and two pence (perhaps pronounced "two shillings and
tuppence").

2 A halfpenny (an abbreviation of "obolus").

3 Secret.

4 A company of infantry.

5 240 paces.

6 Interest.

7 Early.

8 This scene appears to be set in Glendower's own home in Wales.

9 First step in an undertaking; also an introductory speech to a play.

10 Kinsman.

11 Henry IV: Glendower prefers not to recognize Henry as king.

His cheek looks pale, and with a rising sigh
He wisheth you in heaven.
HOTSPUR.   And you in hell,   10
As oft as he hears Owen Glendower spoke of.
GLENDOWER. I cannot blame him. At my nativity
The front of heaven[1] was full of fiery shapes,
Of burning cressets,[2] and at my birth
The frame and huge foundation of the earth   15
Shaked like a coward.
HOTSPUR. Why, so it would have done at the same season if your
mother's cat had but kittened, though yourself had never been
born.
GLENDOWER. I say the earth did shake when I was born.   20
HOTSPUR. And I say the earth was not of my mind,
If you suppose as fearing you it shook.
GLENDOWER. The heavens were all on fire, the earth did tremble.
HOTSPUR. Oh, then the earth shook to see the heavens on fire,
And not in fear of your nativity.   25
Diseasèd nature oftentimes breaks forth
In strange eruptions; oft the teeming° earth   *breeding, fertile*
Is with a kind of colic[3] pinched and vexed
By the imprisoning of unruly wind
Within her womb, which for enlargement striving[4]   30
Shakes the old beldam° earth, and topples down   *grandmother*
Steeples and moss-grown towers. At your birth
Our grandam earth, having this distemperature,[5]
In passion° shook.   *physical suffering*
GLENDOWER.   Cousin, of many men
I do not bear these crossings.° Give me leave   *contradictions* 35
To tell you once again that at my birth
The front of heaven was full of fiery shapes,
The goats ran from the mountains, and the herds

---

1 Heaven's brow, the sky.
2 Vessels holding lighted oil and functioning as lamps.
3 Griping pains in the stomach.
4 Striving to get out.
5 Inclemency; disordered or distempered condition (OED).

Were strangely clamorous to the frighted fields.
40　These signs have marked me extraordinary,
　　And all the courses of my life do show
　　I am not in the roll of common men.
　　Where is he living, clipped in° with the sea　　　　*surrounded by*
　　That chides° the banks of England, Scotland, Wales,　　*punishes*
45　Which calls me pupil or hath read to° me?　　　　*lectured*
　　And bring him out that is but woman's son
　　Can trace me[1] in the tedious ways of art,[2]
　　And hold me pace° in deep experiments.　　　　*keep up with me*
HOTSPUR. I think there's no man speaks better Welsh.[3]
50　I'll to dinner.
MORTIMER. Peace, cousin Percy, you will make him mad.
GLENDOWER. I can call spirits from the vasty deep.
HOTSPUR. Why so can I, or so can any man,
　　But will they come when you do call for them?
55 GLENDOWER. Why, I can teach you, cousin, to command the devil.
HOTSPUR. And I can teach thee, coz, to shame the devil,
　　By telling truth: "Tell truth, and shame the devil."[4]
　　If thou have power to raise him, bring him hither,
　　And I'll be sworn I have power to shame him hence.
60　Oh, while you live, tell truth and shame the devil.
MORTIMER. Come, come, no more of this unprofitable chat.
GLENDOWER. Three times hath Henry Bolingbroke made head[5]
　　Against my power; thrice from the banks of Wye[6]
　　And sandy-bottomed Severn have I sent him
65　Bootless[7] home, and weather-beaten back.
HOTSPUR. Home without boots, and in foul weather too!

1　Follow me.
2　Learning, especially in the arts of magic and necromancy.
3　Synonymous with boasting, unintelligibility, and conversing with devils
(Bevington), hence a thinly-veiled insult.
4　Proverbial (Dent T566).
5　Raised an army.
6　The River Wye flows into the Severn Estuary, which separates Wales and
England.
7　Without booty or success.

How scapes he agues,[1] in the devil's name?

GLENDOWER. Come, here is the map. Shall we divide our right,
According to our threefold order ta'en?

MORTIMER. The Archdeacon[2] hath divided it   70
Into three limits very equally:
England from Trent and Severn hitherto
By south and east is to my part assigned;
All westward, Wales beyond the Severn shore
And all the fertile land within that bound,   75
To Owen Glendower; and, dear coz, to you
The remnant northward lying off from Trent.
And our indentures tripartite[3] are drawn,
Which, being sealèd interchangeably[4]—
A business that this night may execute[5]—   80
Tomorrow, cousin Percy, you and I
And my good lord of Worcester will set forth
To meet your father and the Scottish power,
As is appointed us, at Shrewsbury.
My father[6] Glendower is not ready yet,   85
Nor shall we need his help these fourteen days.
[*To Glendower*] Within that space you may have drawn together
Your tenants, friends, and neighboring gentlemen.

GLENDOWER. A shorter time shall send me to you, lords;
And in my conduct° shall your ladies come,   *escort, safe conduct* 90
From whom you now must steal and take no leave;
For there will be a world of water shed
Upon the parting of your wives and you.

HOTSPUR. Methinks my moiety north from Burton[7] here
In quantity equals not one of yours.   95

---

1   How does he escape fevers.
2   The Archdeacon of Bangor in north-west Wales, one of the oldest bishoprics in
Britain. This Archdeacon does not appear in the play.
3   Three-way contract, made up in triplicate.
4   Each copy would be marked with the seal of each of the three signatories.
5   Can be done this night.
6   I.e., father-in-law.
7   My share north of the river at Burton-upon-Trent.

See how this river comes me cranking in,[1]
And cuts me from the best of all my land
A huge half-moon, a monstrous cantle,° out.   *segment*
I'll have the current in this place dammed up,
100   And here the smug° and silver Trent shall run   *smooth*
In a new channel fair and evenly.
It shall not wind with such a deep indent,
To rob me of so rich a bottom[2] here.
GLENDOWER. Not wind? It shall, it must—you see it doth.
105   MORTIMER. Yea, but mark how he bears his course, and runs me
      up
With like advantage on the other side,
Gelding the opposèd continent as much[3]
As on the other side it takes from you.
WORCESTER. Yea, but a little charge will trench him here,
110   And on this north side win this cape of land,
And then he runs straight and even.
HOTSPUR. I'll have it so; a little charge will do it.
GLENDOWER. I'll not have it altered.
HOTSPUR. Will not you?
115   GLENDOWER. No, nor you shall not.
HOTSPUR. Who shall say me nay?
GLENDOWER. Why, that will I.
HOTSPUR. Let me not understand you, then: speak it in Welsh.
GLENDOWER. I can speak English, lord, as well as you,
120   For I was trained up in the English court,
Where, being but young, I framèd to the harp°   *set to harp music*
Many an English ditty lovely well,
And gave the tongue° a helpful ornament—   *language*
A virtue that was never seen in you.
125   HOTSPUR. Marry, and I am glad of it with all my heart.
I had rather be a kitten and cry "mew"
Than one of these same meter ballad-mongers.[4]

---

1   Comes winding in.
2   Valley, fertile river flats.
3   Cutting off as much from the opposite bank.
4   Sellers of metrical ballads, simple popular verses that were often about scandal-
ous events.

I had rather hear a brazen can'stick[1] turned,[2]
Or a dry wheel grate on the axle-tree,°   *axle*
And that would set my teeth nothing on edge,   130
Nothing so much as mincing[3] poetry.
'Tis like the forced gait of a shuffling nag.
GLENDOWER. Come, you shall have Trent turned.
HOTSPUR. I do not care. I'll give thrice so much land
To any well-deserving friend;   135
But in the way of bargain, mark ye me,
I'll cavil° on the ninth part of a hair.   *debate*
Are the indentures drawn? Shall we be gone?
GLENDOWER. The moon shines fair. You may away by night.
I'll haste the writer,[4] and withal   140
Break with your wives of your departure hence.
I am afraid my daughter will run mad,
So much she doteth on her Mortimer.   *Exit.*
MORTIMER. Fie, cousin Percy, how you cross my father!
HOTSPUR. I cannot choose. Sometime he angers me   145
With telling me of the moldwarp[5] and the ant,
Of the dreamer Merlin[6] and his prophecies,
And of a dragon and a finless fish,
A clip-winged griffin[7] and a molten° raven,   *featherless*
A couching lion and a ramping cat,[8]   150
And such a deal of skimble-skamble[9] stuff
As puts me from my faith.[10] I tell you what,
He held me last night at the least nine hours
In reckoning up the several devils' names

---

1 Brass candle stick.
2 Formed by rotating in a lathe.
3 Overly dainty, effeminate: usually used to describe an affected way of walking.
4 Hurry up the scrivener (who has to write out three copies of their agreement).
5 Mole, associated with blindness. The mole represents Henry IV.
6 The wizard of Arthurian legend, famous for his prophecies.
7 A mythical beast, half eagle and half lion.
8 Hotspur mocks the heraldic terms "couchant" (lying down) and "rampant" (rearing).
9 Confused, nonsensical.
10 Is enough to make me irreligious.

"SKIMBLE-SKAMBLE STUFF"
(TLN 1684)

Hotspur's complaint about Glendower's fanciful stories draws on
the suggestion in Shakespeare's sources that Welsh prophecies fueled
the conspiracy. Holinshed writes, "This was done (as some have said)
through a foolish credit given to a vain prophesy, as though King Henry
was the moldwarp, cursed of God's own mouth, and they three were the
dragon, the lion, and the wolf, which should divide this realm between
them" (see Appendix A1, p. 189). The legendary figure of Merlin—supposedly born in Wales—is brought into the story in Hall and *A Mirror
for Magistrates* (Appendices A3 and A5). Even more so than Holinshed
and other chronicle sources, *A Mirror* is scathing about the destructive-
ness of the prophecies, and suggests that Glendower and his confederates sought out hereditary badges and crests to prove their links with
the prophecy (see Appendix A5, p. 225). The dragon, lion, and white
wolf are the crests respectively of Glendower, Hotspur, and Mortimer
(Bevington). In *Henry IV, Part One*, Hotspur clearly wants to dissociate
himself from this aspect of the conspiracy and his list of heraldic beasts
is delivered in mocking terms.

Coat of arms of Sir Henry Percy (Hotspur).

That were his lackeys.[1] I cried "Hum," and "Well, go to,"   155
But marked him not a word. Oh, he is as tedious
As a tired horse, a railing° wife,   *complaining*
Worse than a smoky house. I had rather live
With cheese and garlic, in a windmill, far,
Than feed on cates° and have him talk to me   *delicacies* 160
In any summer house in Christendom.
MORTIMER. In faith, he is a worthy gentleman,
  Exceedingly well read, and profited°   *proficient*
  In strange concealments,° valiant as a lion,   *occult arts*
  And wondrous affable, and as bountiful   165
  As mines of India. Shall I tell you, cousin?
  He holds your temper in a high respect,
  And curbs himself even of his natural scope
  When you come 'cross his humor, faith, he does.
  I warrant you, that man is not alive   170
  Might so have tempted him as you have done
  Without the taste of danger and reproof.
  But do not use it oft, let me entreat you.
WORCESTER. In faith, my lord, you are too willful-blame,[2]
  And since your coming hither have done enough   175
  To put him quite besides his patience.
  You must needs learn, lord, to amend this fault.
  Though sometimes it show greatness, courage, blood—
  And that's the dearest grace it renders you—
  Yet oftentimes it doth present harsh rage,   180
  Defect of manners, want of government,[3]
  Pride, haughtiness, opinion, and disdain,
  The least of which, haunting[4] a nobleman,
  Loseth men's hearts, and leaves behind a stain
  Upon the beauty of all parts besides,[5]   185
  Beguiling° them of commendation.   *cheating*

---

1 Servants.
2 Blameworthy for being willful.
3 Lack of self-control.
4 Habitually associated with.
5 Other qualities the person might possess.

HOTSPUR. Well, I am schooled. Good manners be your speed![1]
Here come our wives, and let us take our leave.

Enter Glendower with the Ladies.
MORTIMER. This is the deadly spite that angers me:
190 My wife can speak no English, I no Welsh.
GLENDOWER. My daughter weeps; she'll not part with you.
She'll be a soldier too, she'll to the wars.
MORTIMER. Good father, tell her that she and my aunt Percy[2]
Shall follow in your conduct speedily.

Glendower speaks to her in Welsh, and she answers him in the same.
195 GLENDOWER. She is desperate here, a peevish self-willed harlotry,[3]
One that no persuasion can do good upon.

The lady speaks in Welsh.
MORTIMER. I understand thy looks. That pretty Welsh[4]
Which thou pourest down from these swelling heavens
I am too perfect in, and but for shame
200 In such a parley[5] should I answer thee.

The lady [speaks] again in Welsh.
MORTIMER. I understand thy kisses, and thou mine,
And that's a feeling disputation;[6]
But I will never be a truant,° love,   *absent pupil*
Till I have learnt thy language, for thy tongue
205 Makes Welsh as sweet as ditties highly penned,[7]
Sung by a fair queen in a summer's bower
With ravishing division,[8] to her lute.
GLENDOWER. Nay, if you melt, then will she run mad.

---

1 Bring you good fortune (a common saying).
2 I.e., Kate: see p. 100, n. 5, TLN 928.
3 Wantonness, here affectionately implying disobedience.
4 I.e., her tears.
5 Exchange of views. Mortimer is claiming that he could cry too.
6 (1) a heartfelt exchange (2) a debate conducted through touch.
7 Skillfully written.
8 An ornate and rapid passage of notes.

The lady speaks again in Welsh.

MORTIMER. Oh, I am ignorance itself in this!

GLENDOWER. She bids you on the wanton[1] rushes lay you down   210
  And rest your gentle head upon her lap,
  And she will sing the song that pleaseth you,
  And on your eyelids crown the god of sleep,
  Charming your blood with pleasing heaviness,
  Making such difference 'twixt wake and sleep   215
  As is the difference betwixt day and night
  The hour before the heavenly-harnessed team[2]
  Begins his golden progress in the east.

MORTIMER. With all my heart, I'll sit and hear her sing.
  By that time will our book,[3] I think, be drawn.   220

GLENDOWER. Do so, and those musicians that shall play to you
  Hang in the air a thousand leagues from hence,
  And straight they shall be here. Sit and attend.

HOTSPUR. Come, Kate, thou art perfect in lying down.
  Come, quick, quick, that I may lay my head in thy lap.   225

LADY PERCY. Go, ye giddy goose!

The music plays.

HOTSPUR. Now I perceive the devil understands Welsh;
  And 'tis no marvel he is so humorous.°   *capricious*
  By'r Lady, he is a good musician.

LADY PERCY. Then should you be nothing but musical,   230
  For you are altogether governed by humors.
  Lie still, ye thief, and hear the lady sing in Welsh.

HOTSPUR. I had rather hear Lady my brach° howl in Irish.   *bitch*

LADY PERCY. Wouldst thou have thy head broken?

HOTSPUR. No.   235

LADY PERCY. Then be still.°   *silent*

HOTSPUR. Neither, 'tis a woman's fault.

LADY PERCY. Now God help thee!

---

1 Luxuriant.
2 Horses that draw the sun's chariot.
3 Documents: the *indentures tripartite* discussed at 3.1.78, TLN 1608.

HOTSPUR. To the Welsh lady's bed.

240 LADY PERCY. What's that?

HOTSPUR. Peace, she sings.

Here the lady sings a Welsh song.

HOTSPUR. Come, Kate, I'll have your song too.

LADY PERCY. Not mine, in good sooth.

HOTSPUR. Not yours, in good sooth!

245   Heart, you swear like a comfit-maker's° wife: *confectioner's*

    "Not you, in good sooth!" and "As true as I live!"

    And "As God shall mend me!" and "As sure as day!":

    And givest such sarcenet[1] surety for thy oaths

    As if thou never walk'st further than Finsbury.[2]

250   Swear me, Kate, like a lady as thou art,

    A good mouth-filling oath, and leave "in sooth"

    And such protest of pepper gingerbread[3]

    To velvet-guards[4] and Sunday citizens.[5]

    Come sing.

255 LADY PERCY. I will not sing.

HOTSPUR. 'Tis the next way to turn tailor,[6] or be redbreast[7] teacher. An the indentures be drawn, I'll away within these two hours; and so come in when ye will.

Exit.

GLENDOWER. Come, come, Lord Mortimer, you are as slow

260   As hot Lord Percy is on fire to go.

    By this our book is drawn.[8] We'll but seal,

    And then to horse immediately.

MORTIMER. With all my heart.   *Exeunt.*

---

1 A very fine, soft silk.

2 Finsbury fields, a popular walking place for London citizens and their wives (in Shakespeare's time, not Hotspur's).

3 A protestation that, like gingerbread, is sweet, crumbly, and only mildly spicy.

4 Those wearing garments trimmed with velvet.

5 Middle-class folk in their "Sunday best."

6 Another group of citizens: supposedly tailors, like weavers, sang at their work.

7 A bird: the European robin.

8 Documents are drawn up.

[3.2]¹

Enter the king, Prince of Wales, and others.

KING. Lords, give us leave. The Prince of Wales and I
   Must have some private conference; but be near at hand,
   For we shall presently have need of you.   *Exeunt Lords.*
   I know not whether God will have it so
   For some displeasing service I have done,   5
   That in his secret doom° out of my blood   *judgment*
   He'll breed revengement and a scourge² for me,
   But thou dost in thy passages of life³
   Make me believe that thou art only marked
   For° the hot vengeance and the rod of heaven   *as* 10
   To punish my mistreadings. Tell me else,°   *how otherwise*
   Could such inordinate and low desires,
   Such poor, such bare, such lewd, such mean attempts,⁴
   Such barren pleasures, rude society,
   As thou art matched withal and grafted to,   15
   Accompany the greatness of thy blood,
   And hold their level⁵ with thy princely heart?
PRINCE. So please your majesty, I would I could
   Quit° all offenses with as clear excuse   *clear myself of*
   As well as I am doubtless I can purge   20
   Myself of many I am charged withal.
   Yet such extenuation let me beg
   As, in reproof of many tales devised—
   Which oft the ear of greatness needs must hear—
   By smiling pickthanks⁶ and base newsmongers,   25
   I may, for some things true wherein my youth
   Hath faulty wandered and irregular,°   *and been irregular*

1 Prince Hal's comments in 2.4 suggest that this scene takes place somewhere at court.
2 Whip; figuratively a thing or person that is an instrument of divine chastisement (OED).
3 Actions; general behavior.
4 Undertakings.
5 Put themselves on the same level as.
6 Those who pick up thanks by informing against others.

"PRIVATE CONFERENCE"
WITH THE KING (TLN 1818)

Various sources describe an interview between Prince Henry and the king in which father and son are reconciled; however, Shakespeare alters the story significantly. According to Holinshed, the interview took place much later in Henry's reign, around 1412, when the court was at Westminster (Appendix A1, p. 198). In Holinshed, Stow, and *The Famous Victories*, the prince comes to his father with a group of his followers, having heard that his father suspects him of planning to usurp the throne (respectively, Appendix A1, p. 197; Appendix A2, p. 202; and Appendix A9, p. 257). The prince is obliged to leave his followers in the hall and formally meet the king in the presence of three or four trusted advisers. He wears a blue satin gown full of small eyelet holes with needles hanging by silk thread from every hole, and carries a dagger. In an extragavant gesture he hands the dagger to the king and offers his life to relieve the king of suspicion. After this their relationship is re-established.

The interview in *Henry IV, Part One* occurs earlier in Henry's reign (a second interview, at Henry IV's death-bed, appears in *Part Two*), it is more restrained, and crucially it is conducted in private. This means that Henry can talk openly with his son about the past, the tactics he used to gain the crown, and his theories about how his heir should conduct himself in order to consolidate power. In Shakespeare's hands it becomes a serious scene about statecraft and a nuanced representation of the father-son relationship.

Coronation of Henry IV, King of England from Jean Froissart's *Chronicles* (c. 1470). From Wikimedia Commons, http://www.commons.wikimedia.org.

Find pardon on my true submission.[1]
KING. God pardon thee! Yet let me wonder, Harry,
  At thy affections,° which do hold a wing   *inclinations* 30
  Quite from the flight of all thy ancestors.
  Thy place in Council thou hast rudely° lost,   *loutishly*
  Which by thy younger brother is supplied,
  And art almost an alien to the hearts
  Of all the court and princes of my blood.   35
  The hope and expectation of thy time
  Is ruined, and the soul of every man
  Prophetically do forethink thy fall.
  Had I so lavish of my presence been,
  So common-hackneyed in the eyes of men,   40
  So stale and cheap to vulgar company,
  Opinion, that did help me to the crown,
  Had still kept loyal to possession,[2]
  And left me in reputeless[3] banishment,
  A fellow of no mark nor likelihood.   45
  By being seldom seen, I could not stir
  But, like a comet, I was wondered at,
  That men would tell their children "This is he!"
  Others would say "Where, which is Bolingbroke?"
  And then I stole all courtesy from heaven,[4]   50
  And dressed myself in such humility
  That I did pluck allegiance from men's hearts,
  Loud shouts and salutations from their mouths,
  Even in the presence of the crownèd king.
  Thus did I keep my person fresh and new,   55
  My presence, like a robe pontifical,[5]
  Ne'er seen but wondered at, and so my state,[6]
  Seldom but sumptuous, showed like a feast,

---

1 Prince Hal is asking his father to extend the same pardon towards his true
faults as he deserves for the many false accusations which have been brought
against him.
2 (1) the right of possession (2) the then-current possessor (Richard II).
3 Devoid of repute, inglorious.
4 I assumed a bearing of heavenly graciousness (Bevington).
5 Belonging to a bishop, cardinal, or other high-ranking cleric.
6 Display of grandeur.

And won by rareness such solemnity.[1]
60 The skipping king, he ambled up and down
   With shallow jesters and rash bavin wits,[2]
   Soon kindled and soon burnt, carded his state,[3]
   Mingled his royalty with cap'ring[4] fools,
   Had his great name profanèd with their scorns,
65 And gave his countenance,[5] against his name,
   To laugh at gibing° boys, and stand the push[6]   *joking, insulting*
   Of every beardless vain comparative;[7]
   Grew a companion to the common streets,
   Enfeoffed himself to° popularity,   *Surrendered himself up to*
70 That, being daily swallowed by men's eyes,
   They surfeited with honey, and began
   To loathe the taste of sweetness, whereof a little
   More than a little is by much too much.
   So when he had occasion to be seen,
75 He was but as the cuckoo is in June,
   Heard, not regarded—seen, but with such eyes
   As, sick and blunted with community,°   *commonness*
   Afford no extraordinary gaze
   Such as is bent on sun-like majesty[8]
80 When it shines seldom in admiring eyes,
   But rather drowsed and hung their eyelids down,
   Slept in his face,[9] and rendered such aspect°   *demeanor*
   As cloudy° men use to their adversaries,   *sullen*
   Being with his presence glutted, gorged, and full.
85 And in that very line, Harry, standest thou;
   For thou hast lost thy princely privilege
   With vile participation.° Not an eye   *mixing in low company*
   But is a-weary of thy common sight

---

1 The dignity appropriate to a great feast.
2 Wits who, like bavin (brushwood kindling), create only a short-lived blaze.
3 (1) defaced the royal arms (2) vandalized his royal position.
4 Dancing in a frolicsome way.
5 Gave his patronage, but with the added sense of "his face" or "his presence."
6 Take the thrust.
7 Young worthless insult-maker.
8 See extended note on p. 77, TLN 298.
9 His presence.

Save mine, which hath desired to see thee more,
Which now doth that I would not have it do: 90
Make blind itself with foolish tenderness.

                                                      [*He weeps.*]

PRINCE. I shall hereafter, my thrice-gracious lord,
  Be more myself.
KING.   For all the world,
  As thou art to this hour was Richard then,
  When I from France set foot at Ravenspurgh,   95
  And even as I was then is Percy now.
  Now by my scepter, and my soul to boot,°   *as well*
  He hath more worthy interest° to the state   *right*
  Than thou, the shadow of succession;
  For, of no right, nor color like to[1] right,   100
  He doth fill fields with harness° in the realm,   *armor*
  Turns head[2] against the lion's armèd jaws,[3]
  And, being no more in debt to years than thou,
  Leads ancient lords and reverend bishops on
  To bloody battles, and to bruising arms.   105
· What never-dying honor hath he got
  Against renownèd Douglas, whose high deeds,
  Whose hot incursions and great name in arms,
  Holds from all soldiers chief majority[4]
  And military title capital°   *soldierly pre-eminence*   110
  Through all the kingdoms that acknowledge Christ.
  Thrice hath this Hotspur, Mars in swaddling-clothes,[5]
  This infant warrior, in his enterprises
  Discomfited great Douglas; ta'en him once;
  Enlargèd° him, and made a friend of him   *freed*   115
  To fill the mouth of deep defiance up,
  And shake the peace and safety of our throne.
  And what say you to this? Percy, Northumberland,

---

1 Anything resembling.
2 Leads a rebel force.
3 The king's power.
4 Pre-eminance, seniority.
5 Mars = the Roman god of war, in this image still a baby.

The Archbishop's grace of York, Douglas, Mortimer,
120   Capitulate[1] against us, and are up.[2]
But wherefore do I tell these news to thee?
Why, Harry, do I tell thee of my foes,
Which art my near'st and dearest enemy?
Thou that art like enough, through vassal° fear,   *servile, base*
125   Base inclination, and the start of spleen,[3]
To fight against me under Percy's pay,
To dog his heels and curtsy at his frowns,
To show how much thou art degenerate.
PRINCE. Do not think so; you shall not find it so.
130   And God forgive them that so much have swayed
Your majesty's good thoughts away from me.
I will redeem all this on Percy's head,
And in the closing of some glorious day
Be bold to tell you that I am your son,
135   When I will wear a garment all of blood,
And stain my favors[4] in a bloody mask,
Which, washed away, shall scour my shame with it.
And that shall be the day, whene'er it lights,
That this same child of honor and renown,
140   This gallant Hotspur, this all-praisèd knight,
And your unthought-of Harry chance to meet.
For every honor sitting on his helm,
Would they were multitudes, and on my head
My shames redoubled; for the time will come
145   That I shall make this northern youth exchange
His glorious deeds for my indignities.
Percy is but my factor,° good my lord,   *agent*
To engross up° glorious deeds on my behalf;   *buy up*
And I will call him to so strict account
150   That he shall render every glory up,
Yea, even the slightest worship of his time,

---

1 Draw up articles of agreement, arrange or propose terms.
2 Are up in arms.
3 Fit of spite or anger.
4 (1) features (2) battle insignia; see also 5.4.95, TLN 3061.

Or I will tear the reckoning[1] from his heart.
This, in the name of God, I promise here,
The which, if he be pleased I shall perform,
I do beseech your majesty may salve°   *heal*   155
The long-grown wounds of my intemperance;
If not, the end of life cancels all bonds,
And I will die a hundred thousand deaths
Ere break the smallest parcel of this vow.
KING. A hundred thousand rebels die in this.   160
Thou shalt have charge[2] and sovereign trust herein.

Enter Blunt.

How now, good Blunt? Thy looks are full of speed.
BLUNT. So hath the business that I come to speak of.
Lord Mortimer of Scotland hath sent word
That Douglas and the English rebels met   165
The eleventh of this month at Shrewsbury.
A mighty and a fearful head they are,
If promises be kept on every hand,
As ever offered foul play in a state.
KING. The Earl of Westmorland set forth today,   170
With him my son Lord John of Lancaster,
For this advertisement° is five days old.   *information*
On Wednesday next, Harry, you shall set forward,
On Thursday we ourselves will march.
Our meeting is Bridgnorth,[3] and, Harry, you   175
Shall march through Gloucestershire, by which account,
Our business valuèd, some twelve days hence
Our general forces at Bridgnorth shall meet.
Our hands are full of business; let's away.
Advantage[4] feeds him fat while men delay.   *Exeunt.*   180

---

1 What is owed, the account.
2 Command of an armed force.
3 A town 20 miles south-east of Shrewsbury, named after a bridge over the River
Severn.
4 Opportunity.

[3.3]¹

Enter Falstaff and Bardolph.

FALSTAFF. Bardolph, am I not fallen away vilely since this last action? Do I not bate? Do I not dwindle? Why, my skin hangs about me like an old lady's loose gown. I am withered like an old apple-john.² Well, I'll repent, and that suddenly, while I am in
5 some liking.³ I shall be out of heart shortly, and then I shall have no strength to repent. An I have not forgotten what the inside of a church is made of, I am a peppercorn, a brewer's horse.⁴ The inside of a church! Company, villainous company, hath been the spoil of me.
10 BARDOLPH. Sir John, you are so fretful you cannot live long.
FALSTAFF. Why, there is it. Come, sing me a bawdy song, make me merry. I was as virtuously given as a gentleman need to be, virtuous enough: swore little, diced not above seven times—a week, went to a bawdy-house not above once in a quarter—of
15 an hour, paid money that I borrowed—three or four times, lived well, and in good compass.⁵ And now I live out of all order, out of all compass.
BARDOLPH. Why, you are so fat, Sir John, that you must needs be out of all compass, out of all reasonable compass, Sir John.
20 FALSTAFF. Do thou amend thy face, and I'll amend my life. Thou art our admiral, thou bearest the lantern in the poop—but 'tis in the nose of thee. Thou art the Knight of the Burning Lamp.⁶
BARDOLPH. Why, Sir John, my face does you no harm.
FALSTAFF. No, I'll be sworn; I make as good use of it as many a man
25 doth of a death's head, or a *memento mori*.⁷ I never see thy face but

---

1 This scene returns to the tavern in Eastcheap as in 2.4.
2 A long-keeping apple, eaten when its skin shriveled.
3 In the right condition, in the mood.
4 A peppercorn is small and a brewer's horse would be old.
5 The bounds of moderation, reasonable limits.
6 Another reference to Bardolph's alcohol-induced complexion (cf. 2.4.270, TLN 1272), here parodying medieval romance heroes such as Amadis, Knight of the Burning Sword.
7 Reminder of death, like a skull ring.

I think upon hell-fire and Dives[1] that lived in purple—for there
he is in his robes, burning, burning. If thou wert any way given
to virtue, I would swear by thy face; my oath should be "By this
fire that's God's angel!"[2] But thou art altogether given over, and
wert indeed, but for the light in thy face, the son of utter dark-   30
ness. When thou rannest up Gad's Hill in the night to catch my
horse, if I did not think thou hadst been an *ignis fatuus*[3] or a ball of
wildfire, there's no purchase in money. Oh, thou art a perpetual
triumph, an everlasting bonfire-light! Thou hast saved me a thousand marks in links[4] and torches, walking with thee in the night   35
betwixt tavern and tavern—but the sack that thou hast drunk me
would have bought me lights as good cheap at the dearest chan-
dler's[5] in Europe. I have maintained that salamander[6] of yours
with fire any time this two-and-thirty years, God reward me for it.
BARDOLPH. 'Sblood, I would my face were in your belly!   40
FALSTAFF. God-a-mercy! So should I be sure to be heartburnt.

Enter Hostess.

How now, Dame Partlet[7] the hen, have you enquired yet who
picked my pocket?
HOSTESS. Why, Sir John, what do you think, Sir John? Do you think
I keep thieves in my house? I have searched, I have enquired; so   45
has my husband, man by man, boy by boy, servant by servant. The
tithe[8] of a hair was never lost in my house before.
FALSTAFF. Ye lie, hostess: Bardolph was shaved[9] and lost many a
hair, and I'll be sworn my pocket was picked. Go to, you are a
woman, go.   50

---

1 Dives, the rich man from the Lazarus parable, was clothed in purple and fine
linen and dined well every day while the beggar, Lazarus, starved to death at his
gate. After death and under torment in Hell, Dives lifted his eyes and saw Lazarus
in Abraham's bosom (Luke 16.19–31).
2 A reference to the story of Moses and the burning bush, "Then the angel of the
Lord appeared unto him in a flame of fire" (Exodus 3.2).
3 Will o'the wisp, literally "foolish fire."
4 Torches used to light dark streets.
5 Candle-maker's.
6 Kind of lizard, supposedly able to live in fire.
7 Traditional name for a hen.
8 Tenth.
9 (1) shaved by a barber (2) "ripped off."

HOSTESS. Who, I? No, I defy thee! God's light, I was never called so in mine own house before.

FALSTAFF. Go to, I know you well enough.

HOSTESS. No, Sir John, you do not know me, Sir John; I know you,
55   Sir John. You owe me money, Sir John, and now you pick a quarrel to beguile me of it. I bought you a dozen of shirts to your back.

FALSTAFF. Dowlas,[1] filthy dowlas. I have given them away to bakers' wives; they have made bolters[2] of them.

HOSTESS. Now as I am a true woman, holland[3] of eight shillings
60   an ell.[4] You owe money here besides, Sir John: for your diet, and by-drinkings,[5] and money lent you, four-and-twenty pound.

FALSTAFF. [Indicating Bardolph.] He had his part of it, let him pay.

HOSTESS. He? Alas he is poor, he hath nothing.

FALSTAFF. How, poor? Look upon his face. What call you rich? Let
65   them coin his nose, let them coin his cheeks, I'll not pay a denier.[6] What, will you make a younker[7] of me? Shall I not take mine ease in mine inn, but I shall have my pocket picked? I have lost a seal-ring of my grandfather's worth forty mark.[8]

HOSTESS. [To Bardolph] O Jesu, I have heard the prince tell him, I
70   know not how oft, that that ring was copper.

FALSTAFF. How? The prince is a Jack,[9] a sneak-up.[10] 'Sblood, an he were here I would cudgel him like a dog if he would say so.

Enter the prince [with Peto] marching, and Falstaff meets him playing upon his truncheon like a fife.

FALSTAFF. How now, lad, is the wind in that door,[11] i'faith? Must we all march?

75 BARDOLPH. Yea, two and two, Newgate[12] fashion.

---

1 A coarse linen, named after Doulas in Brittany.
2 Cloths used to sift flour.
3 Fine linen.
4 Common measure of textiles, 45 inches or about 114 cm.
5 Drinks between meals.
6 A small French coin, worth very little.
7 Fashionable and gullible young gentleman
8 I.e., worth about 26 pounds (see p. 91, n. 7, TLN 691).
9 Knave.
10 Sneak.
11 Is that the way things are going.
12 A London prison.

"YOUNKER": THE PRODIGAL SON
                    (TLN 2083)

Originally a Dutch term for a youth of high rank, "younker" is probably
an allusion to the parable of the prodigal son (Luke 15.11-31). Naseeb
Shaheen notes that the prodigal son is referred to as "the yonger" in the
parable (148). "Yonger" also appears in the Folio version of *The Merchant
of Venice*, "How like a yonger or a prodigall" (2.6.15, TLN 910). Falstaff
alludes to the story again (see 4.2.30, TLN 2408) and is associated with
the parable in *The Merry Wives of Windsor* (4.5.6-7, TLN 2227-28) and
Henry IV, Part Two (2.1.142-43, TLN 740-41).

In this scene Falstaff has already cast himself as someone led astray
by "villainous company." Ironically, in the broader scheme of the play
it is Prince Hal who most closely resembles the figure of the prodigal
son. The parable tells the story of a younger son who asks his father for
his share of his inheritance, then goes away and squanders everything
through wild living. At his lowest point he finds himself feeding pigs
and wanting to share their food. When he decides to return to his father
he is welcomed with unreserved enthusiasm. As a story about loss and
redemption it intersects in interesting ways with Prince Hal's plan to
redeem himself in the eyes of his father and the world.

Lucas van Leyden, "The Return of the Prodigal Son" (c.1510) print; Baltimore
Museum. From Wikimedia Commons, http://www.commons.wikimedia.org.

HOSTESS. My lord, I pray you hear me.

PRINCE. What sayst thou, Mistress Quickly? How doth thy husband? I love him well, he is an honest man.

HOSTESS. Good my lord, hear me!

80 FALSTAFF. Prithee, let her alone, and list to me.

PRINCE. What sayst thou, Jack?

FALSTAFF. The other night I fell asleep here behind the arras, and had my pocket picked. This house is turned bawdy-house: they pick pockets.

85 PRINCE. What didst thou lose, Jack?

FALSTAFF. Wilt thou believe me, Hal, three or four bonds of forty pound apiece, and a seal-ring of my grandfather's.

PRINCE. A trifle, some eightpenny matter.

HOSTESS. So I told him, my lord; and I said I heard your grace say

90 so; and, my lord, he speaks most vilely of you, like a foul-mouthed man as he is, and said he would cudgel you.

PRINCE. What? He did not!

HOSTESS. There's neither faith, truth, nor womanhood in me else.

FALSTAFF. There's no more faith in thee than in a stewed prune,[1] nor

95 no more truth in thee than in a drawn fox;[2] and, for womanhood, Maid Marian[3] may be the deputy's wife of the ward to thee.[4] Go, you thing, go!

HOSTESS. Say, what thing, what thing?[5]

FALSTAFF. What thing? Why, a thing to thank God on.

100 HOSTESS. I am no thing to thank God on. I would thou shouldst know it, I am an honest man's wife; and setting thy knighthood aside, thou art a knave to call me so.

FALSTAFF. Setting thy womanhood aside, thou art a beast to say otherwise.

105 HOSTESS. Say, what beast, thou knave, thou?

FALSTAFF. What beast? Why an otter.

---

1 Commonly served in brothels, hence associated with bawds and prostitutes.
2 A fox that has been drawn from its lair.
3 A character generally performed by boys in morris dances and associated with clowning and sluttish behavior.
4 May be a respectable woman compared to you.
5 The hostess probably suspects a bawdy quibble here (thing = male or female genitalia).

PRINCE. An otter, Sir John? Why an otter?

FALSTAFF. Why? She's neither fish nor flesh, a man knows not where
to have her.[1]

HOSTESS. Thou art an unjust man in saying so. Thou or any man   110
knows where to have me, thou knave, thou.

PRINCE. Thou sayst true, hostess, and he slanders thee most grossly.

HOSTESS. So he doth you my lord, and said this other day you owed
him a thousand pound.

PRINCE. Sirrah, do I owe you a thousand pound?   115

FALSTAFF. A thousand pound, Hal? A million! Thy love is worth a
million; thou owest me thy love.

HOSTESS. Nay, my lord, he called you Jack, and said he would cudgel
you.

FALSTAFF. Did I, Bardolph?   120

BARDOLPH. Indeed, Sir John, you said so.

FALSTAFF. Yea, if he said my ring was copper.

PRINCE. I say 'tis copper, darest thou be as good as thy word now?

FALSTAFF. Why, Hal, thou knowest as thou art but man I dare, but as
thou art prince, I fear thee as I fear the roaring of the lion's whelp.   125

PRINCE. And why not as the lion?

FALSTAFF. The king himself is to be feared as the lion. Dost thou
think I'll fear thee as I fear thy father? Nay, an I do, I pray God
my girdle break.

PRINCE. Oh, if it should, how would thy guts fall about thy knees!   130
But sirrah, there's no room for faith, truth, nor honesty in this
bosom of thine; it is all filled up with guts and midriff. Charge
an honest woman with picking thy pocket? Why, thou whoreson,
impudent, embossed[2] rascal, if there were anything in thy pocket
but tavern reckonings, memorandums of bawdy-houses, and one   135
poor pennyworth of sugar-candy to make thee long-winded[3]—if
thy pocket were enriched with any other injuries but these, I am
a villain. And yet you will stand to it,[4] you will not pocket up[5]
wrong. Art thou not ashamed?

---

1 How to take her meaning (as well as the obvious bawdy suggestion).
2 Swollen.
3 To give you staying-power.
4 Persist.
5 Accept.

140 FALSTAFF. Dost thou hear, Hal? Thou knowest in the state of innocency[1] Adam fell, and what should poor Jack Falstaff do in the
days of villainy? Thou seest I have more flesh than another man,
and therefore more frailty. You confess, then, you picked my
pocket?

145 PRINCE. It appears so by the story.

FALSTAFF. Hostess, I forgive thee. Go make ready breakfast. Love
thy husband, look to thy servants, cherish thy guests. Thou shalt
find me tractable[2] to any honest reason; thou seest I am pacified
still. [3] Nay, prithee, be gone.

Exit Hostess.

150 Now, Hal, to the news at court. For the robbery, lad, how is that
answered?

PRINCE. Oh, my sweet beef, I must still be good angel to thee. The
money is paid back again.

FALSTAFF. Oh, I do not like that paying back; 'tis a double labor.

155 PRINCE. I am good friends with my father and may do anything.

FALSTAFF. Rob me the exchequer the first thing thou dost, and do
it with unwashed hands[4] too.

BARDOLPH. Do, my lord.

PRINCE. I have procured thee, Jack, a charge of foot.[5]

160 FALSTAFF. I would it had been of horse! Where shall I find one that
can steal well? Oh, for a fine thief of the age of two-and-twenty or
thereabouts! I am heinously unprovided. Well, God be thanked
for these rebels: they offend none but the virtuous. I laud them,
I praise them.

165 PRINCE. Bardolph!

BARDOLPH. My lord?

PRINCE. [*Giving letters*] Go bear this letter to Lord John of
Lancaster,
To my brother John; this to my lord of Westmorland.

[*Exit Bardolph.*]

---

1 While living in the innocence of Eden.
2 Agreeable.
3 As always.
4 I.e., straight away.
5 Command of an infantry unit.

Go, Peto, to horse, to horse, for thou and I
Have thirty miles to ride yet ere dinner time.   [*Exit Peto.*]   170
Jack, meet me tomorrow in the Temple Hall[1]
At two o'clock in the afternoon.
There shalt thou know thy charge, and there receive
Money and order for their furniture.°   *equipment*
The land is burning, Percy stands on high,   175
And either we or they must lower lie.   [*Exit Prince.*]
FALSTAFF. Rare words! Brave world! Hostess, my breakfast, come!
    Oh, I could wish this tavern were my drum!   [*Exit.*]

[4.1][2]

[*Enter Hotspur, Worcester, and Douglas.*]
HOTSPUR. Well said, my noble Scot! If speaking truth
    In this fine age were not thought flattery,
    Such attribution should the Douglas have
    As not a soldier of this season's stamp[3]
    Should go so general current[4] through the world.   5
    By God, I cannot flatter, I do defy
    The tongues of soothers,° but a braver place   *flatterers*
    In my heart's love hath no man than yourself.
    Nay, task me° to my word, approve me,[5] lord.   *test me*
DOUGLAS. Thou art the king of honor.   10
    No man° so potent breathes upon the ground   *nobody else*
    But I will beard him.[6]

Enter [Messenger] with letters.
HOTSPUR.   Do so, and 'tis well.
    What letters hast thou there? [*To Douglas*] I can but thank you.
MESSENGER. These letters come from your father.

---

1 Inner Temple Hall of the Inns of Court, a common meeting place.
2 This scene is located in the rebel camp at Shrewsbury (see 3.2.165–66, TLN
1986–87).
3 This period's currency; minted at this time.
4 Should be so widely acclaimed.
5 Put me to the proof.
6 Challenge him to combat.

15 HOTSPUR. Letters from him? Why comes he not himself?
   MESSENGER. He cannot come, my lord; he is grievous sick.
   HOTSPUR. Zounds, how has he the leisure to be sick
      In such a jostling° time? Who leads his power?   *turbulent*
      Under whose government come they along?
20 MESSENGER. His letters bears his mind, not I, my lord.

                              [*Hotspur reads the letter.*]
   WORCESTER. I prithee tell me, doth he keep his bed?
   MESSENGER. He did, my lord, four days ere I set forth;
      And at the time of my departure thence
      He was much feared by his physicians.[1]
25 WORCESTER. I would the state of time had first been whole
      Ere he by sickness had been visited.
      His health was never better worth than now.
   HOTSPUR. Sick now? Droop now? This sickness doth infect
      The very life-blood of our enterprise.
30   'Tis catching hither, even to our camp.
      He writes me here that inward sickness—
      And that his friends by deputation[2]
      Could not so soon be drawn;[3] nor did he think it meet[4]
      To lay so dangerous and dear a trust
35   On any soul removed but on his own.
      Yet doth he give us bold advertisement°   *advice*
      That with our small conjunction[5] we should on,[6]
      To see how fortune is disposed to us;
      For, as he writes, there is no quailing now,
40   Because the king is certainly possessed
      Of all our purposes. What say you to it?
   WORCESTER. Your father's sickness is a maim to us.
   HOTSPUR. A perilous gash, a very limb lopped off.
      And yet, in faith, it is not. His present want°   *absence*

---

1 I.e., his physicians were fearful his illness could be fatal.
2 Through the requests of his deputies.
3 Mustered.
4 Appropriate.
5 Conjoined force.
6 We should go on.

Seems more than we shall find it. Were it good   45
To set the exact wealth of all our states
All at one cast? To set so rich a main[1]
On the nice hazard[2] of one doubtful hour?
It were not good, for therein should we read
The very bottom and the soul of hope,   50
The very list,° the very utmost bound,   *limit*
Of all our fortunes.

DOUGLAS. Faith, and so we should, where now remains
A sweet reversion[3]—we may boldly spend
Upon the hope of what is to come in.   55
A comfort of retirement[4] lives in this.

HOTSPUR. A rendezvous, a home to fly unto,
If that the devil and mischance look big°   *look threateningly*
Upon the maidenhead[5] of our affairs.

WORCESTER. But yet I would your father had been here.   60
The quality and hair° of our attempt   *character*
Brooks no division.[6] It will be thought
By some that know not why he is away
That wisdom, loyalty, and mere dislike
Of our proceedings kept the earl from hence;   65
And think how such an apprehension
May turn the tide of fearful faction,[7]
And breed a kind of question in our cause.
For, well you know, we of the off'ring side[8]
Must keep aloof from strict arbitrament,[9]   70
And stop all sight-holes, every loop[10] from whence
The eye of reason may pry in upon us.

---

1 (1) principal object, course or undertaking (2) military force (3) stake.
2 Finely poised risk.
3 Prospect of inheritance.
4 Retreat; a fall-back position.
5 The first stage (literally the hymen).
6 Will not allow division among us.
7 Dissension or mutiny through fear.
8 The side which is taking the offensive.
9 Inquiry into a dispute by an arbitrator.
10 An opening in a wall, to look through, or allow the passage of a missile.

This absence of your father's draws° a curtain   *opens*
That shows the ignorant a kind of fear
75   Before not dreamt of.
    HOTSPUR.   You strain too far.
    I rather of his absence make this use:
    It lends a luster, and more great opinion,
    A larger dare to our great enterprise,
80   Than if the earl were here; for men must think
    If we without his help can make a head
    To push against a kingdom, with his help
    We shall o'erturn it topsy-turvy down.
    Yet all goes well, yet all our joints are whole.
    DOUGLAS. As heart can think, there is not such a word
85   Spoke of in Scotland as this term of fear.

Enter Sir Richard Vernon.

HOTSPUR. My cousin Vernon! Welcome, by my soul!
VERNON. Pray God my news be worth a welcome, lord.
    The Earl of Westmorland, seven thousand strong,
    Is marching hitherwards; with him Prince John.
HOTSPUR. No harm. What more?
90   VERNON.   And further I have learned
    The king himself in person is set forth,
    Or hitherwards intended speedily,
    With strong and mighty preparation.
    HOTSPUR. He shall be welcome too. Where is his son,
95   The nimble-footed madcap Prince of Wales,
    And his comrades that daffed° the world aside   *tossed*
    And bid it pass?
    VERNON.   All furnished, all in arms,
    All plumed like ostriches, that with the wind
    Baited[1] like eagles having lately bathed,
100   Glittering in golden coats like images,
    As full of spirit as the month of May,
    And gorgeous as the sun at midsummer;[2]

---

1   Beat their wings, fluttered.
2   Cf. extended note on p. 77, TLN 298–304.

Wanton° as youthful goats, wild as young bulls.   *frisky*
I saw young Harry with his beaver[1] on,
His cuisses° on his thighs, gallantly armed,   *thigh plates* 105
Rise from the ground like feathered Mercury,[2]
And vaulted with such ease into his seat
As if an angel dropped down from the clouds
To turn and wind[3] a fiery Pegasus,[4]
And witch° the world with noble horsemanship.   *bewitch* 110
HOTSPUR. No more, no more! Worse than the sun in March,
This praise doth nourish agues.[5] Let them come!
They come like sacrifices in their trim,
And to the fire-eyed maid of smoky war[6]
All hot and bleeding will we offer them.   115
The mailèd Mars[7] shall on his altars sit
Up to the ears in blood. I am on fire
To hear this rich reprisal° is so nigh,   *reward*
And yet not ours! Come, let me taste my horse,
Who is to bear me like a thunderbolt   120
Against the bosom of the Prince of Wales.
Harry to Harry shall, hot horse to horse,
Meet and ne'er part till one drop down a corse.°   *corpse*
Oh, that Glendower were come!
VERNON.   There is more news,
I learned in Worcester, as I rode along,   125
He cannot draw his power this fourteen days.
DOUGLAS. That's the worst tidings that I hear of yet.
WORCESTER. Ay, by my faith, that bears a frosty sound.
HOTSPUR. What may the king's whole battle reach unto?
VERNON. To thirty thousand.
HOTSPUR.   Forty let it be.   130
My father and Glendower being both away,

---

1 The moveable face-guard of a helmet.
2 The messenger of the Gods (with winged heels and cap).
3 To turn round in a curved direction.
4 Winged horse of Greek mythology.
5 Fevers. The early spring sun was thought to do the sick body more harm than good.
6 Bellona, the Roman goddess of war.
7 Armored god of war.

According to Holinshed, the rebels "marched towards Shrewsbury, upon hope to be aided (as men thought) by Owen Glendower, and his Welshmen" (see Appendix A1, p. 191). Holinshed does not say what happened to Glendower, but notes that during the battle the Welshmen "which before had lain lurking in the woods, mountains, and marshes, hearing of this battle toward, came to the aid of the Percies" (Appendix A1, p. 194). Shakespeare's version of events is closer to Daniel who says that because of the king's unexpected swift approach "The joining with the *Welsh* they had decreed / Was hereby stopp'd" (Appendix A4, p. 218). Shakespeare adds the detail that Glendower "cannot draw his power this fourteen days." This scene provides extensive discussion of Northumberland's absence—perhaps because his story continues in *Henry IV, Part Two*—but, as in Shakespeare's sources, there is no mention of Mortimer. The actors playing Glendower, Northumberland, and Mortimer could usefully be doubled in roles such as Vernon, Douglas, and Lancaster in Acts 4 and 5.

The Seal of Owain Glyndŵr. From Wikimedia Commons, http://www.commons. wikimedia.org.

The powers of us may serve so great a day.
Come, let us take a muster speedily.
Doomsday is near: die all, die merrily.
DOUGLAS. Talk not of dying; I am out of fear   135
Of death or death's hand for this one half year.   *Exeunt.*

[4.2]¹

Enter Falstaff, Bardolph.

FALSTAFF. Bardolph, get thee before to Coventry; fill me a bottle of
sack. Our soldiers shall march through. We'll to Sutton Coldfield²
tonight.
BARDOLPH. Will you give me money, captain?
FALSTAFF. Lay out,³ lay out.   5
BARDOLPH. This bottle makes⁴ an angel.⁵
FALSTAFF. An if it do, take it for thy labor; an if it make twenty, take
them all; I'll answer the coinage.⁶ Bid my lieutenant Peto meet
me at town's end.
BARDOLPH. I will, captain. Farewell.   *Exit.* 10
FALSTAFF. If I be not ashamed of my soldiers, I am a soused gurnet.⁷
I have misused the king's press⁸ damnably. I have got in exchange
of one hundred and fifty soldiers three hundred and odd pounds.
I press me⁹ none but good householders, yeomen's sons,¹⁰ enquire
me out contracted bachelors, such as had been asked twice on   15
the banns,¹¹ such a commodity of warm slaves¹² as had as lief hear

---

1 The scene is located on the road between London and Shrewsbury close to the
town of Coventry.
2 About twenty miles north-west of Coventry.
3 Pay out of your own pocket.
4 Brings the total up to.
5 Gold coin with the archangel Michael stamped on it.
6 I'll be answerable for any coins you fabricate. Falstaff uses a pun on "make" to
deliberately misinterpret and avoid answering Bardolph's request.
7 Pickled fish.
8 Royal commission to conscript recruits.
9 Conscript.
10 Sons of property owners who could presumably buy their way out of service.
11 Proclamations of intention to marry, ordinarily declared in church three times.
12 Bunch of mollycoddled drones.

the devil as a drum, such as fear the report of a caliver[1] worse
than a struck fowl or a hurt wild duck. I pressed me none but
such toasts and butter, with hearts in their bellies no bigger than
20 pins' heads, and they have bought out their services;[2] and now my
whole charge consists of ensigns,[3] corporals, lieutenants, gentlemen of companies[4]—slaves as ragged as Lazarus[5] in the painted
cloth,[6] where the glutton's dogs licked his sores—and such as
indeed were never soldiers, but discarded unjust[7] servingmen,
25 younger sons to younger brothers, revolted tapsters,[8] and ostlers
trade-fallen,[9] the cankers[10] of a calm world and a long peace, ten
times more dishonorable-ragged than an old faz'd ancient.[11] And
such have I to fill up the rooms[12] of them as have bought out their
services, that you would think that I had a hundred and fifty tat-
30 tered prodigals lately come from swine-keeping, from eating
draff and husks.[13] A mad fellow met me on the way and told me I
had unloaded all the gibbets and pressed the dead bodies. No eye
hath seen such scarecrows. I'll not march through Coventry with
them, that's flat. Nay, and the villains march wide betwixt the
35 legs, as if they had gyves[14] on, for indeed I had the most of them
out of prison. There's not a shirt and a half in all my company;
and the half-shirt is two napkins tacked together and thrown
over the shoulders like a herald's coat without sleeves; and the
shirt, to say the truth, stolen from my host at Saint Albans,[15] or

---

1 Light musket.
2 Paid bribes to escape conscription.
3 Standard-bearers.
4 Men of higher rank than ordinary soldiers.
5 Another reference to the parable of the beggar Lazarus and Dives the rich man:
see p. 141, n. 1.
6 A cheap alternative to tapestry, often presenting pictures based on biblical
stories.
7 Dishonest.
8 Barmen who have run away from their apprenticeships (as the prince jokes that
Francis might do in 2.4).
9 Out-of-work stablemen.
10 Cankerworms, parasites.
11 Ragged flag.
12 Take the places.
13 Common food for pigs.
14 Fetters, in this case the leg-irons which prevented convicts from running away.
15 Innkeeper at St Albans, a town just outside London on the way to Coventry.

the red-nose innkeeper of Daventry.[1] But that's all one; they'll   40
find linen enough on every hedge.[2]

Enter the prince, [and the] Lord of Westmorland.

PRINCE. How now, blown[3] Jack? How now, quilt?[4]

FALSTAFF. What, Hal! How now, mad wag? What a devil dost thou
   in Warwickshire? My good lord of Westmorland, I cry you mercy!
   I thought your honor had already been at Shrewsbury.   45

WESTMORLAND. Faith, Sir John, 'tis more than time that I were
   there, and you too; but my powers are there already. The king, I
   can tell you, looks for us all. We must away all night.

FALSTAFF. Tut, never fear me. I am as vigilant as a cat to steal cream.

PRINCE. I think to steal cream indeed, for thy theft hath already   50
   made thee butter. But tell me, Jack, whose fellows are these that
   come after?

FALSTAFF. Mine, Hal, mine.

PRINCE. I did never see such pitiful rascals.

FALSTAFF. Tut, tut, good enough to toss, food for powder,[5] food   55
   for powder. They'll fill a pit as well as better. Tush, man, mortal
   men, mortal men.

WESTMORLAND. Ay, but Sir John, methinks they are exceeding poor
   and bare, too beggarly.

FALSTAFF. Faith, for their poverty, I know not where they had that,   60
   and for their bareness, I am sure they never learned that of me.

PRINCE. No, I'll be sworn, unless you call three fingers in the ribs[6]
   bare. But sirrah, make haste. Percy is already in the field.   *Exit.*

FALSTAFF. What, is the king encamped?

WESTMORLAND. He is, Sir John. I fear we shall stay too long.   65

FALSTAFF. Well, to the latter end of a fray°   *fight*
   And the beginning of a feast
   Fits[7] a dull fighter and a keen guest.   *Exeunt.*

---

1   Less than 20 miles from Coventry.
2   I.e., where the washing was left to dry.
3   (1) bloated (2) short-winded.
4   A thick covering and, by extension, a fat person.
5   Gunpowder.
6   Fat around the ribs measuring three fingers deep (a "finger" conventionally
measured three-quarters of an inch).
7   Suits.

4.2.56:   "THEY'LL FILL A PIT" (TLN 2441)

This is one of many moments where it is possible for Falstaff to disrupt the fictional history of the play by referring directly to the audience. In a production mounted on the replica Elizabethan stage of the New Fortune Theatre at the University of Western Australia in September 2011, the actors implied that the audience was Falstaff's troop of "pitiful rascals." In this context, Falstaff's "They'll fill a pit as well as better" suddenly became a grim joke about the "pit" or audience area closest to the stage: a space probably occupied by apprentices and other poorer members of the audience in Shakespeare's day.

ABOVE: Tom Considine, Chris White, and Bob Pavlich in *Henry IV, Part One*, The New Fortune Stage, UWA, 16 September 2011. Directed by Rob Conkie with a cast from La Trobe University Theatre and Drama, the production was linked to the Australian Research Council (ARC) Centre of Excellence for the History of Emotions collaboratory: "Performing Old Emotions on the New Fortune Stage." The five actors in this experimental production seized every opportunity for interaction with the audience and literally roped in two audience members as the victims of the Gadshill robbery. Photo by Tanya Tuffrey, ARC Centre of Excellence for the History of Emotions.

[4.3]¹

Enter Hotspur, Worcester, Douglas, [and] Vernon.

HOTSPUR. We'll fight with him tonight.

WORCESTER.   It may not be.

DOUGLAS. You give him then advantage.

VERNON.   Not a whit.

HOTSPUR. Why say you so? Looks he not for supply?²

VERNON. So do we.

HOTSPUR.   His is certain; ours is doubtful.

WORCESTER. Good cousin, be advised. Stir not tonight.   5

VERNON. Do not, my lord.

DOUGLAS.   You do not counsel well.

  You speak it out of fear and cold heart.

VERNON. Do me no slander, Douglas. By my life—

  And I dare well maintain it with my life—

  If well-respected honor bid me on,³   10

  I hold as little counsel with weak fear

  As you, my lord, or any Scot that this day lives.

  Let it be seen tomorrow in the battle

  Which of us fears.

DOUGLAS. Yea, or tonight.

VERNON.   Content.

HOTSPUR.   Tonight, say I.   15

VERNON. Come, come, it may not be. I wonder much,

  Being men of such great leading as you are,

  That you foresee not what impediments

  Drag back our expedition. Certain horse°   *cavalry*

  Of my cousin Vernon's are not yet come up.°   *arrived* 20

  Your uncle Worcester's horses came but today,

  And now their pride and mettle is asleep,

  Their courage with hard labor tame and dull,

  That not a horse is half the half of himself.

HOTSPUR. So are the horses of the enemy   25

---

1 Location: the rebel camp.
2 Reinforcements.
3 If well-reasoned honor urges me forward.

In general journey-bated[1] and brought low.
The better part of ours are full of rest.
WORCESTER. The number of the king exceedeth ours.
For God's sake, cousin, stay till all come in.

The trumpet sounds a parley.[2] Enter Sir Walter Blunt.

30 BLUNT. I come with gracious offers from the king,
If you vouchsafe° me hearing and respect.   allow
HOTSPUR. Welcome, Sir Walter Blunt: and would to God
You were of our determination.°   mind
Some of us love you well, and even those some[3]
35 Envy your great deservings and good name,
Because you are not of our quality,°   party, side
But stand against us like an enemy.
BLUNT. And God defend but still I should stand so,
So long as out of limit and true rule
40 You stand against anointed majesty.
But to my charge. The king hath sent to know
The nature of your griefs,° and whereupon[4]   grievances
You conjure from the breast of civil peace
Such bold hostility, teaching his duteous land
45 Audacious cruelty. If that the king
Have any way your good deserts forgot,
Which he confesseth to be manifold,
He bids you name your griefs, and with all speed
You shall have your desires with interest
50 And pardon absolute for yourself and these
Herein misled by your suggestion.[5]
HOTSPUR. The king is kind, and well we know the king
Knows at what time to promise, when to pay.
My father and my uncle and myself
55 Did give him that same royalty he wears;
And when he was not six-and-twenty strong,[6]

---

1 Worn down by their journey.
2 Signal for a conference under truce.
3 Those same people.
4 Upon what grounds.
5 Prompting, incitement to evil.
6 He had fewer than twenty six followers.

Sick in the world's regard,[1] wretched and low,
A poor unminded outlaw sneaking home,
My father gave him welcome to the shore;
And when he heard him swear and vow to God   60
He came but to be Duke of Lancaster,
To sue his livery,[2] and beg his peace[3]
With tears of innocency and terms of zeal,
My father, in kind heart and pity moved,
Swore him assistance, and performed it too.   65
Now when the lords and barons of the realm
Perceived Northumberland did lean to him,
The more and less[4] came in with cap and knee,[5]
Met him in boroughs, cities, villages,
Attended him on bridges, stood in lanes,   70
Laid gifts before him, proffered him their oaths,
Gave him their heirs as pages, followed him
Even at the heels, in golden multitudes.
He presently, as greatness knows itself,
Steps me° a little higher than his vow   *raises himself* 75
Made to my father while his blood was poor[6]
Upon the naked shore at Ravenspurgh,
And now forsooth takes on him° to reform   *takes it on himself*
Some certain edicts and some strait° decrees   *restrictive*
That lie too heavy on the commonwealth,   80
Cries out upon abuses, seems to weep
Over his country's wrongs; and by this face,
This seeming brow of justice, did he win
The hearts of all that he did angle for;
Proceeded further, cut me off the heads   85
Of all the favorites that the absent king
In deputation left behind him here
When he was personal[7] in the Irish war.

---

1 Lacking respect from the world at large.
2 To seek his dukedom by suing for possession.
3 To make peace with the king.
4 Those of high and low rank.
5 Bare-headed and kneeling.
6 While his spirits were low.
7 Was personally involved.

BLUNT. Tut, I came not to hear this.

90 HOTSPUR.   Then to the point.
     In short time after, he deposed the king,
     Soon after that deprived him of his life,
     And in the neck of that tasked[1] the whole state;
     To make that worse, suffered his kinsman March[2]
     (Who is, if every owner were well placed,

95   Indeed his king)[3] to be engaged° in Wales,   *held hostage*
     There without ransom to lie forfeited;
     Disgraced me in my happy victories,
     Sought to entrap me by intelligence,
     Rated[4] mine uncle from the council-board,

100 In rage dismissed my father from the court,
     Broke oath on oath, committed wrong on wrong,
     And in conclusion drove us to seek out
     This head[5] of safety, and withal° to pry   *also*
     Into his title,° the which we find   *right to kingship*

105 Too indirect[6] for long continuance.
     BLUNT. Shall I return this answer to the king?
     HOTSPUR. Not so, Sir Walter. We'll withdraw awhile.
       Go to the king, and let there be impawned°   *pledged*
       Some surety[7] for a safe return again;

110   And in the morning early shall mine uncle
       Bring him our purposes. And so, farewell.
     BLUNT. I would you would accept of grace and love.
     HOTSPUR. And may be so we shall.
     BLUNT.   Pray God you do.   [*Exeunt.*]

---

1 Straight after that taxed.
2 I.e., Mortimer.
3 See 1.3.145, TLN 468.
4 Berated, scolded away.
5 Armed force.
6 (1) not direct in terms of succession (2) deceitful.
7 I.e., a hostage. Westmorland will be sent as *surety* for the safe return of
Worcester: see 5.2.28, TLN 2812.

[4.4]¹

Enter Archbishop of York [and] Sir Michael.²

ARCHBISHOP. Hie, good Sir Michael, bear this sealèd brief³
   With wingèd haste to the Lord Marshal,°   *Thomas Mowbray*
   This to my cousin Scrope,⁴ and all the rest
   To whom they are directed. If you knew
   How much they do import, you would make haste.   5
SIR MICHAEL. My good lord, I guess their tenor.⁵
ARCHBISHOP.   Like enough you do.
   Tomorrow, good Sir Michael, is a day
   Wherein the fortune of ten thousand men
   Must bide the touch.° For, sir, at Shrewsbury,   *be put to the test*
   As I am truly given to understand,   10
   The king with mighty and quick-raisèd power
   Meets with Lord Harry. And I fear, Sir Michael,
   What with the sickness of Northumberland,
   Whose power was in the first proportion,°   *the largest in size*
   And what with Owen Glendower's absence thence,   15
   Who with them was a rated sinew° too,   *highly valued strength*
   And comes not in, overruled by prophecies,
   I fear the power of Percy is too weak
   To wage an instant trial with the king.
SIR MICHAEL. Why, my good lord, you need not fear,   20
   There is Douglas and Lord Mortimer.
ARCHBISHOP. No, Mortimer is not there.
SIR MICHAEL. But there is Mordake, Vernon, Lord Harry Percy;
   And there is my lord of Worcester, and a head
   Of gallant warriors, noble gentlemen.   25
ARCHBISHOP. And so there is. But yet the king hath drawn
   The special head of all the land together:

---

1 Presumably this scene takes place at the Archbishop's palace. It is often cut in
performance.
2 The Archbishop is Richard Scrope, mentioned in 1.3.265, TLN 596; Sir Michael
is probably a priest, for whom the title "Sir" was customary.
3 Letter.
4 It is not clear which member of the Scrope family this is.
5 General meaning.

The Prince of Wales, Lord John of Lancaster,
The noble Westmorland, and warlike Blunt,
30   And many more corrivals,[1] and dear° men   *valuable*
Of estimation and command in arms.
SIR MICHAEL. Doubt not, my lord, they shall be well opposed.
ARCHBISHOP. I hope no less, yet needful 'tis to fear;
And to prevent the worst, Sir Michael, speed.
35   For if Lord Percy thrive not, ere the king
Dismiss his power he means to visit us,[2]
For he hath heard of our confederacy,
And 'tis but wisdom to make strong against him.
Therefore make haste. I must go write again
40   To other friends; and so farewell, Sir Michael.   *Exeunt.*

[5.1][3]

Enter King, Prince of Wales, Lord John of Lancaster, Sir Walter Blunt,
[and] Falstaff.
KING. How bloodily the sun begins to peer
Above yon bulky hill! The day looks pale
At his distemperature.°   *the sun's disorder*
PRINCE.   The southern wind
Doth play the trumpet to his purposes,°   *signals his intentions*
5   And by his hollow whistling in the leaves
Foretells a tempest and a blustering day.
KING. Then with the losers let it sympathize,
For nothing can seem foul to those that win.

                        The trumpet sounds. Enter Worcester [and Vernon].
KING. How now, my lord of Worcester? 'Tis not well
10   That you and I should meet upon such terms
As now we meet. You have deceived our trust,

---

1 Comrades, partners.
2 See 5.5.37, TLN 3173.
3 All of Act 5 is located on or near the Shrewsbury battlefield.

And made us doff° our easy robes of peace   *take off*
To crush our old limbs in ungentle steel.
This is not well, my lord, this is not well.
What say you to it? Will you again unknit   15
This churlish knot of all-abhorrèd war,
And move in that obedient orb¹ again
Where you did give a fair and natural light,
And be no more an exhaled meteor,°   *shooting star*
A prodigy of fear, and a portent   20
Of broachèd° mischief to the unborn times?   *unleashed*
WORCESTER. Hear me, my liege:
   For mine own part, I could be well content
   To entertain the lag-end of my life
   With quiet hours; for I protest,   25
   I have not sought the day of this dislike.
KING. You have not sought it? How comes it, then?
FALSTAFF. Rebellion lay in his way, and he found it.
PRINCE. Peace, chewet,° peace!   *chatterbox*
WORCESTER. It pleased your majesty to turn your looks   30
   Of favor from myself and all our house;
   And yet I must remember° you, my lord,   *remind*
   We were the first and dearest of your friends.
   For you my staff of office did I break
   In Richard's time, and posted° day and night   *rode in haste* 35
   To meet you on the way and kiss your hand
   When yet you were in place and in account°   *reputation*
   Nothing so strong and fortunate as I.
   It was myself, my brother, and his son
   That brought you home, and boldly did outdare   40
   The dangers of the time. You swore to us,
   And you did swear that oath at Doncaster,
   That you did nothing purpose 'gainst the state,
   Nor claim no further than your new-fallen right,²
   The seat of Gaunt, dukedom of Lancaster: 45

---

1 Sphere of obedience, revolving around the king.
2 I.e., his inheritance.

To this we swore our aid. But in short space
It rained down fortune showering on your head,
And such a flood of greatness fell on you,
What with our help, what with the absent king,
50   What with the injuries of a wanton° time,   *unruly, violent*
The seeming sufferances° that you had borne,   *wrongs*
And the contrarious winds that held the king
So long in his unlucky Irish wars
That all in England did repute him dead;
55   And from this swarm of fair advantages
You took occasion to be quickly wooed
To gripe the general sway° into your hand,   *seize the kingdom*
Forgot your oath to us at Doncaster,
And being fed by us, you used us so
60   As that ungentle gull, the cuckoo's bird,°   *chick*
Useth the sparrow—did oppress our nest,
Grew by our feeding to so great a bulk[1]
That even our love durst not come near your sight
For fear of swallowing. But with nimble wing
65   We were enforced for safety sake to fly
Out of your sight, and raise this present head,°   *force*
Whereby we stand opposèd by such means
As you yourself have forged against yourself,
By unkind usage, dangerous countenance,°   *threatening looks*
70   And violation of all faith and troth
Sworn to us in your younger enterprise.
KING. These things indeed you have articulate,°   *set forth*
Proclaimed at market crosses, read in churches,
To face° the garment of rebellion   *trim*
75   With some fine color that may please the eye
Of fickle changelings° and poor discontents,   *waverers*
Which gape and rub the elbow° at the news   *i.e., with delight*
Of hurly-burly innovation;[2]
And never yet did insurrection want°   *lack*

---

1 Cuckoo chicks hatched from eggs laid in the nests of other species generally grow faster than the other young and can force them out of the nest.
2 Tumultuous commotion (Kastan).

Such water-colors to impaint his cause,   80
Nor moody beggars starving for a time
Of pell-mell[1] havoc and confusion.
PRINCE. In both your armies[2] there is many a soul
  Shall pay full dearly for this encounter
  If once they join in trial. Tell your nephew   85
  The Prince of Wales doth join with all the world
  In praise of Henry Percy. By my hopes,
  This present enterprise set off his head,[3]
  I do not think a braver gentleman,
  More active-valiant or more valiant-young,   90
  More daring, or more bold, is now alive
  To grace this latter age° with noble deeds.   *present time*
  For my part—I may speak it to my shame—
  I have a truant been to chivalry,
  And so I hear he doth account me too.   95
  Yet this, before my father's majesty:
  I am content that he shall take the odds
  Of his great name and estimation,
  And will, to save the blood on either side,
  Try fortune with him in a single fight.   100
KING. And, Prince of Wales, so dare we venture thee,
  Albeit[4] considerations infinite
  Do make against it. No, good Worcester, no.
  We love our people well, even those we love
  That are misled upon your cousin's° part,   *Hotspur's* 105
  And will they take the offer of our grace,°   *pardon*
  Both he and they and you, yea, every man
  Shall be my friend again, and I'll be his.
  So tell your cousin, and bring me word
  What he will do. But if he will not yield,   110
  Rebuke and dread correction wait on us,[5]
  And they shall do their office. So be gone.

---

1 Disorderly, without keeping ranks.
2 I.e., the armies of both the king and the rebels.
3 Struck from his record.
4 Although (here perhaps with the sense of "except for the fact that").
5 Are our servants.

We will not now be troubled with reply.
We offer fair; take it advisedly.   *Exit Worcester [and Vernon].*
115 PRINCE. It will not be accepted, on my life.
     The Douglas and the Hotspur both together
     Are confident against the world in arms.
     KING. Hence, therefore, every leader to his charge,
     For on their answer will we set on them,
120 And God befriend us as our cause is just!
                                   Exeunt [all but] Prince [and] Falstaff.

FALSTAFF. Hal, if thou see me down in the battle, and bestride me,[1]
     so; 'tis a point of friendship.
PRINCE. Nothing but a colossus[2] can do thee that friendship. Say
     thy prayers, and farewell.
125 FALSTAFF. I would 'twere bed-time, Hal, and all well.
PRINCE. Why, thou owest God a death.   *[Exit Prince.]*
FALSTAFF. 'Tis not due yet—I would be loath to pay him before his
     day. What need I be so forward with him that calls not on me?
     Well, 'tis no matter, honor pricks[3] me on. Yea, but how if honor
130 prick me off[4] when I come on? How then? Can honor set to a
     leg? No. Or an arm? No. Or take away the grief[5] of a wound? No.
     Honor hath no skill in surgery, then? No. What is honor? A word.
     What is in that word "honor"? What is that "honor"? Air. A trim
     reckoning![6] Who hath it? He that died a'Wednesday. Doth he feel
135 it? No. Doth he hear it? No. 'Tis insensible then? Yea, to the dead.
     But will it not live with the living? No. Why? Detraction[7] will not
     suffer[8] it. Therefore I'll none of it. Honor is a mere scutcheon.[9]
     And so ends my catechism.[10]   *Exit.*

---

1 Stand across my body.
2 Large statue.
3 Spurs.
4 Mark me down (suggesting Death's roll-call).
5 Pain.
6 Account, balance sheet.
7 Defamation.
8 Allow.
9 A panel or shield showing coats of arms and displayed at funerals.
10 A religious lesson constructed as a series of questions and answers.

[5.2]

Enter Worcester, [and] Sir Richard Vernon.

WORCESTER. Oh no, my nephew must not know, Sir Richard,
   The liberal and kind offer of the king.

VERNON. 'Twere best he did.

WORCESTER.   Then are we all undone.
   It is not possible, it cannot be
   The king should keep his word in loving us.   5
   He will suspect us still, and find a time
   To punish this offense in other faults.
   Supposition all our lives shall be stuck full of eyes,[1]
   For treason is but trusted like the fox,
   Who, never so tame, so cherished, and locked up,   10
   Will have a wild trick° of his ancestors.   *trait*
   Look how we can, or sad or merrily,[2]
   Interpretation will misquote our looks,
   And we shall feed like oxen at a stall,
   The better cherished still the nearer death.   15
   My nephew's trespass may be well forgot;
   It hath the excuse of youth and heat of blood,
   And an adopted name of privilege:[3]
   A hare-brained Hotspur, governed by a spleen.[4]
   All his offenses live upon my head,   20
   And on his father's. We did train him on,
   And, his corruption being ta'en° from us,   *taken*
   We as the spring of all shall pay for all.
   Therefore, good cousin, let not Harry know
   In any case the offer of the king.   25

Enter [Hotspur and Douglas].

VERNON. Deliver what you will; I'll say 'tis so.
   Here comes your cousin.

---

1   I.e., like the many-eyed allegorical figures of suspicion or envy.
2   Either sad or merry.
3   A nickname that excuses him.
4   Believed to engender impulsive behavior, see 2.3.71, TLN 927.

HOTSPUR.   My uncle is returned.
Deliver up my lord of Westmorland.[1]
Uncle, what news?

30   WORCESTER. The king will bid you battle presently.

DOUGLAS. Defy him by[2] the Lord of Westmorland.

HOTSPUR. Lord Douglas, go you and tell him so.

DOUGLAS. Marry, and shall, and very willingly.   *Exit Douglas.*

WORCESTER. There is no seeming mercy in the king.

35   HOTSPUR. Did you beg any? God forbid!

WORCESTER. I told him gently of our grievances,
Of his oath-breaking, which he mended° thus,   *amended*
By now forswearing[3] that he is forsworn.°   *perjured*
He calls us rebels, traitors, and will scourge°   *punish by lashing*

40   With haughty arms this hateful name in us.

Enter Douglas.

DOUGLAS. Arm, gentlemen, to arms! For I have thrown
A brave defiance in King Henry's teeth,
And Westmorland that was engaged[4] did bear it,
Which cannot choose but bring him quickly on.[5]

45   WORCESTER. The Prince of Wales stepped forth before the king
And, nephew, challenged you to single fight.

HOTSPUR. Oh, would the quarrel lay upon our heads,
And that no man might draw short breath today
But I and Harry Monmouth![6] Tell me, tell me,

50   How showed his tasking?[7] Seemed it in contempt?

VERNON. No, by my soul, I never in my life
Did hear a challenge urged more modestly,
Unless a brother should a brother dare
To gentle exercise and proof of arms.

---

1   Westmorland has been the *surety* for Worcester's safe return, see 4.3.109,
TLN 2580.
2   Send our defiance through.
3   Falsely denying.
4   Pledged as surety.
5   The defiance must bring King Henry's force quickly.
6   The Welsh town of Prince Hal's birth.
7   Proffering of the challenge.

He gave you all the duties of a man, 55
Trimmed up your praises with a princely tongue,
Spoke your deservings like a chronicle,
Making you ever better than his praise
By still dispraising praise valued with you;
And, which became him like a prince indeed, 60
He made a blushing cital° of himself,   *modest report*
And chid° his truant youth with such a grace   *rebuked*
As if he mastered there a double spirit
Of teaching and of learning instantly.[1]
There did he pause; but let me tell the world, 65
If he outlive the envy of this day,
England did never owe° so sweet a hope,   *own*
So much misconstrued in his wantonness.°   *wildness*
HOTSPUR. Cousin, I think thou art enamorèd
   On° his follies. Never did I hear   *in love with* 70
   Of any prince so wild a liberty.[2]
   But be he as he will, yet once ere night
   I will embrace him with a soldier's arm,
   That° he shall shrink under my courtesy.   *so that*
   Arm, arm, with speed! And fellows, soldiers, friends, 75
   Better consider what you have to do
   Than I, that have not well the gift of tongue,
   Can lift your blood up with persuasion.[3]

Enter a Messenger.
MESSENGER. My lord, here are letters for you.
HOTSPUR. I cannot read them now, 80
   O gentlemen, the time of life is short.
   To spend that shortness basely were too long
   If life did ride upon a dial's point,[4]
   Still ending at the arrival of an hour.
   An if we live, we live to tread on kings; 85

---

1 Showed the capacity to teach and learn in the same instant.
2 Presumptuous behavior; licence.
3 You are better equipped to consider what you have to do than I am able to inspire
you with words.
4 Even if life rode upon the hand of a clock.

If die, brave death when princes die with us!
Now for our consciences: the arms are fair
When the intent of bearing them is just.

Enter another [Messenger].

MESSENGER. My lord, prepare; the king comes on apace.
90 HOTSPUR. I thank him that he cuts me from my tale,
For I profess not° talking, only this: *make no profession out of*
Let each man do his best. And here draw I
A sword whose temper° I intend to stain   *brightness*
With the best blood that I can meet withal
95 In the adventure of this perilous day.
Now *Esperance!*[1] Percy! And set on!
Sound all the lofty instruments of war,
And by that music let us all embrace,
For, heaven to earth,[2] some of us never shall
100 A second time do such a courtesy.
        Here they embrace. The trumpets sound. [Exeunt.]

[5.3]

*The king enters with his power. Alarum to the battle.[3] Then enter Douglas,
and Sir Walter Blunt [disguised as the king].*
BLUNT. What is thy name, that in battle thus thou crossest me?
What honor dost thou seek upon my head?
DOUGLAS. Know then my name is Douglas,
And I do haunt thee in the battle thus
5 Because some tell me that thou art a king.
BLUNT. They tell thee true.
DOUGLAS. The Lord of Stafford dear today hath bought
Thy likeness, for instead of thee, King Harry,
This sword hath ended him. So shall it thee,
10 Unless thou yield thee as my prisoner.
BLUNT. I was not born a yielder, thou proud Scot,
And thou shalt find a king that will revenge

---

1 The Percy family motto: see p. 100, n. 4, TLN 920.
2 I'll bet on heaven against earth.
3 A call to arms, usually by trumpets.

Lord Stafford's death.

They fight, Douglas kills Blunt, then enter Hotspur.
HOTSPUR. O Douglas, hadst thou fought at Holmedon thus,
  I never had triumphed upon a Scot.   15
DOUGLAS. All's done, all's won: here breathless lies the king.
HOTSPUR. Where?
DOUGLAS. Here.
HOTSPUR. This Douglas? No, I know this face full well.
  A gallant knight he was, his name was Blunt,   20
  Semblably furnished[1] like the king himself.
DOUGLAS. [*To the corpse*] Ah fool, go with thy soul, whither it goes!
  A borrowed title hast thou bought too dear.
  Why didst thou tell me that thou wert a king?
HOTSPUR. The king hath many marching in his coats.   25
DOUGLAS. Now by my sword, I will kill all his coats.
  I'll murder all his wardrobe, piece by piece,
  Until I meet the king.
HOTSPUR.   Up and away!
  Our soldiers stand full fairly for the day.[2]
                    [*Exeunt.*] *Alarum. Enter Falstaff alone.*
FALSTAFF. Though I could scape shot-free[3] at London, I fear the   30
  shot here. Here's no scoring[4] but upon the pate.[5] Soft! Who are
  you? Sir Walter Blunt. There's honor for you. Here's no vanity.[6]
  I am as hot as molten lead, and as heavy too. God keep lead out
  of me! I need no more weight than mine own bowels. I have led
  my ragamuffins where they are peppered;[7] there's not three of   35
  my hundred and fifty left alive, and they are for the town's end,[8]
  to beg during life. But who comes here?

---

1 Similarly dressed and armed.
2 Stand in good stead to win the day.
3 Escape without paying the bill, with an obvious pun on *shot*.
4 (1) adding up (of a tavern bill) (2) notching or slashing.
5 Head.
6 Falstaff echoes Ecclesiastes 1.2 and 12.8, "Vanity of vanities, all is vanity."
7 Bombarded, destroyed, or perhaps pelted with shot.
8 The outskirts of a town, where beggars would set themselves up to catch people
passing through.

Enter the prince.

PRINCE. What, stands thou idle here? Lend me thy sword.
Many a noble man lies stark and stiff
40   Under the hoofs of vaunting enemies,
Whose deaths are yet unrevenged. I prithee
Lend me thy sword.

FALSTAFF. O Hal, I prithee give me leave to breathe awhile. Turk
Gregory[1] never did such deeds in arms as I have done this day. I
45   have paid[2] Percy, I have made him sure.[3]

PRINCE. He is indeed, and living to kill thee.
I prithee lend me thy sword.

FALSTAFF. Nay, before God, Hal, if Percy be alive thou gets not my
sword; but take my pistol if thou wilt.

50   PRINCE. Give it me. What, is it in the case?°   *holster*

FALSTAFF. Ay, Hal, 'tis hot, 'tis hot.[4] There's that will sack[5] a city.

The prince draws it out, and finds it to be a bottle of sack.

PRINCE. What, is it a time to jest and dally now?

He throws the bottle at him. Exit.

FALSTAFF. Well, if Percy be alive, I'll pierce him. If he do come in
my way, so. If he do not, if I come in his willingly, let him make
55   a carbonado[6] of me. I like not such grinning honor as Sir Walter
hath. Give me life, which if I can save, so; if not, honor comes
unlooked for, and there's an end.   [*Exit with Blunt's body.*]

[5.4]

*Alarum. Excursions.[7] Enter the king, the prince, Lord John of Lancaster,
Earl of Westmorland.*

KING. I prithee, Harry, withdraw thyself, thou bleed'st too much.

---

1 Falstaff probably has one of the more violent Popes in mind, possibly Pope
Gregory VII or Pope Gregory VIII.
2 Killed.
3 Made sure of him, but Hal picks up a pun on *sure* as secure.
4 I.e., the pistol is hot from constant firing.
5 (1) plunder (2) wine.
6 Piece of meat which has been scored across for grilling.
7 Groups of fighting soldiers that cross the stage to represent the on-going battle.

Lord John of Lancaster, go you with him.

LANCASTER. Not I, my lord, unless I did bleed too.

PRINCE. I beseech your majesty, make up,°   *advance, go forward*

  Lest your retirement do amaze° your friends.   *bewilder* 5

KING. I will do so. My lord of Westmorland,

  Lead him to his tent.

WESTMORLAND. Come, my lord, I'll lead you to your tent.

PRINCE. Lead me, my lord? I do not need your help,

  And God forbid a shallow scratch should drive   10

  The Prince of Wales from such a field as this,

  Where stained nobility lies trodden on,

  And rebels' arms triumph in massacres.

LANCASTER. We breathe[1] too long. Come, cousin Westmorland,

  Our duty this way lies. For God's sake, come.   15

             [*Exit Lancaster and Westmorland.*]

PRINCE. By God, thou hast deceived me, Lancaster;

  I did not think thee lord of such a spirit.

  Before I loved thee as a brother, John,

  But now I do respect thee as my soul.

KING. I saw him hold Lord Percy at the point°   *at sword point* 20

  With lustier maintenance than I did look for

  Of such an ungrown warrior.

PRINCE. Oh, this boy lends mettle to us all!   *Exit* [*Prince*].

[*Enter Douglas.*]

DOUGLAS. Another king! They grow like Hydra's heads.[2]

  I am the Douglas, fatal to all those   25

  That wear those colors[3] on them. What art thou

  That counterfeit'st the person of a king?

KING. The king himself, who, Douglas, grieves at heart

  So many of his shadows thou hast met

  And not the very king. I have two boys   30

  Seek Percy and thyself about the field;

  But seeing thou fall'st on me so luckily,

  I will assay thee;° and defend thyself.   *try you out*

---

1 Pause to catch breath.

2 In Greek myth the Hydra was a many-headed monster which grew new heads
as soon as one was cut off.

3 I.e., the colors of the king.

5.4.10: "A SHALLOW SCRATCH" (TLN 2969)

Hall and Holinshed report that the prince was wounded in the face with an arrow but kept on fighting. This is their only reference to the prince's valor at Shrewsbury. Samuel Daniel adds the detail that the prince rescued his father from Douglas. Prince Hal describes a field of "massacres" and he is not exaggerating. According to Stow, 5000 common men were slain and it seems that the longbow was largely to blame. He writes, "the bowmen of Henry Percy began the battle. Whole arrows fell not upon the ground, but upon the bodies of the king's soldiers, and the king's archers shot as fiercely against their enemies, so that on both sides many were slain" (555).

ABOVE: The Battle of Crecy (1346) from Jean Froissart's *Chronicles* (c. 1470). The British archers in the foreground on the right are using English (or Welsh) longbows against the crossbowmen on the left. From Wikimedia Commons, http://www.commons. wikimedia.org.

DOUGLAS. I fear thou art another counterfeit;
    And yet, in faith, thou bear'st thee like a king.   35
    But mine[1] I am sure thou art, whoe'er thou be,
    And thus I win thee.

                    They fight. The king being in danger, enter Prince of Wales.
PRINCE. Hold up thy head, vile Scot, or thou art like°   likely
    Never to hold it up again! The spirits
    Of valiant Shirley, Stafford, Blunt, are in my arms.   40
    It is the Prince of Wales that threatens thee,
    Who never promiseth but he means to pay.

                                        They fight, Douglas flieth.
    Cheerly, my lord! How fares your grace?
    Sir Nicholas Gawsey hath for succor sent,
    And so hath Clifton. I'll to Clifton straight.   45
KING. Stay and breathe awhile.
    Thou hast redeemed thy lost opinion,°   reputation
    And showed thou mak'st some tender of[2] my life,
    In this fair rescue thou hast brought to me.
PRINCE. O God, they did me too much injury   50
    That ever said I hearkened for° your death.   eagerly wished for
    If it were so, I might have let alone
    The insulting[3] hand of Douglas over you,
    Which would have been as speedy in your end
    As all the poisonous potions in the world,   55
    And saved the treacherous labor of your son.
KING. Make up[4] to Clifton; I'll to Sir Nicholas Gawsey.   *Exit King.*

Enter Hotspur.
HOTSPUR. If I mistake not, thou art Harry Monmouth.
PRINCE. Thou speak'st as if I would deny my name.
HOTSPUR. My name is Harry Percy.

---

1 My victim and prize.
2 Have some regard for.
3 Scornfully triumphing (OED).
4 Go forward.

60 PRINCE.   Why then I see
     A very valiant rebel of the name.
     I am the Prince of Wales; and think not, Percy,
     To share with me in glory any more.
     Two stars keep not their motion in one sphere,
65   Nor can one England brook¹ a double reign
     Of Harry Percy and the Prince of Wales.
HOTSPUR. Nor shall it, Harry, for the hour is come
     To end the one of us, and would to God
     Thy name in arms were now as great as mine.
70 PRINCE. I'll make it greater ere I part from thee,
     And all the budding honors on thy crest²
     I'll crop to make a garland for my head.
HOTSPUR. I can no longer brook thy vanities.

                              They fight. Enter Falstaff.
FALSTAFF. Well said, Hal! To it, Hal! Nay, you shall find no boy's
75   play here, I can tell you.

*Enter Douglas, he fighteth with Falstaff, [who] falls down as if he were
dead. [Exit Douglas.]*

                              The prince killeth Percy.
HOTSPUR. O Harry, thou hast robbed me of my youth.
     I better brook the loss of brittle life
     Than those proud titles thou hast won of me.
     They wound my thoughts worse than thy sword my flesh.
80   But thoughts, the slaves of life, and life, time's fool,
     And time, that takes survey of all the world,
     Must have a stop. Oh, I could prophesy,
     But that the earthy and cold hand of death
     Lies on my tongue. No, Percy, thou art dust,
85   And food for—

                              [*He dies.*]

---

1 Take, tolerate.
2 (1) chivalric insignia on your helmet (2) the reputation for honor you have
begin to accrue.

5.4.76:   THE DEATH OF HOTSPUR (TLN 3041)

Hall, Holinshed, and Daniel do not specify who killed Hotspur, although in *The History of Scotland* Holinshed implies that the king was responsible (2.254). Hotspur's final words are about his loss of honor. It was a common idea that dying men could produce prophetic utterances, as does John of Gaunt in *Richard II* 2.1, but Hotspur is denied the opportunity: tellingly, his final line has to be completed by the prince. For the 1945 Old Vic production of *Henry IV, Part One* Laurence Olivier gave Hotspur a slight stammer on the letter "w," adding extra pathos to his inability to utter his dying word (see also Introduction, p. 37).

ABOVE: Illustration from *A Chronicle of England, B.C. 55 - A.D. 1485* by James William Edmund Doyle, 1864. From Wikimedia Commons, http://www.commons. wikimedia.org.

PRINCE. For worms, brave Percy. Fare thee well, great heart.
Ill-weaved ambition, how much art thou shrunk!
When that this body did contain a spirit,
A kingdom for it was too small a bound,
90 But now two paces of the vilest° earth   *most worthless*
Is room enough. This earth that bears thee dead
Bears not alive so stout° a gentleman.   *brave*
If thou wert sensible° of courtesy,   *aware*
I should not make so dear a show of zeal;[1]
95 But let my favors[2] hide thy mangled face,
And even in thy behalf I'll thank myself
For doing these fair rites of tenderness.
Adieu, and take thy praise with thee to heaven.
Thy ignominy sleep with thee in the grave,
100 But not remembered in thy epitaph.

He spieth Falstaff on the ground.
What, old acquaintance! Could not all this flesh
Keep in a little life? Poor Jack, farewell.
I could have better spared a better man.
Oh, I should have a heavy miss of thee,
105 If I were much in love with vanity.[3]
Death hath not struck so fat a deer today,
Though many dearer[4] in this bloody fray.
Embowelled° will I see thee by and by.   *disemboweled*
Till then, in blood by noble Percy lie.   *Exit.*

Falstaff riseth up.
110 FALSTAFF. Embowelled? If thou embowel me today, I'll give you
leave to powder me,[5] and eat me too, tomorrow. 'Sblood, 'twas
time to counterfeit, or that hot termagant[6] Scot had paid me,[7]

---

1 Strongly felt display of admiration.
2 Token worn as a mark of identity or favor, in this case probably the plumes
from Hal's helmet.
3 Frivolity, worldliness (see p. 171, n. 6, TLN 2926).
4 (1) more noble (2) more valued.
5 Salt me.
6 Violent.
7 I.e., killed me.

scot and lot¹ too. Counterfeit? I lie, I am no counterfeit. To die
is to be a counterfeit, for he is but the counterfeit of a man, who
hath not the life of a man. But to counterfeit dying when a man   115
thereby liveth is to be no counterfeit, but the true and perfect
image of life indeed. The better part of valor is discretion, in the
which better part I have saved my life. Zounds, I am afraid of this
gunpowder Percy, though he be dead. How if he should counterfeit too, and rise? By my faith, I am afraid he would prove the bet-   120
ter counterfeit. Therefore I'll make him sure; yea, and I'll swear
I killed him. Why may not he rise as well as I? Nothing confutes
me but eyes,² and nobody sees me. Therefore, sirrah, [*stabbing
him*] with a new wound in your thigh, come you along with me.

He takes up Hotspur on his back. Enter Prince [and] John of Lancaster.
PRINCE. Come, brother John. Full bravely hast thou fleshed³   125
    Thy maiden sword.
LANCASTER.   But soft; whom have we here?
    Did you not tell me this fat man was dead?
PRINCE. I did, I saw him dead,
  Breathless and bleeding on the ground. Art thou alive?
  Or is it fantasy that plays upon our eyesight?   130
  I prithee speak; we will not trust our eyes
  Without our ears. Thou art not what thou seem'st.
FALSTAFF. No, that's certain: I am not a double man.⁴ But if I be
  not Jack Falstaff, then am I a jack. ⁵

                     [*He puts down the body.*]
There is Percy. If your father will do me any honor, so; if not, let   135
  him kill the next Percy himself. I look to be either earl or duke,
  I can assure you.
PRINCE. Why, Percy I killed myself, and saw thee dead.
FALSTAFF. Didst thou? Lord, Lord, how this world is given to lying!
  I grant you I was down and out of breath, and so was he; but we   140
  rose both at an instant, and fought a long hour by Shrewsbury

---

1 In full.
2 Nobody can contradict my story except an eyewitness.
3 Blooded (*maiden sword* develops the phallic suggestion).
4 (1) phantom (2) two men, Falstaff and Hotspur.
5 Knave.

clock. If I may be believed, so; if not, let them that should reward
valor bear the sin upon their own heads. I'll take it upon my death
I gave him this wound in the thigh. If the man were alive and
145 would deny it, zounds, I would make him eat a piece of my sword.
LANCASTER. This is the strangest tale that ever I heard.
PRINCE. This is the strangest fellow, brother John.
[*To Falstaff*] Come, bring your luggage nobly on your back.
For my part, if a lie may do thee grace,[1]
150 I'll gild[2] it with the happiest terms I have.

A retreat is sounded.
PRINCE. The trumpet sounds retreat; the day is ours.
Come, brother, let us to the highest[3] of the field
To see what friends are living, who are dead.
Exeunt [Prince and Lancaster].
FALSTAFF. I'll follow, as they say, for reward. He that rewards me,
155 God reward him. If I do grow great, I'll grow less; for I'll purge,[4]
and leave sack, and live cleanly, as a nobleman should do.
Exit [with Hotspur's body].

[5.5]

*The Trumpets sound. Enter the king, the Prince of Wales, Lord John of
Lancaster, Earl of Westmorland, with Worcester and Vernon prisoners.*
KING. Thus ever did rebellion find rebuke.
Ill-spirited Worcester, did not we send grace,
Pardon, and terms of love to all of you?
And wouldst thou turn our offers contrary,
5 Misuse the tenor° of thy kinsman's trust?   *underlying substance*
Three knights upon our party slain today,
A noble earl, and many a creature else,
Had been alive this hour,
If like a Christian thou hadst truly borne
10 Betwixt our armies true intelligence.
WORCESTER. What I have done my safety urged me to,

---

1 Good fortune.
2 Give it a fair appearance.
3 Highest point.
4 (1) take purgatives (and therefore lose weight) (2) cleanse my spirit.

And I embrace this fortune patiently,
Since not to be avoided it falls on me.
KING. Bear Worcester to the death, and Vernon too.
Other offenders we will pause upon.°   *consider further* 15

                    [*Worcester and Vernon exit, guarded.*]
How goes the field?°   *battlefield*
PRINCE. The noble Scot, Lord Douglas, when he saw
    The fortune of the day quite turned from him,
    The noble Percy slain, and all his men
    Upon the foot of fear,° fled with the rest;   *fleeing in fear* 20
    And falling from a hill he was so bruised
    That the pursuers took him. At my tent
    The Douglas is, and I beseech your grace
    I may dispose of him.
KING.   With all my heart.
PRINCE. Then, brother John of Lancaster,   25
    To you this honorable bounty shall belong.
    Go to the Douglas, and deliver him
    Up to his pleasure ransomless and free.
    His valors shown upon our crests° today   *helmets*
    Have taught us how to cherish such high deeds   30
    Even in the bosom of our adversaries.
LANCASTER. I thank your grace for this high courtesy,
    Which I shall give away immediately.°   *i.e., to Douglas*
KING. Then this remains, that we divide our power.
    You, son John, and my cousin Westmorland,   35
    Toward York shall bend° you with your dearest speed   *turn*
    To meet Northumberland and the prelate Scrope,
    Who, as we hear, are busily in arms.
    Myself and you, son Harry, will toward Wales,
    To fight with Glendower and the Earl of March.   40
    Rebellion in this land shall lose his sway,°   *its influence*
    Meeting the check of such another day,[1]
    And since this business so fair is done,
    Let us not leave till all our own be won.[2]   *Exeunt.*

---

1 Defeat on another day like this.
2 (1) all our country is won back (2) all our country is united as one.

APPENDIX A: SOURCES AND INFLUENCES

1. FROM RAPHAEL HOLINSHED, *CHRONICLES OF ENGLAND, SCOTLAND, AND IRELAND* (1587)

[Raphael Holinshed's *Chronicles of England, Scotland, and Ireland* (1587 edition) was one of Shakespeare's most frequently consulted sources and provided the main outline for events in *Henry IV, Part One*. The *Chronicles* were produced by a team of around a dozen writers, described by Annabel Patterson as "a syndicate of middle-class entrepreneurs and antiquarians" (3). Raphael Holinshed was a key driving force behind the first edition of 1577, but he died in 1580 well before the substantially revised second edition was published. For convenience, however, the work is commonly referred to via Holinshed's name. As the product of several writers and a wide range of sources, the *Chronicles* is characterized by diverse opinions and attitudes. It reflects an attempt to document or chronicle events as they happened year by year, and as such it provides a wide-ranging and unstructured narrative that acknowledges a degree of uncertainty about the veracity of its materials and often suggests alternative readings of events. For *Henry IV, Part One* Shakespeare selected only a few of the events recorded for the period in the *Chronicles*. The play's depiction of multiple viewpoints does, nevertheless, owe a lot to the characteristic tone of this source. The following modernized selections from Holinshed are based on the online text provided by the Holinshed Project and the facsimiles provided by the Schoenberg Center for Electronic Text and Image, University of Pennsylvania.]

[*Owen Glendower and the Welsh rebellion*]
[1400: vol. 3, p. 518]

In the king's absence, whilst he was forth of the realm in Scotland against his enemies, the Welshmen took occasion to rebel under the conduct of their captain Owen Glendower, doing what mischief they could devise, unto their English neighbors. This Owen Glendower was son to an esquire[1] of Wales, named Griffith Vichan: he dwelled in the

---

1 Belonging to the higher order of English gentry (OED).

parish of Conway, within the county of Merioneth in North Wales, in a place called Glindourwie, which is as much to say in English, as The valley by the side of the water of Dee, by occasion whereof he was surnamed Glindour Dew.

He was first set to study the laws of the realm, and became an utter barrister, or an apprentice of the law (as they term him) and served King Richard at Flint Castle, when he was taken by Henry Duke of Lancaster, though other have written that he served this King Henry the fourth, before he came to attain the crown, in room[1] of an esquire, and after, by reason of variance that rose betwixt him and the Lord Reginald Grey of Ruthen, about the lands which he claimed to be his by right of inheritance: when he saw that he might not prevail, finding no such favor in his suit as he looked for, he first made war against the said Lord Grey, wasting his lands and possessions with fire and sword, cruelly killing his servants and tenants. The king advertised[2] of such rebellious exploits, enterprised by the said Owen, and his unruly [ac]complices, determined to chastise them, as disturbers of his peace, and so with an army entered into Wales; but the Welshmen with their captain withdrew into the mountains of Snowdon, so to escape the revenge, which the king meant towards them. The king therefore did much hurt in the countries with fire and sword, slaying diverse that with weapon in hand came forth to resist him, and so with a great booty of beasts and cattle he returned.

[*The Battle of Shrewsbury*]
[1402–04: vol. 3, pp. 520–24]

Owen Glendower, according to his accustomed manner, robbing and spoiling within the English borders, caused all the forces of the shire of Hereford to assemble together against them, under the conduct of Edmund Mortimer Earl of March.[3] But coming to try the matter by battle, whether by treason or otherwise, so it fortuned, that the English power was discomfited, the Earl taken prisoner, and above a thousand of his people slain in the place. The shameful villainy used by

---

1 The role.
2 Notified.
3 This error is replicated by Shakespeare: Edmund Mortimer was not the Earl of March; the real Earl was his nephew, held in captivity by Henry IV.

the Welshwomen towards the dead carcasses, was such, as honest ears would be ashamed to hear, and continent tongues to speak thereof.[1] The dead bodies might not be buried, without great sums of money given for liberty to convey them away.

The king was not hasty to purchase the deliverance of the Earl of March, because his title to the crown was well enough known, and therefore suffered him to remain in miserable prison, wishing both the said Earl, and all other of his lineage out of this life, with God and his saints in heaven, so they had been out of the way, for then all had been well enough as he thought. But to let these things pass, the king this year sent his eldest daughter Blanche, accompanied with the Earl of Somerset, the Bishop of Worcester, the Lord Clifford, and others, into Almanie,[2] which brought her to Cologne, and there with great triumph she was married to William Duke of Bavaria, son and heir to Lewis the Emperor. About mid of August, the king, to chastise the presumptuous attempts of the Welshmen, went with a great power of men into Wales, to pursue the captain of the Welsh, rebel Owen Glendower, but in effect he lost his labor; for Owen conveyed himself out of the way, into his known lurking places, and (as was thought) through art magic, he caused such foul weather of winds, tempest, rain, snow, and hail to be raised, for the annoyance of the king's army, that the like had not been heard of; in such sort, that the king was constrained to return home, having caused his people yet to spoil and burn first a great part of the country. The same time, the lord Edmund of Langley, Duke of York, departed this life, and was buried at Langley with his brethren. The Scots, under the leading of Patrick Hepborne, of Hales the younger, entering into England, were overthrown at Nesbit,[3] in the marches,[4] as in the Scottish chronicle ye may find more at large. This battle was fought the two and twentieth of June, in this year of our Lord 1402.

Archibald, Earl Douglas, sore displeased in his mind for this overthrow, procured a commission to invade England, and that to his cost, as ye may likewise read in the Scottish histories. For at a place called Holmedon, they were so fiercely assailed by the Englishmen, under

---

1 The grisly practices of the Welshwomen are described in greater detail later in Holinshed; see below, p. 196.
2 Germany.
3 In Northumberland.
4 Areas of England bordering Scotland and Wales.

the leading of the Lord Percy, surnamed Henry Hotspur, and George, Earl of March, that with violence of the English shot they were quite vanquished and put to flight, on the Rood Day[1] in harvest, with a great slaughter made by the Englishmen. We know that the Scottish writers note this battle to have chanced in the year 1403. But we, following Tho[mas] Walsingham in this place, and other English writers, for the accompt of times, have thought good to place it in this year 1402, as in the same writers we find it. There were slain of men of estimation, Sir John Swinton, Sir Adam Gordon, Sir John Leviston, Sir Alexander Ramsey of Dalehousie, and three and twenty knights, besides ten thousand of the commons: and of prisoners among other were these: Mordake, Earl of Fife, son to the Governor;[2] Archibald Earl Douglas, which in the fight lost one of his eyes; Thomas, Earl of Murray; Robert, Earl of Angus; and (as some writers have) the Earls of Atholl & Menteith, with five hundred other of meaner degrees. After this, the Lord Percy, having bestowed the prisoners in sure keeping, entered Tividale, wasting and destroying the whole country, and then besieged the castle of Cocklawes, whereof was captain one Sir John Grenlow, who compounded with the Englishmen, that if the castle were not succored[3] within three months, then he would deliver it into their hands.

The first two months passed, and no likelihood of rescue appeared; but ere the third month was expired, the Englishmen being sent for to go with the king into Wales, raised their siege and departed, leaving the noblemen prisoners with the Earl of Northumberland, and with his son the Lord Percy, to keep them to the king's use. In this meanwhile, such as misliked with the doctrine and ceremonies then used in the church, ceased not to utter their consciences, though in secret, to those in whom they had affiance.[4] But as in the like cases it commonly happeneth, they were betrayed by some that were thought chiefly to favor their cause, as by Sir Lewis Clifford, Knight, who having leaned to the doctrine a long time, did now (as Thomas Walsingham writeth) disclose all that he knew unto the Archbishop of Canterbury, to show himself as it were to have erred rather of simpleness and ignorance,

---

1 Holy Cross day, September 14.
2 The original missing punctuation here led Shakespeare to identify Mordake as son to Douglas.
3 Assisted.
4 Trust.

than of frowardness[1] or stubborn malice. The names of such as taught the articles and conclusions maintained by those which then they called Lollards or heretics, the said Sir Lewis Clifford gave in writing to the said Archbishop. Edmund Mortimer, Earl of March, prisoner with Owen Glendower, whether for irksomness of cruel captivity, or fear of death, or for what other cause, it is uncertain, agreed to take part with Owen, against the king of England, and took to wife the daughter of the said Owen.

Strange wonders happened (as men reported) at the nativity of this man, for the same night he was born, all his father's horses in the stable were found to stand in blood up to their bellies. The morrow after the Feast of Saint Michael,[2] a parliament began at Westminster, which continued the space of seven weeks, in the same was a tenth and a half[3] granted by the clergy, and a fifteenth by the commonalty. Moreover, the commons in this parliament besought the king to have the person of George, Earl of March, a Scottishman, recommended to his majesty, for that the same Earl showed himself faithful to the king & his realm.

There was also a statute made, that the friars beggars[4] should not receive any into their order, under the age of fourteen years. In this fourth year of King Henry's reign, ambassadors were sent over into Brittany, to bring from thence the Duchess of Brittany, the Lady Jane de Navarre, the widow of John de Montford, late Duke of Brittany, surnamed the conqueror, with whom by procurators the king had contracted matrimony. In the beginning of February, those that were sent returned with her in safety, but not without tasting the bitter storms of the wind and weather, that tossed them sore to and fro, before they could get to land. The king met her at Winchester, where, the seventh of February, the marriage was solemnized betwixt them.

Whilst these things were thus in doing in England, Waleran, Earl of Saint Paul, bearing still a deadly and malicious hatred toward King Henry, having assembled sixteen or seventeen hundred men of war, embarked them at Harfleur, and taking the sea, landed in the Isle of Wight, in the which he burned two villages, and four simple cottages, and for a triumph of so noble an act, made four knights. But when he

---

1 Perversity.
2 September 29.
3 I.e., proportion of taxes paid to the king.
4 Religious orders whose members lived on alms; mendicant friars.

heard that the people of the Isle were assembled and approached to fight with him, he hasted to his ships, and returned home: wherewith the noblemen of his company were displeased, considering his provision to be great and his gain small. In the same very season, John, Earl of Clermont, son to the Duke of Bourbon, won in Gascoigne out of the Englishmen's possession, the castles of Saint Peter, Saint Marie, and the New castle; and the Lord de la Bret won the castle of Carlassin, which was no small loss to the English nation.

Henry, Earl of Northumberland, with his brother Thomas, Earl of Worcester, and his son the Lord Henry Percy, surnamed Hotspur, which were to King Henry in the beginning of his reign, both faithful friends, and earnest aiders, began now to envy his wealth and felicity; and especially they were grieved, because the king demanded of the Earl and his son such Scottish prisoners as were taken at Holmedon and Nesbit. For of all the captives which were taken in the conflicts foughten in those two places, there was delivered to the king's possession only Mordake, Earl of Fife, the Duke of Albany's son, though the king did diverse and sundry times require deliverance of the residue, and that with great threatenings: wherewith the Percies being sore offended, for that they claimed them as their own proper prisoners, and their peculiar prize, by the counsel of the Lord Thomas Percy, Earl of Worcester, whose study was ever (as some write) to procure malice, and set things in a broil, came to the king unto Windsor (upon a purpose to prove him) and there required of him, that either by ransom or otherwise, he would cause to be delivered out of prison Edmund Mortimer, Earl of March, their cousin germane,[1] whom (as they reported) Owen Glendower kept in filthy prison, shackled with irons, only for that he took his part, and was to him faithful and true.

The king began not a little to muse at this request, and not without cause: for indeed it touched him somewhat near, since this Edmund was son to Roger, Earl of March,[2] son to the Lady Philippa, daughter of Lionel, Duke of Clarence, the third son of King Edward the third; which Edmund at King Richard's going into Ireland, was proclaimed heir apparent to the crown and realm, whose aunt called Elianor,[3] the Lord Henry Percy had married; and therefore King Henry could not

1 Closely akin.
2 In reality this Edmund was brother to Roger, Earl of March.
3 In reality Elizabeth, but called Kate by Shakespeare.

well hear, that any man should be earnest about the advancement of that lineage. The king when he had studied on the matter, made answer, that the Earl of March was not taken prisoner for his cause, nor in his service, but willingly suffered himself to be taken, because he would not withstand the attempts of Owen Glendower, and his [ac]complices, & therefore he would neither ransom him, nor relieve him.

The Percies with this answer and fraudulent excuse were not a little fumed, insomuch that Henry Hotspur said openly: "Behold, the heir of the realm is robbed of his right, and yet the robber with his own will not redeem him." So in this fury the Percies departed, minding nothing more than to depose King Henry from the high type of his royalty, and to place in his seat their cousin Edmund, Earl of March, whom they did not only deliver out of captivity, but also (to the high displeasure of King Henry) entered in league with the foresaid Owen Glendower. Herewith, they by their deputies in the house of the Archdeacon of Bangor, divided the realm amongst them, causing a tripartite indenture to be made and sealed with their seals, by the covenants whereof, all England from Severn and Trent, south and eastward, was assigned to the Earl of March; all Wales, & the lands beyond Severn westward, were appointed to Owen Glendower; and all the remnant from Trent northward, to the Lord Percy.

This was done (as some have said) through a foolish credit given to a vain prophecy, as though King Henry was the moldwarp,[1] cursed of God's own mouth, and they three were the dragon, the lion, and the wolf, which should divide this realm between them. Such is the deviation (saith Hall) and not divination of those blind and fantastical dreams of the Welsh prophesiers. King Henry not knowing of this new confederacy, and nothing less minding than that which after happened, gathered a great army to go again into Wales, whereof the Earl of Northumberland and his son were advertised by the Earl of Worcester, and with all diligence raised all the power they could make, and sent to the Scots which before were taken prisoners at Holmedon, for aid of men, promising to the Earl of Douglas the town of Berwick, and a part of Northumberland, and to other Scottish lords, great lordships and seigniories,[2] if they obtained the upper hand. The Scots in hope of

---

1 Mole.
2 Territories.

gain, and desirous to be revenged of their old griefs, came to the Earl with a great company well appointed.

The Percies, to make their part seem good, devised certain articles, by the advice of Richard Scroop, Archbishop of York, brother to the Lord Scroop, whom King Henry had caused to be beheaded at Bristol. These articles being showed to diverse noblemen, and other states of the realm, moved them to favor their purpose, in so much that many of them did not only promise to the Percies aid and succor by words, but also by their writings and seals confirmed the same. Howbeit when the matter came to trial, the most part of the confederates abandoned them, and at the day of the conflict left them alone. Thus after that the conspirators had discovered themselves, the Lord Henry Percy, desirous to proceed in the enterprise, upon trust to be assisted by Owen Glendower, the Earl of March, & other, assembled an army of men of arms and archers forth of Cheshire and Wales. Incontinently, his uncle Thomas Percy, Earl of Worcester, that had the government of the Prince of Wales, who as then lay at London in secret manner, conveyed himself out of the prince's house, and coming to Stafford (where he met his nephew) they increased their power by all ways and means they could devise. The Earl of Northumberland himself was not with them, but being sick, had promised upon his amendment to repair unto them (as some write) with all convenient speed.

These noble men, to make their conspiracy to seem excusable, besides the articles above mentioned, sent letters abroad, wherein was contained, that their gathering of an army tended to none other end, but only for the safeguard of their own persons, and to put some better government in the commonwealth. For whereas taxes and tallages[1] were daily levied, under pretense to be employed in defense of the realm, the same were vainly wasted, and unprofitably consumed: and where through the slanderous reports of their enemies, the king had taken a grievous displeasure with them, they durst not appear personally in the king's presence, until the prelates[2] and barons of the realm had obtained of the king license for them to come and purge themselves before him, by lawful trial of their peers, whose judgment (as they pretended) they would in no wise refuse. Many that saw and heard these

---

1   Taxes levied on feudal dependants (OED).
2   High-ranking clergymen.

letters, did commend their diligence, and highly praised their assured fidelity and trustiness towards the commonwealth.

But the king, understanding their cloaked drift, devised (by what means he might) to quiet and appease the commons, and deface their contrived forgeries; and therefore he wrote an answer to their libels, that he marveled much, since the Earl of Northumberland, and the Lord Henry Percy his son, had received the most part of the sums of money granted to him by the clergy and commonalty, for defense of the marches, as he could evidently prove, what should move them to complain and raise such manifest slanders. And whereas he understood, that the Earls of Northumberland and Worcester, and the Lord Percy, had by their letters signified to their friends abroad, that by reason of the slanderous reports of their enemies, they durst not appear in his presence, without the mediation of the prelates and nobles of the realm, so as they required pledges, whereby they might safely come afore him, to declare and allege what they had to say in proof of their innocency, he protested by letters sent forth under his seal, that they might safely come and go, without all danger, or any manner of indamagement to be offered to their persons.

But this could not satisfy those men, but that resolved to go forwards with their enterprise, they marched towards Shrewsbury, upon hope to be aided (as men thought) by Owen Glendower, and his Welshmen, publishing abroad throughout the countries on each side, that King Richard was alive, whom if they wished to see, they willed them to repair in armor unto the castle of Chester, where (without all doubt) he was at that present, and ready to come forward. This tale being raised, though it were most untrue, yet it bred variable motions in men's minds, causing them to waver, so as they knew not to which part they should stick; and verily, diverse were well affected towards King Richard, specially such as had tasted of his princely bountifulnes, of which there was no small number. And to speak a truth, no marvel it was, if many envied the prosperous state of King Henry, since it was evident enough to the world, that he had with wrong usurped the crown, and not only violently deposed King Richard, but also cruelly procured his death; for the which undoubtedly, both he and his posterity tasted such troubles, as put them still in danger of their states, till their direct succeeding line was quite rooted out by the contrary faction, as in Henry the sixth and Edward the fourth it may appear.

But now to return where we left. King Henry, advertised of the proceedings of the Percies, forthwith gathered about him such power as
he might make, and being earnestly called upon by the Scot, the Earl
of March,[1] to make haste and give battle to his enemies, before their
power by delaying of time should still too much increase, he passed
forward with such speed, that he was in sight of his enemies, lying in
camp near to Shrewsbury, before they were in doubt of any such thing,
for the Percies thought that he would have stayed at Burton-upon-Trent,
till his council had come thither to him to give their advice what he
were best to do. But herein the enemy was deceived of his expectation,
since the king had great regard of expedition and making speed for
the safety of his own person, whereunto the Earl of March incited him,
considering that in delay is danger, & loss in lingering, as the poet in
the like case saith:

Tolle moras, nocuit semper differre paratis,
Dum trepidant nullo firmatae robore partes.[2]

By reason of the king's sudden coming in this sort, they stayed from
assaulting the town of Shrewsbury, which enterprise they were ready
at that instant to have taken in hand, and forthwith the Lord Percy (as
a captain of high courage) began to exhort the captains and soldiers to
prepare themselves to battle, since the matter was grown to that point,
that by no means it could be avoided, so that (said he), "This day shall
either bring us all to advancement & honor, or else if it shall chance
us to be overcome, shall deliver us from the king's spiteful malice and
cruel disdain: for playing the men (as we ought to do), better it is to
die in battle for the commonwealth's cause, than through cowardlike
fear to prolong life, which after shall be taken from us, by sentence
of the enemy."

Hereupon, the whole army being in number about fourteen thousand
chosen men, promised to stand with him so long as life lasted. There
were with the Percies as chieftains of this army, the Earl of Douglas,
a Scottish man, the Baron of Kinderton, Sir Hugh Browne, and Sir

---

1 I.e., Dunbar, the Scottish Earl of March.
2 "While the other side in panic has not fortified its strength / end delay!
Procrastination always harms the men prepared for action." From Lucan's *Civil War*
(*Pharsalia*), trans. Susan H. Braund (Oxford: Oxford UP, 1992), 1.280–81.

Richard Vernon, Knights, with diverse other stout and right valiant captains. Now when the two armies were encamped, the one against the other, the Earl of Worcester and the Lord Percy with their [ac]complices sent the articles (whereof I spake before) by Thomas Caton, and Thomas Salvain esquires to King Henry, under their hands and seals, which articles in effect charged him with manifest perjury, in that (contrary to his oath received upon the evangelists[1] at Doncaster, when he first entered the realm after his exile) he had taken upon him the crown and royal dignity, imprisoned King Richard, caused him to resign his title, and finally to be murdered. Diverse other matters they laid to his charge, as levying of taxes and tallages, contrary to his promise, infringing of laws & customs of the realm, and suffering the Earl of March to remain in prison, without travailing[2] to have him delivered. All which things they as procurors & protectors of the commonwealth, took upon them to prove against him, as they protested unto the whole world.

King Henry after he had read their articles, with the defiance which they annexed to the same, answered the esquires, that he was ready with dint of sword and fierce battle to prove their quarrel false, and nothing else than a forged matter, not doubting, but that God would aid and assist him in his righteous cause, against the disloyal and false forsworn traitors. The next day in the morning early, being the even of Mary Magdalene,[3] they set their battles in order on both sides, and now whilst the warriors looked when the token of battle should be given, the Abbot of Shrewsbury, and one of the clerks of the privy seal, were sent from the king unto the Percies, to offer them pardon, if they would come to any reasonable agreement. By their persuasions, the Lord Henry Percy began to give ear unto the king's offers, & so sent with them his uncle, the Earl of Worcester, to declare unto the king the causes of those troubles, and to require some effectual reformation in the same.

It was reported for a truth, that now when the king had condescended unto all that was reasonable at his hands to be required, and seemed to humble himself more than was meet for his estate, the Earl of Worcester (upon his return to his nephew) made relation clean contrary to that the king had said, in such sort that he set his nephew's heart more in

---

1 The writers of the Four Gospels, Matthew, Mark, Luke, and John; hence also a copy of the Gospels.
2 Working.
3 The eve before the feast day of Mary Magdalene. The feast day is July 22.

displeasure towards the king, than ever it was before, driving him by that means to fight whether he would or not. Then suddenly blew the trumpets, the king's part crying, "S[aint] George! Upon them!" The adversaries cried, "Esperance![1] Percy!" and so the two armies furiously joined. The archers on both sides shot for the best game, laying on such load with arrows, that many died, and were driven down that never rose again.

The Scots (as some write) which had the foreward[2] on the Percies' side, intending to be revenged of their old displeasures done to them by the English nation, set so fiercely on the king's foreward, led by the Earl of Stafford, that they made the same draw back, and had almost broken their adversaries' array. The Welshmen also, which before had lain lurking in the woods, mountains, and marshes, hearing of this battle toward, came to the aid of the Percies, and refreshed the wearied people with new succors. The king, perceiving that his men were thus put to distress, what with the violent impression of the Scots, and the tempestuous storms of arrows, that his adversaries discharged freely against him and his people, it was no need to will him to stir: for suddenly with his fresh battle, he approached and relieved his men; so that the battle began more fierce than before. Here the Lord Henry Percy, and the Earl Douglas, a right stout and hardy captain, not regarding the shot of the king's battle, nor the close order of the ranks, pressing forward together bent their whole forces towards the king's person, coming upon him with spears and swords so fiercely, that the Earl of March the Scot, perceiving their purpose, withdrew the king from that side of the field (as some write) for his great benefit and safegard (as it appeared) for they gave such a violent onset upon them that stood about the king's standard, that slaying his standard-bearer, Sir Walter Blunt, and overthrowing the standard, they made slaughter of all those that stood about it, as the Earl[3] of Stafford, that day made by the king constable of the realm, and diverse other.

The prince that day helped his father like a lusty young gentleman: for although he was hurt in the face with an arrow, so that diverse noble men that were about him, would have conveyed him forth of the field, yet he would not suffer them so to do, least his departure from amongst

---

1   "Esperance ma comforte" (in hope is my strength) is a Percy family motto. Shakespeare gives the cry to Hotspur in 5.2.

2   Vanguard.

3   Including the Earl.

his men might happily[1] have stricken some fear into their hearts: and so without regard of his hurt, he continued with his men, & never ceased, either to fight where the battle was most hot, or to encourage his men where it seemed most need. This battle lasted three long hours, with indifferent fortune on both parts, till at length, the king crying, "Saint George! Victory!" brake the array of his enemies, and adventured so far, that (as some write) the Earl Douglas strake him down; & at that instant slew Sir Walter Blunt, and three other, appareled in the king's suit and clothing, saying: "I marvel to see so many kings thus suddenly arise one in the neck of another." The king indeed was raised, & did that day many a noble feat of arms, for as it is written, he slew that day with his own hands six and thirty persons of his enemies. The other on his part,[2] encouraged by his doings, fought valiantly, and slew the Lord Percy, called Sir Henry Hotspur. To conclude, the king's enemies were vanquished, and put to flight, in which flight, the Earl of Douglas, for haste, falling from the crag of a high mountain, brake one of his cullions,[3] and was taken, and for his valiantness, of the king frankly and freely delivered.

There was also taken the Earl of Worcester, the procuror and setter forth of all this mischief, Sir Richard Vernon, and the Baron of Kinderton, with diverse other. There were slain upon the king's part, beside the Earl of Stafford, to the number of ten knights, Sir Hugh Shirley, Sir John Clifton, Sir John Cokaine, Sir Nicholas Gawsey, Sir Walter Blunt, Sir John Calverley, Sir John Macy of Podington, Sir Hugh Mortimer, and Sir Robert Gawsey, all the which received the same morning the order of knighthood: Sir Thomas Wendesley was wounded to death, and so passed out of this life shortly after. There died in all upon the king's side sixteen hundred, and four thousand were grievously wounded. On the contrary side were slain, besides the Lord Percy, the most part of the knights and esquires of the county of Chester, to the number of two hundred, besides yeomen and footmen; in all there died of those that fought on the Percies' side, about five thousand. This battle was fought on Mary Magdalene even, being Saturday. Upon the Monday following, the Earl of Worcester, the Baron of Kinderton, and Sir Richard Vernon, Knights, were condemned and beheaded. The Earl's head was sent to London, there to be set on the bridge.

---

1 Perhaps.
2 Others on the king's side, not necessarily the prince.
3 Testicles.

[*Welshwomen and English corpses*]
[1405: vol. 3, p. 528]

This was a shrewd discomfiture to the Welsh by the English, on whom sinister lot loured,[1] at such time as more than a thousand of them were slain in a hot skirmish; and such shameful villainy executed upon the carcasses of the dead men by the Welshwomen; as the like (I do believe) hath never or seldom been practiced. For though it was a cruel deed of Tomyris, Queen of the Massagetae in Scythia, against whom when Cyrus, the great king of Persia came and had slain her son, she by her policy trained him into such straits, that she slew him and all his host; and causing a great vessel to be filled with the blood of Cyrus and other Persians, did cast his head thereinto, saying, "Blood thou hast thirsted and now drink thereof thy fill." Again, though it was a cruel deed of Fulvia, the wife of Marcus Antonius (at whose commandment Popilius cut off the head and hands of that golden mouthed orator, Tully,[2] which afterwards were nailed up over the place of common pleas at Rome), to hold in her hands the tongue of that father of eloquence, cut out of his head after the same was parted from his shoulders, and to prick it all over with pins and needles. Yet neither the cruelty of Tomyris nor yet of Fulvia is comparable to this of the Welshwomen, which is worthy to be recorded to the shame of a sex pretending the title of weak vessels, and yet raging with such force of fierceness and barbarism. For the dead bodies of the Englishmen, being above a thousand lying upon the ground imbrued[3] in their own blood, was a sight (a man would think) grievous to look upon, and so far from exciting and stirring up affections of cruelty that it should rather have moved the beholders to commiseration and mercy. Yet did the women of Wales cut off their privities, and put one part thereof into the mouths of every dead man, in such sort that the cullions hung down to their chins; and not so contented, they did cut off their noses and thrust them into their tails as they lay on the ground, mangled and defaced. This was a very ignominious deed, and a worse not committed among the barbarous, which though it make the reader to read it, and

---

1 Frowned.
2 Marcus Tullius Cicero, (106–43 BCE), commonly called Cicero, one of Rome's greatest orators and prose writers.
3 Stained.

the hearer to hear it, ashamed. Yet because it was a thing done in open sight, and left testified in history; I see little reason why it should not be imparted in our mother tongue to the knowledge of our own countrymen, as well as unto strangers in a language unknown. And thus, much by way of notifying the inhumanity and detestable demeanor of those Welshwomen, after the conflict between the English and the Welsh, whereof desultory mention is made before pag. 520, where Edmund Mortimer, Earl of March, was taken prisoner.

[An interview between the prince and the king]
[1412: vol. 3, pp. 538–39]

Whilst these things were a doing in France, the Lord Henry, Prince of Wales, eldest son to King Henry, got knowledge that certain of his father's servants were busy to give informations against him, whereby discord might arise betwixt him and his father: for they put into the king's head, not only what evil rule (according to the course of youth) the prince kept to the offense of many, but also what great resort of people came to his house, so that the court was nothing furnished with such a train as daily followed the prince. These tales brought no small suspicion into the king's head, lest his son would presume to usurp the crown, he being yet alive, through which suspicious jealousy, it was perceived that he favored not his son, as in times past he had done.

The prince, sore offended with such persons, as by slanderous reports, sought not only to spot his good name abroad in the realm, but to sow discord also betwixt him and his father, wrote his letters into every part of the realm, to reprove all such slanderous devises of those that sought his discredit. And to clear himself the better, that the world might understand what wrong he had to be slandered in such wise: about the feast of Peter and Paul, to wit, the nine and twentieth day of June, he came to the court with such a number of noble men and other his friends that wished him well, as the like train had been seldom seen repairing to the court at any one time in those days. He was appareled in a gown of blue satin, full of small eyelet holes, at every hole the needle hanging by a silk thread with which it was sewed. About his arm he wore a hound's collar set full of ss of gold, and the tirets[1] likewise being of the same metal.

---

1 Rings on a dog's collar.

The court was then at Westminster, where he, being entered into the hall, not one of his company durst once advance himself further than the fire in the same hall, notwithstanding they were earnestly requested by the lords to come higher. But they, regarding what they had in commandment of the prince, would not presume to do in anything contrary thereunto. He himself, only accompanied with those of the king's house, was straight admitted to the presence of the king his father, who being at that time grievously diseased, yet caused himself in his chair to be born into his privy chamber, where in the presence of three or four persons, in whom he had most confidence, he commanded the prince to show what he had to say concerning the cause of his coming.

The prince kneeling down before his father said: "Most redoubted and sovereign lord and father, I am at this time come to your presence as your liege man, and as your natural son, in all things to be at your commandment. And where I understand you have in suspicion my demeanor against your grace, you know very well, that if I knew any man within this realm, of whom you should stand in fear, my duty were to punish that person, thereby to remove that grief from your heart. Then how much more ought I to suffer death, to ease your grace of that grief which you have of me, being your natural son and liege man. And to that end, I have this day made myself ready by confession and receiving of the sacrament. And therefore I beseech you, most redoubted lord and dear father, for the honor of God, to ease your heart of all such suspicion as you have of me, and to dispatch me here before your knees, with this same dagger (and withal, he delivered unto the king his dagger, in all humble reverence, adding further that his life was not so dear to him that he wished to live one day with your displeasure) and therefore in thus ridding me out of life, and your self from all suspicion, here in presence of these lords, and before God at the day of the general judgment, I faithfully protest clearly to forgive you."

The king moved herewith, cast from him the dagger, and embracing the prince kissed him, and with shedding tears confessed that indeed he had him partly in suspicion, though now (as he perceived) not with just cause, and therefore from thenceforth no misreport should cause him to have him in mistrust, and this he promised of his honor. So by his great wisdom was the wrongful suspicion, which his father had conceived against him, removed, and he restored to his favor. And further, where he could not but grievously complain of them that had slandered him so greatly, to the defacing not only of his honor, but also putting him in danger of his life, he humbly besought the king that they might answer their unjust accusation; and in case they were found to have forged such matters upon a malicious purpose, that then they might suffer some punishment for their faults, though not to the full of that they had deserved. The king, seeming to grant his reasonable desire, yet told him that he must tarry[1] a parliament, that such offenders might be punished by judgment of their peers. And so, for that time he was dismissed, with great love and signs of fatherly affection.

Thus were the father and the son reconciled, betwixt whom the said pickthanks[2] had sewn division, insomuch that the son, upon a vehement conceit of unkindness sprung in the father, was in the way to be worn out of favor. Which was the more likely to come to pass, by their informations that privily charged him with riot and other uncivil demeanor unseemly for a prince. Indeed, he was youthfully given, grown to audacity, and had chosen him companions agreeable to his age with whom he spent the time in such recreations, exercises, and delights as he fancied. But yet (it should seem by the report of some writers) that his behavior was not offensive or at least tending to the damage of anybody, since he had a care to avoid doing of wrong, and to tender his affections within the tract of virtue, whereby he opened unto himself a ready passage of good liking among the prudent sort, and was beloved of such as could discern his disposition, which was in no degree so excessive, as that he deserved in such vehement manner to be suspected. In whose dispraise I find little, but to his praise very much, parcel whereof I will deliver by the way as a metyard[3] whereby the residue may be measured.

2. FROM JOHN STOW, *CHRONICLES OF ENGLAND* (1580)

[As well as contributing to the revised 1587 edition of Holinshed's *Chronicles of England, Scotland, and Ireland,* John Stow published his own shorter historical works, including the *Chronicles of England* (1580) and the *Annales of England* (1592). Although Shakespeare's debt to Stow for the materials of *Henry IV, Part One* is uncertain, Stow's work did

---

1 Wait for.
2 Flatterers, telltales.
3 Yardstick.

contribute to popular conceptions about the reign of Henry IV and the king's relationship with his son. According to *The Oxford Dictionary of National Biography*, Stow's chronicles "were more widely read than those of any other historian of his era." The modern-spelling excerpts presented here are based on a facsimile of *The Chronicles of England* available through the *Early English Books Online* database.]

[*The Battle of Shrewsbury*]
[1403: pp. 553–56]

Henry Percy the younger did suddenly show himself to be the king's enemy, unto whom joined Thomas Percy Earl of Worcester, uncle to the said Henry: and to make their conspiracy excusable, they did write unto the Shires about, that they pretended nothing against the allegiance nor fidelity which they ought[1] to the king, neither to gather to any other end an army, but only for the saving of their persons, and for the better government of the common wealth, because the payments and taxes granted to the king for the safe custody of the realm, were put to such uses as they ought not to be, and were unprofitably consumed and wasted.

Moreover they complained, that because of the evil slanders which their enemies had made of them, they durst not personally appear in the king's presence, until the prelates and barons had entreated for them, that they might be permitted to purge themselves before the king, and be lawfully judged by their peers, so that many that saw these letters, did praise their diligence, and extol their fidelity towards the common wealth. But the king being disquieted with these doings, that he might appease the commonalty, he wrote to them, that he marveled much, that seeing the Earl of Northumberland, and Henry his son had received the most part of the payments and sums granted to him by the clergy and commonalty, for the defense of the Marches of Scotland, what occasion they had to make such manifest slanders &c. But the young Henry Percy putting his confidence in the aid of Owen Glendower, and Edmund Mortimer Earl of March, with the Welshmen, and men of Cheshire, published that King Richard was alive, and was with them, whom if any man would see, they should without delay come

---

1 Owed.

in armor to the Castle of Leicester, which declaration made diverse variable motions in the hearts of many, and caused them to waver. King Henry considering all things wisely, gathered together as many as he could, and came suddenly in to the parts where the rebels kept their rage, and when Henry [Percy] saw upon a sudden the king's banner, and was even ready to have scaled the town of Shrewsbury he straight away desisted from the assault of the town, and said to his men: "We must now needs turn our weapons upon them that come against us. Ye see the king's standard: neither can we, though we would, seek any starting-hole. Stand to it manfully therefore, for this day shall either bring us all to promotion and honor, if we overcome, or else if we be overcome, it shall deliver us from the king's malice. For it is a more comely thing to die in battle for the common wealth, than after battle to die by the sentence of condemnation by the enemy."

And with that, 14000 of the best men that were with Henry, made vow and promised to stand by him so long as breath would serve, and they took the field that was commodious for them, and the king and his men lay in the field right against them. The bowmen of Henry Percy began the battle. Whole arrows fell not upon the ground, but upon the bodies of the king's soldiers, and the king's archers shot as fiercely against their enemies, so that on both sides many were slain, and many thousands fled, thinking the king had been slain. But the Earl of Dunbar withdrew the king the place that he stood in, which was a good turn for him, for the foresaid Henry Percy, and Earl Douglas the Scot (than whom was never man more stout) raged so, that the king's standard was overthrown, and those about it slain, among whom was slain Humphrey Earl of Stafford, Sir Walter Blunt the king's standard-bearer, Sir Nicholas Langford, Sir John Clifton, and the two brethren Genetels, with many other knights and gentlemen, and of the commons on both sides about 5000 slain. Henry the prince was wounded in the face with an arrow. In the mean season, Henry Percy, whilst he went before his men in the battle, pressing upon his enemies, was suddenly slain, which being known, the king's enemies fled, but the Earl Douglas was taken, and also Thomas Percy Earl of Worcester, with Sir Richard Vernon, and the Baron of Kinderton, and many other were taken. This battle was fought on Mary Magdalen eve, near unto Shrewsbury, in a place called Old field, alias Bull field. On the Monday following, were condemned and beheaded at Shrewsbury the Earl of Worcester, the

Baron of Kinderton, and Sir Richard Vernon. The body of Henry Percy was delivered to the L. of Furnivale to be buried, but the king caused the same body to be taken up, and to be reposed between two millstones in the Town of Shrewsbury, there to be kept with armed men, and afterward to be headed and quartered, commanding his head and quarters to be carried unto diverse cities of the kingdom.

[An interview between the prince and his father]
[1412: pp. 576–81]

King Henry kept his Christmas at his manor of Eltham, being so sore sick, that sometime men thought that he had been dead: notwithstanding it pleased God that he recovered his strength again a little.

After Christmas he called the nobles of the realm together to a parliament at London, but he lived not to the end thereof, for now after the great and fortunate chances happened to him and being delivered of all civil division, he was taken with sickness, of the which he languished till his appointed hour, during which sickness, some evil disposed people labored to make dissension between the king and the prince his son, by reason whereof, and by the act of youth, which he exercised more than meanly, and for the great recourse of people unto him, of whom his court was at all times more abundant than the king his father, the king suspected that he would presume to usurp the crown, he being alive: which suspicious jealousy was occasion that he in part withdrew his affection and singular love from the prince. But when this noble prince was advertised of his father's jealousy, he disguised himself in a gown of blue satin, made full of small eyelet holes, and at every eyelet the needle wherewith it was made hanging still by a thread of silk. And about his arm he wore a dog's collar set full of ss of gold, and the tirets[1] of the same also of fine gold. Thus appareled, with a great company of lords and other noblemen of his court, he came to the king his father, who at that time lay at Westminster, where at his coming (by his own commandment) not one of his company advanced himself further than the fire in the hall, notwithstanding that they were greatly and oft desired to the contrary, by the lords and great estates of the king's court. And that the prince had commanded, to give the less occasion

---

1 See p. 197, n. 1.

of mistrust to the king his father, but he himself only accompanied of the king's house, passed forth to the king his father, to whom (after due salutation) he desired to show the intent of his mind in secret manner.

Then the king caused himself to be borne in his chair into his secret chamber (because he was diseased and might not go) where in the presence of three or four persons, in whom the king had most confidence, he commanded the prince to show the effect of his mind. Then the prince kneeling down before his father, said to him these words: "Most redoubted lord and father, I am this time come to your presence, as your liegeman, and as your son natural, in all things to obey your grace as my sovereign lord and father. And whereas I understand you have me suspect of my behavior against your grace, and that you fear I would usurp your crown against the pleasure of your highness, of my conversation your grace knoweth that if you were in fear of any man, of what estate so ever he were, my duty were to the endangering of my life to punish that person, thereby to raze that sore from your heart. And then how much rather ought I to suffer death to bring your grace from the fear that you have of me that am your natural son, and your liegeman. And to that intent I have this day by confession and receiving the sacrament, prepared myself, and therefore most redoubted lord and father, I beseech you in the honor of God, for the easing of your heart, heretofore[1] your knees to slay me with this dagger." And at that word with all reverence he delivered to the king his dagger, saying: "My lord and father my life is not so desirous to me, that I would live one day that should be to you displeasure, nor I covet not so much my life as I do your pleasure and welfare, and in your thus doing, here in the presence of these lords, and tofore God at the day of judgment I clearly forgive you my death." At these words of the prince, the king taken with compassion of heart, cast from him the dagger, and embracing the prince kissed him, and with effusion of tears said unto him: "My right dear and heartily beloved son, it is of truth that I had you partly suspect, and as I now perceive, undeserved on your part: but seeing this your humility and faithfulness, I shall neither slay you, nor from henceforth have you any more in mistrust, for no report that shall be made unto me, and thereof I assure you upon mine honor." Thus by his

---

1 Before.

great wisdom was the wrongful imagination of his father's hate utterly avoided, and himself restored to the king's former grace and favor.

3. FROM EDWARD HALL, *UNION OF THE TWO NOBLE AND ILLUSTRIOUS FAMILIES OF LANCASTER AND YORK* (1548)

[While this work may not have been a direct source for *Henry IV, Part One*, it does provide an important example of the official Tudor perspective on the century preceding the reign of Henry VII. Its full title is *The Union of the two noble and illustrious families of Lancaster and York being long in continual dissension for the crown of this noble realm, with all the acts done in both the times of the Princes, both of the one lineage and of the other, beginning at the time of king Henry the fourth, the first author of this division, and so successively proceeding to the reign of the high and prudent prince, king Henry the eighth, the indubitable flower and very heir of both the said lineages.* As this title indicates, Hall presents a providential view of history, which sees Henry IV's usurpation of the throne as leading directly to the Wars of the Roses: a crisis finally resolved through the union of the houses of Lancaster and York through the marriage of the Lancastrian Henry Tudor with Elizabeth of York. Holinshed draws on Hall extensively and it is interesting to note how much both Holinshed and Stow owe to Hall. This modern-spelling excerpt is based on the facsimile provided by the *Early English Books Online* database.]

The Third Year
In this year appeared a comet or blazing Star of a huge quantity by a long season which, as the Astronomers affirmed, signified great effusion of man's blood, which judgment was not frustrate, as you shall perceive. For Henry, Earl of Northumberland and Thomas, Earl of Worcester, his brother, and his son Lord Henry Percy called Hotspur, which were to King Henry in the beginning of his reign both fautors,[1] friends and aiders, perceiving now that he had pacified all domestical sedition and repressed his enemies, and reduced his realm to a convenient quietness, began somewhat to envy the glory of him, and grudged against his wealth and felicity. And specially grieved, because

---

1 Supporters.

the king demanded of the Earl and his son such Scottish prisoners as they had taken at the conflicts fought at Holmedon and Nesbit, as you before have heard. For of all the captives which were there taken, there was delivered to the king's possession only Mordake, Earl of Fife, son to the Duke of Albany, Governor of Scotland, for the king them diverse and sundry times of the Earl and his son required. But the Percies, affirming them to be their own proper prisoners and their peculiar praies,[1] and to deliver them utterly denied, in so much that the king openly said that if they would not deliver them, he would take them without deliverance. Wherewith they, being sore discontent, by the counsel of Lord Thomas Percy, Earl of Worcester, whose study was ever to procure malice, and to set all things in broil and uncertainty, feigning a cause to prove and tempt the king, came to him to Windsor, requiring him by ransom or otherwise to cause to be delivered out of prison Edmund Mortimer, Earl of March, their cousin germain,[2] whom (as they reported) Owen Glendower kept in filthy prison shackled with irons, only for that cause that he took his part, and was to him faithful and true. The king began not a little to muse on this request, and not without a cause, for indeed it touched him as near as his shirt, as you well may perceive by the genealogy rehearsed in the beginning of this story. For this Edmund was son[3] to Earl Roger, which was son to Lady Philippa, daughter to Lionel, Duke of Clarence, the third son to King Edward the third, which Edmund, at King Richard's going to Ireland, was proclaimed heir apparent to the crown and realm, whose Aunt, called Elinor,[4] this Lord Henry Percy had married. And therefore the king little forced, although that that lineage were clearly subverted and utterly extinct.

When the king had long digested and studied on this matter, he made answer and said that the Earl of March was not taken prisoner neither for his cause nor in his service, but willingly suffered himself to be taken, because he would take no part against Owen Glendower and his [ac]complices, and therefore he would neither ransom nor relieve him, which fraud the king caused openly to be published and divulged, with which answer, if the parties were angry, doubt you not.

---

1 Prey.
2 Closely akin.
3 In reality brother; this error is replicated in Holinshed, Daniel, and Shakespeare.
4 In reality Elizabeth, but called Kate by Shakespeare.

But with the publishing of the cautell[1] that the Earl of March was willingly taken, they ten times more fumed and raged, in so much that Sir Henry Hotspur said openly: "Behold the heir of the realm is robbed of his right, and yet the robber, with his own, will not redeem him." So in this fury the Percies departed, nothing more minding than to depose King Henry from the high type of his regality, and to deliver and set in his throne their cousin, friend & confederate, Edmund, Earl of March, whom they not only delivered out of the captivity of Owen Glendower, but also entered into a league and amity with the said Owen against King Henry and all his friends and fautors, to the great displeasure and long unquieting of King Henry and his partakers. Here, I pass over to declare how a certain writer writeth that this Earl of March, the Lord Percy and Owen Glendower were unwisely made [to] believe by a Welsh Prophesier, that King Henry was the Moldwarp,[2] cursed of God's own mouth, and that they three were the Dragon, the Lion and the Wolf, which should divide this realm between them, by the deviation and not divination of that mawmet[3] Merlin.

I will not rehearse how they, by their deputies in the house of the Archdeacon of Bangor, seduced with that false feigned Prophesy, divided the realm amongst them, nor yet write how by a tripartite indenture sealed with their seals, all England from Severn and Trent South and Eastward, was assigned to the Earl of March: Nor how all Wales and the lands beyond Severn Westward, were appointed to Owen Glendower, and all the remnant from Trent Northward to the Lord Percy. But I will declare to you that which was not prophesized: that is, the confusion, destruction and perdition of these persons, not only giving credit to such a vain fable, but also setting it forward and hoping to attain to the effect of the same, which was especial of the Lord Percy and Owen Glendower. For the Earl of March was ever kept in the court under such a keeper that he could neither do or attempt anything against the king without his knowledge,[4] and died without issue, leaving his right title and interest to Anne, his sister and heir, married to Richard, Earl of Cambridge, father to the Duke of York,

---

1 Deceit.
2 Mole.
3 False god.
4 Hall is correct here, but fails to note that this contradicts his assertions about the Earl of March above.

whose offspring, in continuance of time, obtained the game and got the garland. O, ye wavering Welshmen, call you these prophecies? Nay, call them unprofitable practices. Name you them divinations? Nay, name them diabolical devices. Say you they be prognostications? Nay, they be pestiferous publishings. For by declaring & credit giving to their subtle & obscure meanings, princes have been deceived, many a noble man hath suffered, and many an honest man hath been beguiled & destroyed.

King Henry, knowing of this new confederacy, and nothing less minding then that that happened after, gathered a great army to go again into Wales, whereof the Earl of Northumberland and his son were advertised, by Lord Thomas, Earl of Worcester, and with all diligence raised all the power that they could make and sent to the Scots which before were taken prisoners at Holmedon for aid and men, promising the Earl Douglas the town of Berwick and a part of Northumberland, and to other Scottish lords great lordships and seigniories,[1] if they obtained the upper hand and superiority. The Scots, allured with desire of gain, and for no malice that they bare to King Henry, but somewhat desirous to be revenged of their old grieves, came to the Earl with great company, and to make their cause seem good and just, they devised certain articles by the advice of Richard Scroop, Archbishop of York, brother to the Lord Scroop, whom King Henry caused to be beheaded at Bristow, as you have heard before. Which articles they showed to diverse noblemen and prelates[2] of the realm, which, favoring and consenting to their purpose, not only promised them aid and succor by words, but by their writing and seals confirmed the same. Howbeit, whether it were for fear, either for that they would be lookers-on and no deed-doers, neither promise by word or by writing was performed. For all their confederates them abandoned, & at the day of the conflict left alone, the Earl of Stafford only except, which being of a haughty courage and high stomach, kept his promise & joined with the Percies, to his destruction.

The Lord Percy, with the Earl Douglas and other earls of Scotland with a great army, departed out of the Northparties, leaving his father sick (which promised upon his amendment & recovery without delay to follow) and came to Stafford where his uncle the Earl of Worcester

---

1   Territories.
2   High-ranking clergymen.

and he met, and there began to consult upon their great affairs and high attempted enterprise. There they exhorted their soldiers and companions to refuse no pain for the advancement of the commonwealth, nor to spare no travail for the liberty of their country: protesting openly that they made war only to restore the noble realm of England to his accustomed glory and freedom, which was governed by a tyrant and not by his lawful and right king. The captains swore and the soldiers promised to fight, yea & to die for the liberty of their country. When all things were prepared, they set forward toward Wales, looking every hour for new aid and succors, noising abroad that they came to aid the king against Owen Glendower. The king, hearing of the earls approaching, thought it policy to encounter with them before that the Welshmen should join with their army, and so include him on both parts, and therefore returned suddenly to the town of Shrewsbury. He was scantly entered into the town, but he was by his posts advertised that the earls, with banners displayed and battles ranged, were coming toward him, and were so hot and so courageous, that they with light horses began to skirmish with his host. The king, perceiving their doings, issued out and encamped himself without the East gate of the town. The earls nothing abashed, although their succors them deceived, embattled themselves not far from the king's army. And the same night they sent the articles whereof I spake before, by Thomas Caton and Thomas Salvain, esquires to King Henry, signed with their hands and sealed with their seals, which articles (because no Chronicler save one maketh mention what was the very cause and occasion of this great bloody battle, in the which on both parts were above forty thousand men assembled) I, word for word, according to my copy, do here rehearse.

We Henry Percy, Earl of Northumberland, High Constable of England, and Warden of the West Marches[1] of England toward Scotland, Henry Percy our eldest son, Warden of the East Marches of England toward Scotland, and Thomas Percy, Earl of Worcester, being proctors and protectors of the commonwealth, before our Lord Jesu Christ our supreme judge, do allege, say and intend to prove with our hands personally this instant day, against the Henry, Duke of Lancaster, thy [ac]complices and favorers, unjustly presuming and named king of England without title of right, but only of thy guile and by force

---

1 Border areas.

of thy fautors: that when thou, after thine exile, didst enter England, thou madest an oath to us upon the holy Gospels, bodily touched and kissed by thee at Doncaster, that thou wouldest never claim the crown, kingdom or state royal but only thine own proper inheritance, and the inheritance of thy wife in England, and that Richard our sovereign lord the king and thine, should reign during the term of his life, governed by the good counsel of the lords spiritual and temporal. Thou hast imprisoned the same thy sovereign lord and our king within the Tower of London, until he had, for fear of death, resigned his kingdoms of England and France, and had renounced all his right in the foresaid kingdoms, and others his dominions and lands of beyond the sea. Under color of which resignation and renunciation, by the counsel of thy friends and [ac]complices, and by the open noising of the rascal people by thee and thy adherents assembled at Westminster, thou hast crowned thyself king of the realms aforesaid, and hast seized and entered into all the castles and lordships pertaining to the king's crown, contrary to thine oath. Wherefore thou art forsworn and false.

Also we do allege, say and intend to prove, that where thou sworest upon the same Gospels in the same place and time to us, that thou wouldest not suffer any dismes[1] to be levied of the Clergy, nor fifteens[2] on the people, nor any other tallagies[3] and taxes to be levied in the realm of England to the behoffe[4] of the realm during thy life, but by the consideration of the three estates[5] of the realm, except for great need in causes of importance or for the resistance of our enemies, only and none otherwise. Thou, contrary to thine oath so made, hast done to be levied right many dismes and fifteens, and other impositions and tallagies, as well of the Clergy as of the commonalty of the realm of England, & of the Merchants, for fear of thy majesty royal. Wherefore thou art perjured and false.

Also we do allege, say & intend to prove, that w[h]ere thou sworest to us upon the same Gospels in the foresaid place and time, that our sovereign lord and thine, King Richard, should reign during the term of his life in his royal prerogative and dignity: thou hast caused the

---

1 Taxes amounting to one tenth of held property.
2 Taxes amounting to one fifteenth of held property.
3 Taxes levied on feudal dependants (OED).
4 Behalf.
5 I.e., the clergy, nobles, and commons.

same our sovereign lord and thine, traitorously within the castle of Pomfret, without the consent or judgment of the lords of the realm, by the space of fifteen days and so many nights (which is horrible among Christian people to be heard) with hunger, thirst and cold to perish, to be murdered. Wherefore thou art perjured and false.

Also we do allege, say & intend to prove, that thou at that time when our sovereign lord and thine, King Richard, was so by that horrible murder dead, as above said, thou by extort power, didst usurp and take the kingdom of England, and the name and the honor of the kingdom of France, unjustly and wrongfully, contrary to thine oath, from Edmund Mortimer, Earl of March and of Ulster, then next and direct heir of England and of France, immediately by due course of inheritance after the decease of the foresaid Richard. Wherefore thou art perjured and false.

Also we do allege, say & intend to prove as aforesaid, that where thou madest an oath in the same place and time, to support and maintain the laws and good customs of the realm of England, and also afterward at the time of thy coronation thou madest an oath, the said laws and good customs to keep and conserve inviolate. Thou fraudulently and contrary to the law of England and thy fautors, have written almost through every shire in England to choose such knights for to hold a parliament as shall be for thy pleasure and purpose, so that in thy parliaments no justice should be ministered against thy mind in these our complaints now moved and showed by us, whereby at any time we might have any perfect redress, notwithstanding that we, according to our conscience (as we trust ruled by God), have often times thereof complained, as well can testify and bear witness the right reverend fathers in God, Thomas Arundell, Archbishop of Canterbury, and Richard Scroop, Archbishop of York. Wherefore now, by force and strength of hand before our Lord Jesu Christ, we must ask our remedy and help.

Also we do allege, say and intend to prove, that where Edmund Mortimer, Earl of March and Ulster, was taken prisoner by Owen Glendower in a pitched and foughten field, and cast into prison and laden with iron fetters, for thy matter and cause, whom falsely thou hast proclaimed willingly to yield himself prisoner to the said Owen Glendower, and neither wouldest deliver him thyself, nor yet suffer us his kinsmen to ransom and deliver him. Yet notwithstanding, we have not only concluded and agreed with the same Owen for his ransom at our proper charges and expenses, but also for a peace between thee and the said Owen. Why hast thou then not only published and declared us as traitors, but also craftily and deceitfully imagined, purposed and conspired the utter destruction and confusion of our persons? For the which cause we defy thee, thy fautors and [ac]complices as common traitors and destroyers of the realm, and the invaders, oppressors and confounders of the very true and right heirs to the Crown of England, which thing we intend with our hands to prove this day, almighty God helping us.

When King Henry had overseen their articles and defiance, he answered the esquires that he was ready with dent of sword and fierce battle to prove their quarrel false and feigned, and not with writing nor slanderous words, and so in his righteous cause and just quarrel he doubted not but God would both aid and assist him, against untrue persons and false forsworn traitors: with which answer the messengers departed. The next day in the morning early, which was the vigil[1] of Mary Magdalene,[2] the king, perceiving that the battle was nearer than he either thought or looked for, lest that long tarrying might be a [di]minishing of his strength, set his battles in good order. Likewise did his enemies, which both in puissance[3] and courage were nothing to him inferior. Then suddenly the trumpets blew, the king's part cried "Saint George! Upon them!" The adversaries cried "Esperance[4] Percie!" and so furiously the armies joined. The Scots, which had the forward on the lords' side, intending to be revenged of their old displeasures done to them by the English nation, set so fiercely on the king's forward, that they made them draw back, and had almost broken their array. The Welshmen also, which, since the king's departure out of Wales, had lurked and lain in woods, mountains and marshes, hearing of this battle toward, came to the aid of the earls, and refreshed the weary people with new succors. When a fearful messenger had declared to the king, that his people were beaten down on every side, it was no need to bid him stir, for suddenly he approached with his fresh battle, and comforted, heartened and encouraged his part so, that they took their hearts to them, and manly fought with their enemies.

---

1 Eve.
2 A feast day, July 22.
3 Strength.
4 See p. 194, n. 1.

The prince Henry that day helped much his father, for although he were sore wounded in the face with an arrow, yet he never ceased either to fight where the battle was most strongest, or to courage his men where their hearts was most daunted. This great battle continued three long hours with indifferent fortune on both parts. That at the last the king, crying "Saint George! Victory!" brake the array and entered into the battle of his enemies and fought fiercely, and adventured so far into the battle, that the Earl Douglas strake him down and slew Sir Walter Blunt, and three other appareled in the king's suit and clothing, saying, "I marvel to see so many kings so suddenly rise again." The king was raised and did that day many a noble feat of arms. For as the Scots write and Frenchmen affirm, although that Englishmen keep silence, that he himself slew with his hands that day xxxvi. persons of his enemies, the other of his part,[1] encouraged by his doings, fought valiantly and slew the Lord Percy called Sir Henry Hotspur, the best captain on the part adverse. When his death was known, the Scots fled, the Welshmen ran, the traitors overcome. Then neither woods letted,[2] nor hills stopped the fearful hearts of them that were vanquished to fly, and in that flight the Earl Douglas, which for hast[e], falling from the crag of a mountain, brake one of his genitals and was taken, and for his valiantness, of the king freely & frankly delivered. There was taken also Sir Thomas Percy, Earl of Worcester, & diverse other. On the king's part were slain Sir Walter Blunt and 1600 other persons, but on the part of the rebels were slain the Earl of Stafford, the Lord Percy and above five thousand other, and as for the Scots, few or none escaped alive.

After this glorious victory by the king obtained, he rendered to almighty God his humble and hearty thanks, and caused the Earl of Worcester, the morrow after Mary Magdalene, at Shrewsbury to be drawn, hanged and quartered, and his head to be sent to London, at which place many more captains were executed. After this great battle, he like a triumphant conqueror returned with great pomp to London, where he was by the senate and magistrates solemnly received, not a little rejoicing of his good fortune and fortunate victory. But before his departure from Shrewsbury, he, not forgetting his enterprise against Owen Glendower, sent into Wales with a great army Prince Henry, his

---

1 Others on his side.
2 Impeded.

eldest son, against the said Owen and his seditious fautors, which being dismayed and in manner desperate of all comfort by the reason of the king's late victory, fled in desert places and solitary caves, where he received a final reward, meet and prepared by God's providence for such a rebel and seditious seducer. For being destitute of all comfort, dreading to show his face to any creature, lacking meat to sustain nature, for pure hunger and lack of food miserably ended his wretched life.

This end was provided for such as gave credence to false prophecies. This end had they that by diabolical divinations were promised great possessions and seigniories. This end happeneth to such as believing such fantastical follies, aspire and gape for honor and high promotions. When the prince with little labor and less loss, had tamed & bridled the furious rage of the wild and savage Welshmen, and left governors to rule and govern the country, he returned to his father with great honor & no small praise. The Earl of Northumberland, hearing of the overthrow of his brother and son, came of his own free will to the king, excusing himself as one neither party [to] nor knowing of their doing nor enterprise. The king neither accused him nor held him excused, but dissimulated the matter for ii. causes: one was he had Berwick in his possession, which the king rather desired to have by policy than by force; the other was that the earl had his castles of Alnwick, Warkworth and other fortified with Scots, so that if the earl were apprehended, all Northumberland were in jeopardy to become Scottish. For these causes the king gave him fair words & let him depart home, where he continued in peace a while, but after he rebelled, as you shall perceive by the sequel of this story.

4. FROM SAMUEL DANIEL, *THE CIVIL WARS BETWEEN THE TWO HOUSES OF LANCASTER AND YORK* (1595)

[Samuel Daniel's verse account was first published in 1595 under the title *The First Four Books of the Civil Wars*. It is written in *ottava rima* stanzas and draws on classical models to present English history in epic form. Some details from the third book of Daniel's work seem to have influenced the shape of Shakespeare's *Henry IV, Part One*, most notably in relation to the figure of Henry Percy (Hotspur). Daniel describes him as "young Hotspur" even though historically he was two years older than Henry IV, and he is characterized as rash, courageous, and perverse. Although Daniel does not claim that the prince killed Hotspur, the narrator of the poem imagines them meeting on the field as equally fierce opponents. Holinshed reports that the prince helped his father on the battlefield and that he was hurt in the face with an arrow, but in Daniel the prince saves his father from a ferocious encounter with Douglas. Such small touches of color in Daniel's account were expanded in Shakespeare's *Henry IV, Part One* into vividly realized dramatic events, and the rivalry between Hal and Hotspur gave the story focus, suspense, and a satisfying dramatic shape. This modern spelling version is based on the facsimile of the 1595 edition provided by the *Early English Books Online* database.]

[From Book 3, Verses 85–115, pp. 59–63]

85
And thus one king most near in blood allied
Is made th'oblation[1] for the other's peace:
Now only one, both name and all beside
Entirely hath, plurality doth cease:
He that remains, remains unterrified
With others' right; this day doth all release:
And henceforth he is absolutely king,
No crowns, but one, this deed confirms the thing.

86
And yet new Hydras[2] lo, new heads appear
T'afflict that peace reputed then so sure,
And gave him much to do, and much to fear,
And long and dangerous tumults did procure,
And those even of his chiefest followers were
Of whom he might presume him most secure,
Who whether not so grac'd or so prefer'd
As they expected, these new factions stirr'd.

---

1 Sacrifice.
2 In Greek mythology, the Hydra was a many-headed snake that speedily grew new heads for those cut off.

87

The Percies were the men, men of great might,
Strong in alliance, and in courage strong
That thus conspire, under pretense to right
The crooked courses they had suffered long:
Whether their conscience urg'd them or despite,[1]
Or that they saw the part they took[2] was wrong,
Or that ambition hereto did them call,
Or others envied grace, or rather all.

88

What cause soever were, strong was their plot,
Their parties great, means good, th'occasion fit:
Their practice close, their faith suspected not,
Their states far off and they of wary wit
Who with large promises draw in the Scot
To aid their cause, he likes, and yields to it,
Not for the love of them or for their good,
But glad hereby of means to shed our blood.

89

Then join they with the Welsh, who fitly train'd
And all in arms under a mighty head
Great Glendower, who long warr'd, and much attain'd,
Sharp conflicts made, and many vanquished:
With whom was Edmund Earl of March[3] retain'd
Being first his prisoner, now confedered,[4]
A man the king much fear'd, and well he might
Lest he should look whether his crown stood right.

90

For Richard, for the quiet of the state,
Before he took those Irish wars in hand

---

1 Contempt.
2 I.e., in helping to depose Richard II.
3 Like Shakespeare, Daniel replicates Holinshed in conflating Sir Edmund
Mortimer with his nephew the Earl of March.
4 Allied.

About succession doth deliberate,
And finding how the certain right did stand,
With full consent this man did ordinate[1]
The heir apparent in the crown and land:
Then judge if this the king might nearly[2] touch,
Although his might were small, his right being much.

91
With these the Percies them confederate
And as three heads they league in one intent,
And instituting a triumvirate
Do part the land in triple government:
Dividing thus among themselves the state,
The Percies should rule all the North from Trent
And Glendower Wales, the Earl of March should be
Lord of the South from Trent; and thus they [a]gree.

92
Then those two helps which still such actors find,
Pretense of common good, the king's disgrace,
Doth fit their course, and draw the vulgar mind
To further them and aid them in this case:
The king they accus'd for cruel, and unkind
That did the state, and crown, and all deface;
A perjured man that held all faith in scorn,
Whose trusted oaths had others made forsworn.

93
Besides the odious detestable act
Of that late murdered king they aggravate,
Making it his that so had will'd the fact
That he the doers did remunerate:
And then such taxes daily doth exact
That were against the orders of the state,
And with all these or worse they him assail'd

---

1 Appoint.
2 Closely.

Who late of others with the like prevail'd.

94
Thus doth contentious proud mortality[1]
Afflict each other and itself torment:
And thus, O thou mind-tort[u]ring misery
Restless ambition, born in discontent,
Turn'st and retossest with iniquity
The unconstant courses frailty did invent:
And foul'st fair order and defil'st the earth
Fost[e]ring up war, father of blood and dearth.

95
Great seem'd the cause, and greatly to, did add
The people's love thereto, these crimes rehears'd,
That many gathered to the troops they had
And many more do flock from coasts dispers'd:
But when the king had heard these news so bad,
Th'unlooked-for dangerous toil more nearly pers'd;[2]
For bent t[o]wards Wales t'appease those tumults there,
H[e] is forc'd divert his course, and them forbear.

96
Not to give time unto th'increasing rage
And gathering fury, forth he hastes with speed,
Lest more delay or giving longer age
To th'evil grown, it might the cure exceed:
All his best men at arms, and leaders sage
All he prepar'd he could, and all did need;
For to a mighty work thou goest, O king,
To such a field that power to power shall bring.

97
There shall young Hotspur with a fury led
Meet with thy forward son as fierce as he:

---

1 Mortals.
2 Pierced.

There warlike Worcester, long experienced
In foreign arms, shall come t'encounter thee:
There Douglas to thy Stafford shall make head:
There Vernon for thy valiant Blunt shall be:
There shalt thou find a doubtful bloody day,
Though sickness keep Northumberland away.

98
Who yet reserv'd, though after quit[1] for this,
Another tempest on thy head to raise,
As if still wrong revenging Nemesis[2]
Did mean t'afflict all thy continual days:
And yet this field he happily[3] might miss
For thy great good, and therefore well he stays:
What might his force have done being join'd thereto
When that already gave so much to do?

99
The swift approach and unexpected speed
The king had made upon this new-raised force
In th'unconfirmed troops much fear did breed,
Untimely hindring their intended course;
The joining with the Welsh they had decreed
Was hereby stopp'd, which made their part the worse,
Northumberland, with forces from the North
Expected to be there, was not set forth.

100
And yet undaunted Hotspur seeing the king
So near approach'd, leaving the work in hand,
With forward speed his forces marshaling,
Sets forth his farther coming to withstand:
And with a cheerful voice encouraging
By his great spirit his well-emboldened band,

---

1 Unpunished. After the battle, Northumberland claimed that he was not involved
in the conspiracy and was granted pardon.
2 Greek goddess of divine retribution.
3 Haply, by chance.

Brings a strong host of firm-resolved might
And plac'd his troops before the king in sight.

101
"This day" (saith he), "O faithful valiant friends,
Whatever it doth give, shall glory give:
This day with honor frees our state, or ends
Our misery with fame, that still shall live.
And do but think how well this day he spends
That spends his blood his country to relieve:
Our holy cause, our freedom, and our right,
Sufficient are to move good minds to fight.

102
"Besides th'assured hope of victory
That we may even promise on our side
Against this weak-constrained company,
Whom force and fear, not will, and love, doth guide
Against a prince whose foul impiety
The heavens do hate, the earth cannot abide,
Our number being no less, our courage more,
What need we doubt if we but work therefore?"

103
This said, and thus resolv'd, even bent[1] to charge
Upon the king, who well their order view'd
And careful noted all the form at large
Of their proceeding, and their multitude:
And deeming better if he could discharge
The day with safety, and some peace conclude,
Great proffers sends of pardon, and of grace
If they would yield, and quietness embrace.

104
But this refus'd, the king, with wrath incens'd,
Rage against fury doth with speed prepare:

---

1 Eager.

And "O," saith he, "though I could have dispens'd
With this day's blood, which I have sought to spare
That greater glory might have recompens'd
The forward worth of these that so much dare,
That we might honor had by th'overthrown
That th'wounds we make, might not have been our own.

105
"Yet since that other men's iniquity
Calls on the sword of wrath against my will,
And that themselves exact this cruelty,
And I constrained am this blood to spill:
Then on, my masters, on courageously,
True-hearted subjects against traitors ill,
And spare not them who seek to spoil us all,
Whose foul confused end soon see you shall."

106
Straight moves with equal motion equal rage
The like incensed armies unto blood,
One to defend, another side to wage
Foul civil war. Both vows their quarrel good:
Ah, too much heat to blood doth now enrage
Both who the deed provokes and who withstood,
That valor here is vice, here manhood sin,
The forward'st hands doth, O, least honor win.[1]

107
But now begin these fury-moving sounds
The notes of wrath that music brought from hell,
The rattling drums which trumpets' voice confounds,
The cries, th'encouragements, the shouting shrill;
That all about the beaten air rebounds,
Thundring confused, murmurs horrible,
To rob all sense except the sense to fight,
Well hands may work, the mind hath lost his sight.

---

1 Those most eager to fight win the least honor in civil war.

108

O war! begot in pride and luxury,
The child of wrath and of dissension,
Horrible good; mischief necessary,
The foul reformer of confusion,
Unjust-just scourge of our iniquity,
Cruel recurer of corruption:
O, that these sin-sick states in need should stand
To be let blood[1] with such a boisterous hand!

109

And O, how well thou hadst been spar'd this day
Had not wrong-counsel'd Percy been perverse,
Whose young undanger'd hand now rash makes way
Upon the sharpest fronts of the most fierce:
Where now an equal fury thrusts to stay
And rebeat-back that force and his disperse,
Then these assail, then those chase back again,
Till stayed with new-made hills of bodies slain.

110

There lo that new-appearing glorious star
Wonder of arms, the terror of the field
Young Henry, laboring where the stoutest are
And even the stoutest forces back to yield,
There in that hand, boldened to blood and war,
That must the sword in wondrous actions wield:
But better hadst thou learn'd with others' blood
A less expense to us, to thee more good.

111

Hadst thou not there lent present speedy aid
To thy endanger'd father nearly tired,
Whom fierce encountering Douglas overlaid,
That day had there his troublous life expired:
Heroical courageous Blunt arrayed

---

1 Bloodletting was a standard medical treatment.

In habit like as was the king attir'd
And deem'd for him, excus'd that fate with his,
For he had what his Lord did hardly miss.[1]

112

For thought a king he would not now disgrace
The person then suppos'd, but princelike shows
Glorious effects of worth that fit his place,
And fighting dies, and dying overthrows:
Another of that forward name and race[2]
In that hot work his valiant life bestows,
Who bare the standard of the king that day,
Whose colors overthrown did much dismay.

113

And dear it cost, and O, much blood is shed
To purchase thee this losing victory
O travail'd[3] king: yet hast thou conquered
A doubtful day, a mighty enemy:
But O, what wounds, what famous worth lies dead!
That makes the winner look with sorrowing eye,
Magnanimous Stafford lost that much had wrought,
And valiant Shirley who great glory got.

114

Such wrack of others' blood thou didst behold
O furious Hotspur, ere thou lost thine own!
Which now, once lost, that heat in thine wax'd cold,
And soon became thy army overthrown;
And O, that this great spirit, this courage bold,
Had in some good cause been rightly shown!
So had not we thus violently then
Have term'd that rage, which valor should have been.

---

1   Barely escape.
2   Another Blunt—the king's standardbearer—also died.
3   Wearied.

115
But now the king retires him to his peace,
A peace much like a feeble sickman's sleep,
(Wherein his waking pains do never cease
Though seeming rest his closed eyes doth keep)
For O, no peace could ever so release
His intricate turmoils, and sorrows deep,
But that his cares kept waking all his life
Continue on till death conclude the strife.

5. FROM *A MIRROR FOR MAGISTRATES* (1559)

[*A Mirror for Magistrates* is a collection of verse accounts of the lives of various key historical figures from the fourteenth and fifteenth centuries. The work of several writers under the editorship of William Baldwin, it pursues a clear aim to shape history into a series of moral and political lessons. Geoffrey Bullough suggests that *Henry IV, Part One* may owe something to *A Mirror for Magistrates* "if only by contraries" (165). The selection here, Thomas Phaer's portrait of Owen Glendower, intersects with Shakespeare in interesting ways. It is narrated by Glendower himself, supposedly starving in the mountains. This modern-spelling excerpt was prepared using a facsimile of the 1559 edition from *Early English Books Online*.]

How Owen Glendower seduced by false prophecies took upon him to be prince of Wales, and was by Henry then prince thereof, chased to the mountains, where he miserably died for lack of food.

...

The king pursued us, greatly to his cost,
From hills to woods, from woods to valley's plain:
And by the way his men and stuff he lost.
And when he saw he gained naught save pain,
He blew retreat, and got him home again.
Then with my power I boldly came abroad
Taken in my country for a very God.

Immediately after fell a jolly jar[1]
Between the king, and Percies worthy bloods,
Which grew at last unto a deadly war.
For like as drops engender mighty floods,
And little seeds sprout forth great leaves and buds,
Even so small strifes, if they be suffered run
Breed wrath and war, and death or they be done.

The king would have the ransom of such Scots
As these the Percies had taken in the field.
But see how strongly Lucre[2] knits her knots,
The king will have, the Percies will not yield.
Desire of goods soon craves, but granteth seld.[3]
O cursed goods, desire of you hath wrought
All wickedness, that hath or can be thought.

The Percies deemed it meeter[4] for the king
To have redeemed their cousin Mortimer,
Who in his quarrel all his power did bring
To fight with me, that took him prisoner,
Than of their pray[5] to rob his soldier,[6]
And therefore willed him see some mean were found,
To quit forth him whom I kept vilely bound.

Because the king misliked their request,
They came themselves and did accord with me,
Complaining how the kingdom was oppressed,
By Henry's rule, wherefore we did agree
To put him down, and part the realm in three:
The North part theirs, Wales wholly to be mine
The rest to rest to the Earl of March's line.

---

1 Discord.
2 Gain, profit.
3 Seldom.
4 Fitter, more appropriate.
5 Booty.
6 Perhaps a reference to Henry's ransom of Grey of Ruthin.

And for to set us hereon more agog
A prophet came (a vengeance take them all)
Affirming Henry to be Gogmagog[1]
Whom Merlin doth a mouldwarp[2] ever call,
Accursed of god, that must be brought in thrall[3]
By a wolf, a dragon, and a lion strong,
Which should divide his kingdom them among.

This crafty dreamer made us three such beasts
To think we were these foresaid beasts indeed,
And for that cause our badges and our crests
We searched out, which scarcely well agreed,
Howbeit the heralds ready at such a need,
Drew down such issues from old ancestors,
As proved these ensigns to be surely ours.

Ye crafty Welshmen, wherefore do you mock
The noble men thus with your feigned rhymes?
Ye noble men why fly you not the flock
Of such as have seduced so many times?
False prophecies are plagues for diverse crimes
Which god doth let the devilish sort devise
To trouble such as are not godly wise.

And that appeared by us three beasts in deed,
Through false persuasion highly born in hand
That in our feat we could not choose but speed
To kill the king, and to enjoy his land.
For which exploit we bound our selves in band
To stand contented each man with his part,
So fully folly assured our foolish heart.

But such they say as fish before the net
Shall seldom surfeit of the prey they take,

---

1 In British folklore, a fearsome giant. In the Bible, Gog and Magog are agents of
Satan associated with Armageddon (Revelation 20:8).
2 Mole.
3 Bondage, captivity.

Of things to come the haps[1] be so unset
That none but fools may warrant of them make.
The full assured, success doth oft forsake.
For Fortune findeth none so fit to flout,
As suresby sots[2] which cast no kind of doubt.

How sayest thou Henry Hotspur, do I lie?
For thou right manly gavest the king a field,
And there was slain because thou wouldest not fly.
Sir Thomas Percy thine uncle (forced to yield)
Did cast his head (a wonder seen but seld[3])
From Shrewsbury town to the top of London bridge.
Lo thus fond hope did their both lives abridge.

When Henry king this victory had won,
Destroyed the Percies, put their power to flight,
He did appoint Prince Henry his eldest son
With all his power to meet me if he might.
But I discomfort through my partners' fight
Had not the heart to meet him face to face,
But fled away, and he pursued the chase.

Now Baldwin mark, for I, called prince of Wales,
And made believe I should be he indeed,
Was made to fly among the hills and dales,
Where all my men forsook me at my need.
Who trusteth loiterers seld hath lucky speed,[4]
And when the captain's courage doth him fail
His soldiers' hearts a little thing may quail.

And so Prince Henry chased me, that lo
I found no place wherein I might abide,
For as the dogs pursue the sely[5] doe,

---

1   Chances.
2   Overly-sure blockheads.
3   Seldom.
4   Seldom has good luck.
5   Feeble.

The brach[1] behind the hounds on every side,
So traced they me among the mountains wide,
Whereby I found I was the heartless hare
And not the beast colprophet[2] did declare.

And at the last: like as the little roach[3]
Must either be eat, or leap upon the shore
When as the hungry pickrel[4] doth approach,
And there find death which it escaped before,
So double death assaulted me so sore
That either I must unto my enemy yield,
Or starve for hunger in the barren field.

Here shame and pain a while were at a strife,
Pain prayed me yield, shame bade me rather fast.
The one bade spare, the other spend my life,
But shame (shame have it) overcame at last.
Than hunger gnew,[5] that doth the stone wall brast[6]
And made me eat both gravel, dirt and mud,
And last of all, my dung, my flesh, and blood.

This was mine end too horrible to hear,
Yet good enough for a life that was so ill.
Whereby (O Baldwin) warn all men to bear
Their youth such love, to bring them up in skill
Bid princes fly colprophets' lying bill,[7]
And not presume to climb above their states,
For they be faults that foil men, not their fates.

---

1 Bitch.
2 False prophet.
3 A freshwater fish.
4 Pike.
5 Gnawed.
6 Burst.
7 Pronouncement.

6. FROM *AN HOMILY AGAINST DISOBEDIENCE AND WILLFUL REBELLION* (1571)

[This homily was printed in *The Second Tome of Homilies* (1571), a collection of sermons edited by Bishop John Jewel (1522–71). Homilies were delivered weekly in church and this one would have been very familiar to Shakespeare's audience. The *Homily against Disobedience and Willful Rebellion* reflects the Elizabethan state's deep anxiety about the possibility of further rebellion after the 1569 Northern uprising. The fact that the rebellion was instigated by descendants of the Percies depicted in *Henry IV, Part One* added an extra layer of topicality to Shakespeare's play. This modern-spelling excerpt is based on a facsimile of *The Second Tome of Homilies* (1571), available through *Early English Books Online*.]

The third part of the homily against disobedience and willful rebellion

As I have in the first part of this treatise showed unto you the doctrine of the holy scriptures, as concerning the obedience of true subjects to their princes, even as well to such as be evil as unto the good, and in the second part of the same treaty confirmed the same doctrine by notable examples, likewise taken out of the holy scriptures, so remaineth it now that I partly do declare unto you in this third part, what an abominable sin against God and man rebellion is, and how dreadfully the wrath of God is kindled and inflamed against all rebels, and what horrible plagues, punishments, and deaths, and finally eternal damnation, doth hang over their heads; as how on the contrary part, good and obedient subjects are in God's favor, and be partakers of peace, quietness, and security, with other God's manifold blessings in this world, and by his mercies through our Savior Christ, of life everlasting, also in the world to come. How horrible a sin against God and man rebellion is, cannot possibly be expressed according unto the greatness thereof. For he that nameth rebellion, nameth not a singular or one only sin, as is theft, robbery, murder, and such like, but he nameth the whole puddle and sink of all sins against God and man, against his prince, his country, his countrymen, his parents, his children, his kinfolk, his friends, and against all men universally, all sins I say against God and all men heaped together nameth he, that nameth rebellion. For concerning the offense of God's majesty, who seeth not that rebellion riseth first by contempt of God and of his holy ordinances and laws, wherein he so straightly commandeth obedience, forbiddeth disobedience and rebellion? And besides the dishonor done by rebels unto God's holy name, by their breaking of their oath made to their prince, with the attestation of God's name, and calling of his majesty to witness, who heareth not the horrible oaths and blasphemies of God's holy name, that are used daily amongst rebels, that is either amongst them, or heareth the truth of their behavior? Who knoweth not that rebels do not only themselves leave all works necessary to be done upon workdays undone, whiles they accomplish their abominable work of rebellion, and to compel others that would gladly be well occupied, to do the same, but also how rebels do not only leave the sabbath day of the Lord unsanctified, the temple and church of the Lord unresorted unto, but also do by their works of wickedness most horribly profane and pollute the sabbath day, serving Satan, and by doing of his work, making it the devil's day, instead of the Lord's day? Besides that, they compel good men that would gladly serve the Lord assembling in his temple and church upon his day, as becometh the Lord's servants, to assemble and meet armed in the field, to resist the furies of such rebels. Yea, and many rebels, lest they should leave any part of God's commandments in the first table[1] of his law unbroken, or any sin against God undone, do make rebellion for the maintenance of their images and idols, and of their idolatry committed, or to be committed by them, and in despite of God, cut and tear in sunder his holy word, and tread it under their feet, as of late ye know was done.

As concerning the second table of God's law, and all sins that may be committed against man, who seeth not that they be not contained in rebellion? For first the rebels do not only dishonor their prince, the parent of their country, but also do dishonor and shame their natural parents, if they have any, do shame their kindred and friends, do disinherit and undo forever their children and heirs. Thefts, robberies, and murders, which of all sins are most loathed of most men, are in no men so much nor so perniciously and mischievously, as in rebels. For the most errant thieves and cruelest murderers that ever were, so long as they refrain from rebellion, as they are not many in number,

---

1 The first of the two stone tablets or "tables" on which the Ten Commandments were inscribed.

so spreadeth their wickedness and damnation unto a few, they spoil but a few, they shed the blood but of few in comparison. But rebels are the cause of infinite robberies, and murders of great multitudes, and of those also whom they should defend from the spoil and violence of others; and as rebels are many in number, so doth their wickedness and damnation spread itself unto many. And if whoredom and adultery amongst such persons as are agreeable to such wickedness, are (as they indeed be) most damnable, what are the forcible oppressions of matrons and men's wives, and the violating and deflowering of virgins and maids, which are most rife with rebels? How horrible and damnable, think you, are they? Now besides that, rebels by breach of their faith given, and oath made to their prince, be guilty of most damnable perjury: it is wondrous to see what false colors and feigned causes, by slanderous lies made upon their prince, and the counselors, rebels will devise to cloak their rebellion withal, which is the worst and most damnable of all false witness-bearing that may be possible. For what should I speak of coveting or desiring of other men's wives, houses, lands, goods and servants in rebels, who by their wills would leave unto no man anything of his own?

Thus you see that all good laws are by rebels violated and broken, and that all sins possible to be committed against God or man be contained in rebellion: which sins if a man list to name by the accustomed names of the seven capital or deadly sins, as pride, envy, wrath, covetousness, sloth, gluttony, and lechery, he shall find them all in rebellion, and amongst rebels. For first, as ambition and desire to be aloft, which is the property of pride, stirreth up many men's minds to rebellion, so cometh it of a Luciferian pride and presumption, that a few rebellious subjects should set themselves up against the majesty of their prince, against the wisdom of the counselors, against the power and force of all nobility, and the faithful subjects and people of the whole realm. As for envy, wrath, murder, and desire of blood, and covetousness of other men's goods, lands, and livings, they are the inseparable accidents of all rebels, and peculiar properties that do usually stir up wicked men unto rebellion.

Now such as by riotousness, gluttony, drunkenness, excess of apparel, and unthrifty games, have wasted their own goods unthriftily, the same are most apt unto, and most desirous of rebellion, whereby they trust to come by other men's goods unlawfully and violently. And where other gluttons and drunkards take too much of such meats and drinks as are served to tables, rebels waste and consume in short space, all corn in barns, fields, or elsewhere, whole garners,[1] whole storehouses, whole cellars, devour whole flocks of sheep, whole droves of oxen and kine.[2] And as rebels that are married, leaving their own wives at home, do most ungraciously, so much more do unmarried men, worse than any stallions or horses, being now by rebellion set at liberty from correction of laws which bridled them before, which abuse by force other men's wives and daughters, and ravish virgins and maidens, most shamefully, abominably, and damnably.

Thus all sins, by all names that sins may be named, and by all means that sins may be committed and wrought, do all wholly upon heaps follow rebellion, and are to be found altogether amongst rebels. Now whereas pestilence, famine, and war, are by the holy scriptures declared to be the greatest worldly plagues and miseries that likely can be, it is evident, that all the miseries that all these plagues have in them, do wholly altogether follow rebellion, wherein, as all their miseries be, so is there much more mischief than in them all. For it is known that in the resorting of great companies of men together, which in rebellion happeneth both upon the part of true subjects, and of the rebels, by their close lying together, and corruption of the air and place where they do lie, with ordure[3] and much filth, in the hot weather, and by unwholesome lodging, and lying often upon the ground, specially in cold and wet weathers in winter, by their unwholesome diet, and feeding at all times, and often by famine and lack of meat and drink in due time, and again by taking too much at other times: it is well known, I say, that as well plagues and pestilences, as all other kinds of sicknesses and maladies by these means grow upon and amongst men, whereby more men are consumed at the length, than are by dint of sword suddenly slain in the field. So that not only pestilences, but also all other sicknesses, diseases, and maladies, do follow rebellion, which are much more horrible than plagues, pestilences, and diseases sent directly from God, as hereafter shall appear more plainly.

And as for hunger and famine, they are the peculiar companions of rebellion: for while rebels do in short time spoil and consume all corn and necessary provision, which men with their labors had gotten and

---

1 Granaries.
2 Cattle.
3 Dung.

appointed upon, for their finding the whole year after, and also do let all other men, husbandmen and others, from their husbandry, and other necessary works, whereby provision should be made for times to come, who seeth not that extreme famine and hunger must needs shortly ensue and follow rebellion? Now whereas the wise king and godly prophet David judged war to be worse than either famine or pestilence, for that these two are often suffered by God, for man's amendment, and be not sins of themselves; but wars have always the sins and mischiefs of men upon the one side or other joined with them, and therefore is war the greatest of these worldly mischiefs. But of all wars, civil war is the worst, and far more abominable yet is rebellion than any civil war, being unworthy the name of any war, so far it exceedeth all wars in all naughtiness, in all mischief, and in all abomination. And therefore our savior Christ denounceth desolation and destruction to that realm, that by sedition and rebellion is divided in itself.

Now as I have showed before, that pestilence and famine, so is it yet more evident that all the calamities, miseries, and mischiefs of war be more grievous and do more follow rebellion, than any other war, as being far worse than all other wars. For not only those ordinary and usual mischiefs and miseries of other wars do follow rebellion, as corn and other things necessary to man's use to be spoiled, houses, villages, towns, cities, to be taken, sacked, burned, and destroyed, not only many very wealthy men, but whole countries to be impoverished, and utterly beggared, many thousands of men to be slain and murdered, women and maids to be violated and deflowered: which things when they are done by foreign enemies, we do much mourn, as we have great causes, yet are all these miseries without any wickedness wrought by any of our own countrymen. But when these mischiefs are wrought in rebellion by them that should be friends, by countrymen, by kinsmen, by those that should defend their country and countrymen from such miseries, the misery is nothing so great, as is the mischief and wickedness when the subjects unnaturally do rebel against their prince, whose honor and life they should defend, though it were with the loss of their own lives: countrymen to disturb the public peace and quietness of their country, for defense of whose quietness they should spend their lives; the brother to seek, and often to work the death of his brother, the son of the father, the father to seek or procure the death of his sons, being at man's age, and by their faults to disinherit their innocent children and kinsmen their heirs forever, for whom they might purchase livings and lands, as natural parents do take care and pains, and be at great costs and charges; and universally instead of all quietness, joy, and felicity, which do follow blessed peace and due obedience, to bring in all trouble, sorrow, disquietness of minds and bodies and all mischief and calamity, to turn all good order upside down, to bring all good laws in contempt, and to tread them under feet, to oppress all virtue and honesty, and all virtuous and honest persons, and to set all vice and wickedness, and all vicious and wicked men at liberty, to work their wicked wills, which were before bridled by wholesome laws, to weaken, to overthrow, and to consume the strength of the realm their natural country, as well by the spending and wasting of money and treasure of the prince and realm, as by murdering of the people of the same, their own countrymen, who should defend the honor of their prince, and liberty of their country, against the invasion of foreign enemies: and so finally, to make their country thus by their mischief weakened, ready to be a prey and spoil to all outward enemies that will invade it, to the utter and perpetual captivity, slavery, and destruction of all their countrymen, their children, their friends, their kinsfolk left alive, whom by their wicked rebellion they procure to be delivered into the hands of foreign enemies, as much as in them doth lie.

In foreign wars our countrymen in obtaining the victory win the praise of valiantness, yea and though they were overcome and slain, yet win they an honest commendation in this world, and die in a good conscience for serving God, their prince, and their country, and be children of eternal salvation. But in rebellion how desperate and strong soever they be, yet win they shame here in fighting against God, their prince and country, and therefore justly do fall headlong into hell if they die, and live in shame and fearful conscience, though they escape. But commonly they be rewarded with shameful deaths, their heads and carcasses set upon poles, or hanged in chains, eaten with kites[1] and crows, judged unworthy the honor of burial, and so their souls, if they repent not (as commonly they do not) the devil harrieth them into hell, in the midst of their mischief. For which dreadful execution Saint Paul showeth the cause of obedience, not only for fear of death,

---

1   Birds of prey.

but also in conscience to God-ward, for fear of eternal damnation in the world to come.

Wherefore good people, let us, as the children of obedience, fear the dreadful execution of God, and live in quiet obedience to be the children of everlasting salvation. For as heaven is the place of good obedient subjects, and hell the prison and dungeon of rebels against God and their prince, so is that realm happy where most obedience of subjects doth appear, being the very figure of heaven; and contrariwise where most rebellions and rebels be, there is the express similitude[1] of hell, and the rebels themselves are the very figures of fiends and devils, and their captain the ungracious pattern of Lucifer and Satan, the prince of darkness, of whose rebellion as they be followers, so shall they of his damnation in hell undoubtedly be partakers, and as undoubtedly children of peace the inheritors of heaven with God the father, God the son, and God the holy ghost, to whom be all honor and glory for ever and ever, Amen.

7. WILLIAM ELDERTON, *A BALLAD ENTITLED NORTHUMBERLAND NEWS* (1570)

[*A ballad entitled Northumberland News, Wherein you may see what Rebels do use* was printed in 1570, as a response to the 1569 Northern Rebellion. It reflects the author's protestant patriotism and shows that in 1570 Elizabethans still saw a connection between contemporary rebellion and the conflict between the Percys and Henry IV. Key figures involved in the Northern Rebellion—notably Thomas Percy, seventh earl of Northumberland, and Charles Neville, sixth earl of Westmorland— were descendants of nobles represented in Shakespeare's play. This modern-spelling version of the ballad is adapted from a facsimile from *Early English Books Online.*]

A ballad entitled Northumberland news
Wherein you may see what Rebels do use

Come tumbling down, come tumbling down.
That will not yet be true to the crown.

---

1   Exact representation.

You north-country noddies,[1] why be ye so bragge[2]
To rise and raise honor to Romish[3] renown
You know ye at Tyburn[4] there standeth a nag
For such as will never be true to the crown.
Come tumbling. &c.

What mean ye to follow the man in the moon,
With batts,[5] bows and arrows and billes[6] very brown.
His shining with shame will be shadowed so soon,
It will grieve him that ever he troubled the crown.
Come tumbling. &c.

Though popery wrought a great while ago,
That Percy provoked King Harry to frown.
Yet who would have thought there were any more,
That would not yet be true to the crown.
Come tumbling. &c.

Our queen is the daughter of Henry th'eight,
Who brought every altar and imagery down.
He left her and taught her a remedy great,
For any that would not be true to the crown.
Come tumbling. &c.

And though you do greet her like traitors with treason
To whom you owe honor with cap and knee down.
I am sure that Saint Peter will say it is reason,
To rule ye that will not be true to the crown.
Come tumbling. &c.

And though you do say there is matter amiss,
Which you would redress by noble renown,

---

1 Fools.
2 Arrogant.
3 Roman Catholic.
4 Place of execution, west of London.
5 Clubs.
6 Weapon with varnished handle; like a halberd (OED).

What any way worse than rebellion is,
Of any that will not be true to the crown.
Come tumbling. &c.

What strangers can be, more stranger than ye,
That gather together both carter and clown.
And study to stir to seek and to see,
Which way to devise to trouble the crown.
Come tumbling. &c.

Sir John Shorn, your morrow mass priest,
Saith to Lobbe,[1] look about will ye kneel down.
We will have a mass before Jesus Christ,
And that is the way to trouble the crown.
Come tumbling. &c.

The knights to their knaves say stick and be stout,
Our banners and staves shall bring us renown.
We have nobles and others that be as devout,
To help us at this time of trouble the crown.
Come tumbling. &c.

The rebels come slinging but what cometh after,
A long worth the singing hey down a down down.
A Tyburn tippet,[2] a coope,[3] or a halter,
For any that will not be true to the crown.
Come tumbling. &c.

For though ye spoil churches and burn up the bible,
And worship gay crosses in every town.
Your idols, you asses, are never possible,
To save ye that will not be true to the crown.
Come tumbling. &c.

And though ye do carry the banner of force,

---

1 Country bumpkin.
2 Jocular name for hangman's rope (OED).
3 Like a tippet, a vestment worn round the neck.

And jolly round robin[1] under your gown.
You know that Saint George hath a prancing host,
Can make any rebel to stoop to the crown.
Come tumbling. &c.

The Westmorland bull must come to the stake,
The Lion will roar still till he be down.
Northumberland then will tremble and quake,
For woe that he was to false to the crown.
Come tumbling. &c.

And catholics old that hold with the pope,
And carry dead images up and down.
To take better hold they shall have a rope,
To teach them once to be true to the crown.
Come tumbling. &c.

Let every priest that sayeth any mass,
Either choose to take the crucifix down.
Or hang as high as the crucifix was,
Except he will be true to the crown.
Come tumbling. &c.

For God is a God of jealousy such,
He looks to have his holy renown.
Or else he will mislike very much,
To give anyone his excellent crown.
Come tumbling. &c.

God prosper the queen as I trust that He shall,
And grant of His mercy with blessed renown.
The north, and the west country, the south, east, and all,
The people of England may cleave to the crown.
Come tumbling. &c.

And I wish the good preachers & other true teachers,
Would visit the vineyard whose branches be down.

---

1 Disparaging name for the consecrated host (see OED quoting this passage).

That all the north country yet nuzzled[1] in popery,
Might know their duty to God and the crown.
Come tumbling. &c.

8. FROM NICCOLÒ MACHIAVELLI, *THE PRINCE* (1513)

[Machiavelli's *The Prince* provided pragmatic advice on statecraft and politics, and his analysis of power had a significant influence on the way Elizabethans interpreted the actions of historical figures. Elizabethan writers frequently allude to his works and many stage villains express Machiavellian ideas: in Christopher Marlowe's *The Jew of Malta*, for example, a figure named "Machiavel" enters to speak the prologue. Although *The Prince* was not published in English until 1640, an Italian version was printed in London in 1584, and manuscript translations were also circulated widely. In *Henry IV, Part One*, both King Henry and the prince show an acute awareness of the need to control their public image—an awareness that accords with Machiavelli's advice. This excerpt is based on the 1640 English translation by Edward Dacres, available through *Early English Books Online*.]

Chapter XVIII
In what manner princes ought to keep their words [pp. 135–41].

How commendable in a prince it is to keep his word and live with integrity, not making use of cunning and subtlety, everyone knows well. Yet we see by experience in these our days that those princes have effected great matters who have made small reckoning of keeping their words and have known by their craft to turn and wind men about and in the end have overcome those who have grounded upon the truth. You must then know there are two kinds of combating or fighting: the one by right of the laws, the other merely by force. That first way is proper to men, the other is also common to beasts. But because the first many times suffices not, there is a necessity to make recourse to the second, wherefore it behooves a prince to know how to make good use of that part which belongs to a beast as well as that which is proper to a man. This path hath been covertly showed to princes by ancient writers who say that Achilles and many others of

---

1 Nurtured.

those ancient princes were entrusted to Chiron[1] the centaur to be brought up under his discipline. The moral of this, having for their teacher one that was half a beast and half a man, was nothing else but that it was needful for a prince to understand how to make his advantage of the one and the other nature because neither could subsist without the other. A prince, then, being necessitated to know how to make use of that part belonging to a beast, ought to serve himself of the conditions of the fox and the lion, for the lion cannot keep himself from snares nor the fox defend himself against the wolves. He had need then be a fox that he may beware of the snares, and a lion that he may scare the wolves. Those that stand wholly upon the lion understand not well themselves.

And therefore a wise prince cannot nor ought not keep his faith given, when the observance thereof turns to disadvantage and the occasions that made him promise are past. For if men were all good, this rule would not be allowable; but being they are full of mischief and would not make it good to thee, neither art thou tied to keep it with them, nor shall a prince ever want[2] lawful occasions to give color to this breach. Very many modern examples hereof might be alleged wherein might be showed how many peaces concluded and how many promises made have been violated and broken by the infidelity of princes, and ordinarily things have best succeeded with him that hath been nearest the fox in condition. But it is necessary to understand how to set a good color upon this disposition, and to be able to feign and dissemble thoroughly. And men are so simple, and yield so much to the present necessities, that he who hath a mind to deceive shall always find another that will be deceived.

I will not conceal any one of the examples that have been of late. Alexander the sixth[3] never did anything else than deceive men and never meant otherwise, and always found whom to work upon. Yet never was there man would protest more effectually nor aver anything with more solemn oaths and observe them less than he. Nevertheless, his cozenages all thrived well with him, for he knew how to play this part cunningly. Therefore is there no necessity for a prince to be endowed with all these above-written qualities, but it behoves well that he seem to be so. Or rather I will boldly say this, that having these qualities and

---

1 In Greek mythology, a centaur distinguished by wisdom and kindness.
2 Lack.
3 From the notorious Borgia family, elected Pope in 1492.

always regulating himself by them, they are hurtful, but seeming to have them, they are advantageous. As to seem pitiful, faithful, mild, religious, and of integrity and indeed to be so, provided withal thou beest of such a composition that if need require thee to use the contrary, thou canst and knowest how to apply thyself thereto. And it suffices to conceive this, that a prince, and especially a new prince, cannot observe all those things for which men are held good, he being often forced for the maintenance of his state to do contrary to his faith, charity, humanity, and religion. And therefore, it behoves him to have a mind so disposed as to turn and take the advantage of all winds and fortunes, and, as formerly I said, not forsake the good while he can, but to know how to make use of the evil upon necessity. A prince, then, ought to have a special care that he never let fall any words but what are all seasoned with the five above-written qualities, and let him seem to him that sees and hears him, all pity, all faith, all integrity, all humanity, all religion. Nor is there anything more necessary for him to seem to have than this last quality, for all men in general judge thereof rather by the sight than by the touch. For every man may come to the sight of him, few come to the touch and feeling of him; every man may come to see what thou seemest, few come to perceive and understand what thou art; and those few dare not oppose the opinion of many, who have the majesty of state to protect them. And in all men's actions, especially those of princes wherein there is no judgment to appeal unto, men forbear to give their censures till the events and ends of things. Let a prince therefore take the surest courses he can to maintain his life and state. The means shall always be thought honorable and commended by everyone, for the vulgar is overtaken with the appearance and event of a thing. And for the most part of people, they are but the vulgar. The others that are but few, take place where the vulgar have no subsistence. A prince there is in these days, whom I shall not do well to name, that preaches nothing else but peace and faith, but had he kept the one and the other, several times had they taken from him his state and reputation.

9. FROM *THE FAMOUS VICTORIES OF HENRY THE FIFTH* (c. 1587)

[An anonymous play, *The Famous Victories of Henry the Fifth, Containing the Honorable Battle of Agincourt* was first printed in 1598, but it was written and performed well before Shakespeare's *Henry IV, Part One*.

It was entered in the Stationers' Register in 1594, and was probably staged before 1588 when the famous comic actor Richard Tarleton died (an anecdote in *Tarleton's Jests* (1613) indicates that he played Derick the clown). The 1598 title page describes *The Famous Victories* as being performed by the Queen's Majesty's Players, but unfortunately it does not supply the name of an author.

The Famous Victories is regarded as a key source for the rich comedy of the tavern scenes in *Henry IV, Part One* and as possible inspiration for the overall shape of Shakespeare's three plays about the figure of Henry V. It begins with the prince's rebellious exploits, then goes on to show his sudden reformation, his assumption of the crown, and his campaign against the French. In the play's early scenes the prince shows no intention to reform. He is presented as a seasoned thief who has robbed the receivers himself and who intimidates them into remaining silent about the crime. He insists on spending the money in the old tavern in Eastcheap because of the wine and the pretty wench that waits there. He tells his companions, "if the old king, my father, were dead, we would be all kings." As in Holinshed and Stow he visits his father wearing a cloak full of needles, but this time his strange attire is emblematic of his impatience for the crown, and it is only when he is confronted with the tears of his sick father that he suddenly repents and resolves to abandon his old companions.

The Famous Victories obviously presents a vastly different prince, yet some of its knockabout humor intersects with *Henry IV, Part One* in intriguing ways. At one point, for example, an improvised play is performed in which two comic figures, Derick and John Cobbler, replay the previous scene where the prince boxed the Lord Chief Justice's ear. Derick directs: "thou shalt sit in the chair / And I'll be the young prince." The success of this scene in the theater may well have inspired 2.4 of *Henry IV, Part One*. Falstaff's original name, too, seems to have come from *The Famous Victories*: Sir John Oldcastle (generally called "Jockey," a version of "Jack") is one of the prince's companions. This Sir John is a fairly minor figure in the play, however, with little in common with the gargantuan figure of Shakespeare's Falstaff.

This modern-spelling excerpt is based on the facsimile of the Huntington Library copy of Q1 published for the Malone Society in 2007. It reproduces the first nineteen pages of Q1—a little under half the play. Speech headings have been regularized, but Q1's idiosyncratic arrangement of verse and prose is retained.]

[*SCENE 1*]

Enter the young prince, Ned, and Tom.

HENRY V. [1] Come away, Ned and Tom.

BOTH. Here, my lord.

HENRY V. Come away, my lads.

Tell me, sirs, how much gold have you got?

NED. Faith, my lord, I have got five hundred pound.

HENRY V. But tell me, Tom, how much hast thou got?

TOM. Faith, my lord, some four hundred pound.

HENRY V. Four hundred pounds! Bravely spoken, lads. But tell me, sirs, think you not that it was a villainous part of me to rob my father's receivers?[2]

NED. Why no, my lord, it was but a trick of youth.

HENRY V. Faith, Ned, thou sayest true.

But tell me, sirs, whereabouts are we?

TOM. My lord, we are now about a mile off London.

HENRY V. But, sirs, I marvel that Sir John Oldcastle

Comes not away. Zounds,[3] see where he comes.

Enter Jockey [Sir John Oldcastle].

How now Jockey, what news with thee?

JOCKEY. Faith, my lord, such news as passeth;

For the town of Deptford is risen

With hue and cry after your man,

Which parted from us the last night

And has set upon and hath robbed a poor carrier.

HENRY V. Zounds! The villain that was wont to spy out our booties?

JOCKEY. Ay, my lord; even the very same.

HENRY V. Now, base-minded rascal, to rob a poor carrier.

Well, it skills not; I'll save the base villain's life.

Ay, I may. But tell me, Jockey, whereabout be the receivers?

JOCKEY. Faith, my lord, they are hard by;

But the best is, we are a-horseback and they be a-foot,

So we may escape them.

---

1 The prince is referred to as "Hen. 5" in speech prefixes throughout the play.

2 Officials appointed to collect tolls, rents, or other monies (OED).

3 An oath: by God's wounds.

HENRY V. Well, if the villains come, let me alone with them.
   But tell me, Jockey, how much got thou from the knaves?
   For I am sure I got something; for one of the villains
   So belammed[1] me about the shoulders,
   As I shall feel it this month.
JOCKEY. Faith, my lord, I have got a hundred pound.
HENRY V. A hundred pound! Now, bravely spoken, Jockey.
   But come, sirs, lay all your money before me.
   Now, by heaven, here is a brave show.
   But, as I am true gentleman, I will have the half
   Of this spent tonight. But, sirs, take up your bags;
   Here comes the receivers. Let me alone.

Enter two Receivers.
ONE. Alas, good fellow, what shall we do?
   I dare never go home to the Court, for I shall be hanged.
   But look, here is the young prince. What shall we do?
HENRY V. How now, you villains, what are you?
ONE. Speak you to him.
OTHER. No, I pray. Speak you to him.
HENRY V. Why, how now, you rascals; why speak you not?
ONE. Forsooth, we be—Pray, speak you to him.
HENRY V. Zounds, villains, speak, or I'll cut off your heads.
OTHER. Forsooth, he can tell the tale better than I.
ONE. Forsooth, we be your father's receivers.
HENRY V. Are you my father's receivers?
   Then I hope ye have brought me some money.
ONE. Money? Alas, sir, we be robbed.
HENRY V. Robbed? How many were there of them?
ONE. Marry, sir, there were four of them;
   And one of them had Sir John Oldcastle's bay hobby,[2]
   And your black nag.
HENRY V. Gog's wounds![3] How like you this Jockey?
   Blood,[4] you villains; my father robbed of his money abroad,

---

1 Beat.
2 A small horse.
3 An oath: God's wounds.
4 An oath: by Christ's blood.

And we robbed in our stables!
But tell me, how many were of them?

ONE. If it please you, there were four of them;
And there was one about the bigness of you.
But I am sure I so belammed him about the shoulders
That he will feel it this month.

HENRY V. Gog's wounds, you 'lammed them fairly,
So that they have carried away your money.
But come, sirs, what shall we do with the villains?

BOTH RECEIVERS. I beseech your grace, be good to us.

NED. I pray you, my Lord, forgive them this once.

[HENRY V.] Well, stand up and get you gone.
And look that you speak not a word of it;
For if there be, Zounds, I'll hang you and all your kin.

                                              [*Exit Receivers.*]

Now, sirs, how like you this?
Was not this bravely done?
For now the villains dare not speak a word of it,
I have so feared them with words.
Now, whither shall we go?

ALL. Why, my lord, you know our old hostess
At Faversham?

HENRY V. Our hostess at Faversham? Blood, what shall we do there?
We have a thousand pound about us
And we shall go to a petty ale-house?
No, no; you know the old tavern in Eastcheap;
There is good wine. Besides, there is a pretty wench
That can talk well, for I delight as much in their tongues
As any part about them.

ALL. We are ready to wait upon your grace.

HENRY V. Gog's wounds, wait? We will go altogether;
We are all fellows. I tell you, sirs, and[1] the king,
My father, were dead, we would be all kings.
Therefore, come away.

NED. Gog's wounds, bravely spoken Harry!

                                              [*Exeunt.*]

---

1 If.

[SCENE 2]

Enter John Cobbler, Robin Pewterer, Lawrence Costermonger. [1]

JOHN. All is well here; all is well, masters.

LAWRENCE. How say you, neighbor John Cobbler?
  I think it best that my neighbor,
  Robin Pewterer, went to Pudding Lane End,
  And we will watch here at Billingsgate Ward. [2]
  How say you, neighbor Robin? How like you this?

ROBIN. Marry well, neighbors;
  I care not much if I go to Pudding Lane's End.
  But, neighbors, and you hear any ado about me,
  Make haste; and if I hear any ado about you,
  I will come to you.

                                        Exit Robin.

LAWRENCE. Neighbor, what news hear you of the young prince?

JOHN. Marry, neighbor, I hear say he is a toward young prince;
  For, if he meet any by the highway,
  He will not let [3] to talk with him.
  I dare not call him thief, but sure he is one of these taking fellows.

LAWRENCE. Indeed, neighbor, I hear say he is as lively
  A young prince as ever was.

JOHN. Ay, and I hear say if he use it long,
  His father will cut him off from the crown.
  But, neighbor, say nothing of that!

LAWRENCE. No, no, neighbor, I warrant you!

JOHN. Neighbor, methinks you begin to sleep.
  If you will, we will sit down;
  For I think it is about midnight.

LAWRENCE. Marry, content, neighbor; let us sleep.

Enter Derick, roving. [4]

DERICK. Whoa! Whoa, there! Whoa, there!   *Exit Derick.*

---

1 Seller of fruit and vegetables (from "costard apples").
2 These citizens are watchmen, charged with keeping order in the streets.
3 Not hesitate.
4 Roaming around, searching.

Enter Robin.

ROBIN. Oh, neighbors, what mean you to sleep
    And such ado in the streets?
BOTH. How now, neighbor, what's the matter?

Enter Derick again.

DERICK. Whoa, there! Whoa, there! Whoa, there!
JOHN. Why, what ailst thou? Here is no horses.
DERICK. O, alas, man, I am robbed! Whoa, there! Whoa, there!
ROBIN. Hold him, Neighbor Cobbler.
ROBIN. Why, I see thou art a plain clown.
DERICK. Am I a clown? Zounds, masters,
    Do clowns go in silk apparel?
    I am sure all we gentlemen-clowns in Kent scant go so
    Well. Zounds! You know clowns very well!
    Hear you, are you Master Constable? And you be, speak,
    For I will not take it at his hands.[1]
JOHN. Faith, I am not Master Constable;
    But I am one of his bad[2] officers, for he is not here.
DERICK. Is not Master Constable here?
    Well, it is no matter. I'll have the law at his hands.
JOHN. Nay, I pray you, do not take the law of us.
DERICK. Well, you are one of his beastly officers.
JOHN. I am one of his bad officers.
DERICK. Why then, I charge thee, look to him!
JOHN. Nay, but hear ye, sir; you seem to be an honest
    Fellow, and we are poor men; and now 'tis night,
    And we would be loath to have anything ado;
    Therefore, I pray thee, put it up.[3]
DERICK. First, thou sayst true; I am an honest fellow
    And a proper handsome fellow, too!
    And you seem to be poor men; therefore I care not greatly.
    Nay, I am quickly pacified.
    But and you chance to spy the thief,
    I pray you, lay hold on him.

---

1   From his underlings.
2   Sworn.
3   Put away your weapon (probably a dagger).

ROBIN. Yes, that we will, I warrant you.

DERICK. 'Tis a wonderful thing to see how glad the knave
    Is, now I have forgiven him.

JOHN. Neighbors, do ye look about you.
    How now, who's there?

Enter the Thief.

THIEF. Here is a good fellow. I pray you, which is the
    Way to the old tavern in Eastcheap?

DERICK. Whoop hollo! Now, Gadshill,[1] knowest thou me?

THIEF. I know thee for an ass.

DERICK. And I know thee for a taking fellow
    Upon Gad's Hill in Kent.
    A bots[2] light upon ye!

THIEF. The whoreson villain would be knocked.

DERICK. Masters, villain! And ye be men, stand to him
    And take his weapon from him. Let him not pass you!

JOHN. My friend, what make you abroad now?
    It is too late to walk now.

THIEF. It is not too late for true men to walk.

LAWRENCE. We know thee not to be a true man.

THIEF. Why, what do you mean to do with me?
    Zounds! I am one of the king's liege people.[3]

DERICK. Hear you, sir, are you one of the king's liege people?

THIEF. Ay, marry am I, sir! What say you to it?

DERICK. Marry, sir, I say you are one of the king's filching people.

JOHN. Come, come, let's have him away.

THIEF. Why, what have I done?

ROBIN. Thou hast robbed a poor fellow,
    And taken away his goods from him.

THIEF. I never saw him before.

DERICK. Masters, who comes here?

Enter the Vintner's Boy.

---

1 Like Shakespeare's Gadshill, he is nicknamed after the spot on the highway where
hold-ups take place.
2 A case of worms, commonly in horses.
3 Loyal subjects.

BOY. How now, Goodman Cobbler!

JOHN. How now, Robin, what makes thou abroad
    At this time of night?

BOY. Marry, I have been at the Counter;[1]
    I can tell such news as never you have heard the like.

JOHN. What is that, Robin? What is the matter?

BOY. Why, this night, about two hours ago, there came the young
    prince and three or four more of his companions, and called for
    wine good store; and then they sent for a noise[2] of musicians,
    and were very merry for the space of an hour; then, whether their
    music liked them not, or whether they had drunk too much wine
    or no, I cannot tell, but our pots flew against the walls; and then
    they drew their swords and went into the street and fought, and
    some took one part and some took another; but for the space of
    half an hour there was such a bloody fray as passeth! And none
    could part them until such time as the Mayor and Sheriff were
    sent for; and then, at the last, with much ado, they took them;
    and so the young prince was carried to the Counter; and then,
    about one hour after, there came a messenger from the court in
    all haste from the king for my Lord Mayor and the Sheriff, but for
    what cause I know not.

JOHN. Here is news indeed, Robert![3]

LAWRENCE. Marry, neighbor, this news is strange, indeed! I think it
    best, neighbor, to rid our hands of this fellow first.

THIEF. What mean you to do with me?

JOHN. We mean to carry you to the prison, and there to remain till
    the sessions day.

THIEF. Then, I pray you, let me go to the prison where my master is.

JOHN. Nay, thou must go to the country prison, to Newgate.
    Therefore, come away.

THIEF. I prithee, be good to me, honest fellow.

DERICK. Ay, marry, will I; I'll be very charitable to thee,
    For I will never leave thee, till I see thee on the gallows.

                                                            [*Exeunt.*]

---

1   A London prison.
2   A company or band of musicians.
3   John is probably addressing Robin Pewterer here. The situation is further complicated by the fact that the Vintner's boy is also called Robin.

[SCENE 3]

Enter [King] Henry the Fourth, with the Earl of Exeter, and the Lord of Oxford.

OXFORD. And please your Majesty, here is my Lord Mayor and the Sheriff of London to speak with your Majesty.

HENRY IV. Admit them to our presence.

Enter the Mayor and the Sheriff.

Now, my good Lord Mayor of London, the cause of my sending for you at this time is to tell you of a matter which I have learned of my Council. Herein, I understand that you have committed my son to prison without our leave and license. What, although he be a rude youth and likely to give occasion, yet you might have considered that he is a prince, and my son, and not to be hauled to prison by every subject.

MAYOR. May it please your Majesty to give us leave to tell our tale?

HENRY IV. Or else God forbid; otherwise you might think me an unequal judge, having more affection to my son than to any rightful judgment.

MAYOR. Then I do not doubt but we shall rather deserve commendations at your Majesty's hands than any anger.

HENRY IV. Go to; say on.

MAYOR. Then, if it please your Majesty; this night, betwixt two and three of the clock in the morning, my lord the young prince, with a very disordered company, came to the old tavern in Eastcheap, and whether it was that their music liked them not, or whether they were overcome with wine, I know not, but they drew their swords and into the street they went; and some took my lord the young prince's part, and some took the other. But betwixt them there was such a bloody 'fray for the space of half an hour that neither watchmen, nor any other, could stay them till my brother the Sheriff of London and I were sent for, and at the last, with much ado, we stayed them; but it was long first, which was a great disquieting to all your loving subjects thereabouts. And then, my good Lord, we knew not whether your Grace had sent them to try us whether we would do justice, or whether it were of their own voluntary will or not; we cannot tell. And therefore, in such a case, we knew not what to do, but for our own safeguard we sent him to ward,[1] where he wanteth nothing that is fit for his grace and your Majesty's son. And thus most humbly beseeching your Majesty to think of our answer.

HENRY IV. Stand aside until we have further deliberated on your answer.

Exit Mayor [and Sheriff].

Ah, Harry, Harry! Now thrice accursed Harry,
That hath gotten a son which with grief
Will end his father's days.
Oh my son! A prince thou art, ay, a prince indeed;
And to deserve imprisonment.
And well have they done, and like faithful subjects.
Discharge them, and let them go.

EXETER. I beseech your Grace, be good to my lord, the young prince.

HENRY IV. Nay, nay. 'Tis no matter; let him alone.

OXFORD. Perchance the Mayor and the Sheriff have been too precise in this matter.

HENRY IV. No, they have done like faithful subjects.
I will go myself to discharge them and let them go.

Ex[eunt] omnes.

[SCENE 4]

Enter Lord Chief Justice, Clerk of the Office, the Jailer, John Cobbler, Derick, and the Thief.

JUDGE. Jailer, bring the prisoner to the bar.

DERICK. Hear you, my lord; I pray you, bring the bar to the prisoner.

JUDGE. Hold thy hand up at the bar.

THIEF. Here it is, my lord.

JUDGE. Clerk of the Office, read his indictment.

CLERK. What is thy name?

THIEF. My name was known before I came here,
And shall be when I am gone, I warrant you.

---

1 Custody.

JUDGE. Ay, I think so; but we will know it better before thou go.

DERICK. Zounds, and you do but send to the next jail,
We are sure to know his name;
For this is not the first prison he hath been in, I'll warrant you.

CLERK. What is thy name?

THIEF. What need you to ask, and have it in writing?

CLERK. Is not thy name Cutbert Cutter?

THIEF. What the devil need you ask, and know it so well?

CLERK. Why then, Cutbert Cutter, I indict thee, by the name of
Cutbert Cutter, for robbing a poor carrier the twentieth day of
May last past, in the fourteenth year of the reign of our sovereign
Lord, King Henry the Fourth, for setting upon a poor carrier
upon Gad's Hill in Kent, and having beaten and wounded the
said carrier, and taken his goods from him.

DERICK. Oh, masters, stay there! Nay, let's never belie the man, for
he hath not beaten and wounded me also, but he hath beaten
and wounded my pack, and hath taken the great rase[1] of ginger
that bouncing Bess with the jolly buttocks should have had. That
grieves me most.

JUDGE. Well, what sayest thou? Art thou guilty or not guilty?

THIEF. Not guilty, my lord.

JUDGE. By whom wilt thou be tried?

THIEF. By my lord the young prince, or by myself, whether you will.

Enter the young prince, with Ned and Tom.

HENRY V. Come away, my lads. Gog's wounds, ye villain, what make
you here? I must go about my business myself and you must
stand loitering here?

THIEF. Why, my lord, they have bound me and will not let me go.

HENRY V. Have they bound thee, villain? Why, how now, my lord?

JUDGE. I am glad to see your grace in good health.

HENRY V. Why, my lord, this is my man.
'Tis marvel you knew him not long before this.
I tell you, he is a man of his hands.[2]

THIEF. Ay, Gog's wounds, that I am! Try me who dare!

---

1 Root.
2 A brave man, but with a pun on his dexterity as a thief.

JUDGE. Your grace shall find small credit by acknowledging him to
  be your man.
HENRY V. Why, my lord, what hath he done?
JUDGE. And it please your majesty, he hath robbed a poor carrier.
DERICK. Hear you, sir; marry, it was one Derick,
  Goodman Hobling's man, of Kent.
HENRY V. What! Was't you, button-breech?
  Of my word, my lord, he did it but in jest.
DERICK. Hear you, sir, is it your man's quality to rob folks in jest? In
  faith, he shall be hanged in earnest.
HENRY V. Well, my lord, what do you mean to do with my man?
JUDGE. And please your grace, the law must pass on him
  According to justice; then he must be executed.
HENRY V. Why, then, belike you mean to hang my man?
JUDGE. I am sorry that it falls out so.
HENRY V. Why, my lord, I pray ye, who am I?
JUDGE. And please your grace, you are my lord the young prince,
  our king that shall be after the decease of our sovereign Lord,
  King Henry the Fourth, whom God grant long to reign!
HENRY V. You say true, my lord.
  And you will hang my man?
JUDGE. And like your grace, I must needs do justice.
HENRY V. Tell me, my lord, shall I have my man?
JUDGE. I cannot, my lord.
HENRY V. But will you not let him go?
JUDGE. I am sorry that his case is so ill.
HENRY V. Tush! Case me no casings, shall I have my man?
JUDGE. I cannot, nor I may not, my lord.
HENRY V. Nay? And I shall not say, and then I am answered?
JUDGE. No.
HENRY V. No! Then I will have him.

He giveth him a box on the ear.
NED. Gog's wounds, my lord, shall I cut off his head?
HENRY V. No. I charge you, draw not your swords.
  But get you hence. Provide a noise of musicians.
  Away, be gone!
Exeunt [Ned and Tom].

JUDGE. Well, my lord, I am content to take it at your hands.

HENRY V. Nay, and you be not, you shall have more.

JUDGE. Why, I pray you, my lord, who am I?

HENRY V. You! Who knows not you?
Why, man, you are Lord Chief Justice of England.

JUDGE. Your grace hath said truth; therefore, in striking me in this
place you greatly abuse me; and not me only but also your father,
whose lively[1] person here in this place I do represent. And therefore to teach you what prerogatives mean, I commit you to the
Fleet[2] until we have spoken with your father.

HENRY V. Why, then, belike you mean to send me to the Fleet?

JUDGE. Ay, indeed; and therefore carry him away.

Exeunt HENRY V *with the Officers.*
Jailer, carry the prisoner to Newgate again, until the next 'sizes.[3]

JAILER. At your commandment, my lord, it shall be done.

[*Exeunt all except Derick and John Cobbler.*]

DERICK. Zounds, masters, here's ado
When princes must go to prison!
Why, John didst ever see the like?

JOHN. O Derick, trust me, I never saw the like!

DERICK. Why, John, thou may'st see what princes be in choler.
A judge a box on the ear! I'll tell thee, John, O John,
I would not have done it for twenty shillings.

JOHN. No, nor I. There had been no way but one with us
We should have been hanged.

DERICK. Faith, John, I'll tell thee what; thou shalt be my
Lord Chief Justice, and thou shalt sit in the chair,
And I'll be the young prince, and hit thee a box on the ear,
And then thou shalt say, "To teach you what prerogatives
Mean, I commit you to the Fleet."

JOHN. Come on; I'll be your judge!
But thou shalt not hit me hard.

DERICK. No, no.

JOHN. What hath he done?

DERICK. Marry, he hath robbed Derick.

---

1 Living.
2 Prison on the bank of the River Fleet.
3 I.e., assizes: sessions for administering justice.

JOHN. Why, then, I cannot let him go.

DERICK. I must needs have my man.

JOHN. You shall not have him.

DERICK. Shall I not have my man? Say "No" and you dare!
How say you? Shall I not have my man?

JOHN. No, marry, shall you not.

DERICK. Shall I not, John?

JOHN. No, Derick.

DERICK. Why, then, take you that [*Boxes his ear.*] till more come!
Zounds, shall I not have him?

JOHN. Well, I am content to take this at your hand.
But, I pray you, who am I?

DERICK. Who art thou? Zounds, dost not know thyself?

JOHN. No.

DERICK. Now away, simple fellow.
Why, man, thou art John the Cobbler.

JOHN. No, I am my Lord Chief Justice of England.

DERICK. Oh, John, Mass,[1] thou sayst true, thou art indeed.

JOHN. Why, then, to teach you what prerogatives mean,
I commit you to the Fleet.

DERICK. Well, I will go; but, i'faith, you gray-beard knave, I'll
course you.[2]

Exit. And straight enters again.

Oh John, come, come out of thy chair. Why, what a clown wert
thou to let me hit thee a box on the ear! And now thou seest they
will not take me to the Fleet. I think that thou art one of these
worenday[3] clowns.

JOHN. But I marvel what will become of thee.

DERICK. Faith, I'll be no more a carrier.

JOHN. What wilt thou do, then?

DERICK. I'll dwell with thee and be a cobbler.

JOHN. With me? Alas, I am not able to keep thee.
Why, thou wilt eat me out of doors.

---

1 An oath: by the mass.
2 Chase you with blows.
3 Workaday, ordinary (Bullough 311).

DERICK. Oh, John, no, John; I am none of these great slouching
    fellows that devour these great pieces of beef and brews.[1] Alas, a
    trifle serves me: a woodcock, a chicken, or a capon's[2] leg, or any
    such little thing serves me.
JOHN. A capon! Why, man, I cannot get a capon once a year, except
    it be at Christmas, at some other man's house; for we cobblers be
    glad of a dish of roots.
DERICK. Roots! Why, are you so good at rooting?
    Nay, cobbler, we'll have you ringed.[3]
JOHN. But, Derick, though we be so poor,
    Yet will we have in store a crab[4] in the fire,
    With nut-brown ale, that is full stale,[5]
    Which will a man quail,[6] and lay in the mire.
DERICK. A bots on you! And be but[7] for your ale,
    I'll dwell with you. Come, let's away as fast as we can.

                                                    Exeunt.

                        [*SCENE 5*]

Enter the young prince, with Ned and Tom.
HENRY V. Come away, sirs. Gog's wounds, Ned,
    Didst thou not see what a box on the ear
    I took my Lord Chief Justice?
TOM. By Gog's blood, it did me good to see it.
    It made his teeth jar in his head!

Enter Sir John Oldcastle.
HENRY V. How now, Sir John Oldcastle!
    What news with you?
JOCKEY. I am glad to see your grace at liberty.
    I was come, I, to visit you in prison.

---

1 Broths.
2 A castrated rooster.
3 Ringed through the nose, as pigs were to stop them rooting.
4 Crab-apple.
5 Old and strong.
6 Overpower.
7 If only.

HENRY V. To visit me? Didst thou not know that I am a prince's son? Why, 'tis enough for me to look into a prison, though I come not in myself. But here's such ado nowadays, here's prisoning, here's hanging, whipping, and the devil and all! But I tell you, sirs, when I am king we will have no such things. But, my lads, if the old king, my father, were dead, we would be all kings.

JOCKEY. He is a good old man; God take him to his mercy the sooner!

HENRY V. But, Ned, so soon as I am king, the first thing
I will do shall be to put my Lord Chief Justice out of office,
And thou shalt be my Lord Chief Justice of England.

NED. Shall I be Lord Chief Justice?
By Gog's wounds, I'll be the bravest Lord Chief Justice
That ever was in England.

HENRY V. Then, Ned, I'll turn all these prisons into fence-schools,[1] and I will endue thee with them, with lands to maintain them withal. Then I will have a bout with my Lord Chief Justice. Thou shalt hang none but pick-purses, and horse-stealers, and such base-minded villains; but that fellow that will stand by the highway side courageously with his sword and buckler and take a purse, that fellow, give him commendations. Beside that, send him to me, and I will give him an annual pension out of my exchequer to maintain him all the days of his life.

JOCKEY. Nobly spoken, Harry! We shall never have a merry world till the old king be dead.

NED. But whither are ye going now?

HENRY V. To the court; for I hear say my father lies very sick.

TOM. But I doubt he will not die.

HENRY V. Yet will I go thither; for the breath shall be no sooner out of his mouth but I will clap the crown on my head.

JOCKEY. Will you go to the court with that cloak so full of needles?

HENRY V. Cloak, eyelet-holes, needles,[2] and all was of mine own devising; and therefore I will wear it.

TOM. I pray you, my lord, what may be the meaning thereof?

---

1 Fencing schools.
2 Evidently echoing Holinshed and Stow: see above, p. 197 and p. 202.

HENRY V. Why, man, 'tis a sign that I stand upon thorns till the crown be on my head.

JOCKEY. Or that every needle might be a prick to their hearts that repine at your doings?

HENRY V. Thou say'st true, Jockey. But there's some will say the young prince will be "a well toward young man" and all this gear, that I had as lief they would break my head with a pot, as to say any such thing. But we stand prating here too long. I must needs speak with my father; therefore, come away.

[*They knock at the court-gate. Enter a Porter.*]

PORTER. What a rapping keep you at the king's court-gate?

HENRY V. Here's one that must speak with the king.

PORTER. The king is very sick, and none must speak with him.

HENRY V. No? You rascal, do you not know me?

PORTER. You are my lord, the young prince.

HENRY V. Then go and tell my father that I must, and will, speak with him.

NED. Shall I cut off his head?

HENRY V. No, no. Though I would help you in other places, yet I have nothing to do here. What, you are in my father's court.

NED. I will write him in my tables; for so soon as I am made Lord Chief Justice I will put him out of his office.

The trumpet sounds.

HENRY V. Gog's wounds, sirs, the king comes. Let's all stand aside.

Enter the king, with the Lord of Exeter.

HENRY IV. And is it true, my lord, that my son is already sent to the Fleet? Now, truly, that man is more fitter to rule the realm than I; for by no means could I rule my son, and he, by one word, hath caused him to be ruled. Oh, my son! My son! No sooner out of one prison but into another. I had thought once, whiles I had lived, to have seen this noble realm of England flourish by thee, my son; but now I see it goes to ruin and decay.   *He weepeth.*

Enter Lord of Oxford.

OXFORD. And please your Grace, here is my lord, your son, That cometh to speak with you.

He saith he must and will speak with you.

HENRY IV. Who? My son Harry?

OXFORD. Ay, and please your Majesty.

HENRY IV. I know wherefore he cometh.
But look that none come with him.

OXFORD. A very disordered company, and such as make
Very ill rule in your Majesty's house.

HENRY IV. Well, let him come;
But look that none come with him.

He goeth.

OXFORD. And please your grace,
My lord the king sends for you.

HENRY V. Come away, sirs; let's go all together.

OXFORD. And please your grace, none must go with you.

HENRY V. Why I must needs have them with me;
Otherwise I can do my father no countenance.[1]
Therefore, come away.

OXFORD. The king your father commands
There should none come.

HENRY V. Well, sirs, then be gone,
And provide me three noise of musicians.

Exeunt Knights.

[SCENE 6]

[*The king discovered, attended by Oxford and Exeter.*] Enter the prince,
with a dagger in his hand.

HENRY IV. Come, my son; come on, a' God's name!
I know wherefore thy coming is.
Oh, my son, my son, what cause hath ever been
That thou shouldst forsake me, and follow this vile and
Reprobate company, which abuseth youth so manifestly?
Oh, my son, thou knowest that these thy doings will end thy
father's days. *He weeps.* Ay, so, so, my son, thou fearest not to
approach the presence of thy sick father in that disguised sort. I
tell thee, my son, that there is never a needle in thy cloak but it is

---

1 Show due dignity.

a prick to my heart, and never an eyelet-hole but it is a hole to my soul; and wherefore thou bringest that dagger in thy hand I know not, but by conjecture. *He weeps.*

HENRY V. My conscience accuseth me. Most Sovereign Lord, and well-beloved father, to answer first to the last point, that is whereas you conjecture that this hand and this dagger shall be armed against your life: no. Know, my beloved father, far be the thoughts of your son—"son," said I? an unworthy son for so good a father—but far be the thoughts of any such pretended mischief. And I most humbly render it to your majesty's hand; and live, my lord and sovereign, for ever. And with your dagger-arm show like vengeance upon the body of that—"your son," I was about say, and dare not, ah, woe is me therefore—that, your wild slave. 'Tis not the crown that I come for, sweet father, because I am unworthy. And those vile and reprobate company I abandon and utterly abolish their company for ever. Pardon, sweet father, pardon: the least thing and most desir'd. And this ruffianly cloak I here tear from my back, and sacrifice it to the devil, which is master of all mischief. Pardon me, sweet father, pardon me. Good my lord of Exeter speak for me. Pardon me, pardon good father. Not a word? Ah, he will not speak one word! Ah, Harry, now thrice-unhappy Harry. But what shall I do? I will go take me into some solitary place, and there lament my sinful life; and when I have done, I will lay me down and die.

Exit.

HENRY IV. Call him again. Call my son again.

[*Re-enter the prince.*]

HENRY V. And doth my father call me again? Now Harry,
Happy be the time that thy father calleth thee again.

[*He kneels.*]

HENRY IV. Stand up, my son; and do not think thy father,
But at the request of thee, my son, I will pardon thee.
And God bless thee, and make thee his servant.

HENRY V. Thanks, good my Lord. And no doubt but this day,
Even this day, I am born new again.

HENRY IV. Come, my son and lords, take me by the hands.

Exeunt omnes.

10. FROM MICHAEL DRAYTON ET AL., *SIR JOHN OLDCASTLE, PART ONE* (1600)

[The play *Sir John Oldcastle, Part One* by Michael Drayton, Richard Hathway, Anthony Munday, and Robert Wilson was first printed in quarto form in 1600. Strangely, it was also included in the third and fourth folios of Shakespeare's works. *Part Two* has not survived. *Part One* was performed by the Admiral's Men towards the end of 1599. The full title for Q1 is *The First Part of the True and Honorable History of the Life of Sir John Oldcastle, the Good Lord Cobham*. This, along with the prologue reproduced here, indicates that the play was written as a response to Shakespeare's two *Henry IV* plays, to set the record straight with regard to the character of John Oldcastle. It shows that, although Shakespeare's knight had been renamed Falstaff, the association with Oldcastle and concern about his portrayal persisted. The full play is available in *The Oldcastle Controversy: Sir John Oldcastle, Part 1 and The Famous Victories of Henry V*, edited by Peter Corbin and Douglas Sedge (Manchester: Manchester UP, 1991). The complete old-spelling text of the play is published on the Internet Shakespeare Editions site.]

The Prologue

The doubtful title,[1] gentlemen, prefixed
Upon the argument[2] we have in hand,
May breed suspense and wrongfully disturb
The peaceful quiet of your settled thoughts.
To stop this scruple let this brief suffice:
It is no pampered glutton we present,
Nor agèd counselor to youthful sins;
But one whose virtues shone above the rest,
A valiant martyr and a virtuous peer,
In whose true faith and loyalty expressed
To his true sovereign and his country's weal,[3]
We strive to pay that tribute of our love
Your favors merit.[4] Let fair truth be graced,
Since forged invention former time defaced.[5]

---

1 The play's title.
2 Subject matter.
3 Welfare.
4 We try to give you the true representation you deserve.
5 Because (Shakespeare's) fake creation vandalized history.

APPENDIX B: HISTORICAL FIGURES
IN *HENRY IV, PART ONE*

[Although Prince Hal's tavern companions in *Henry iv, Part One* are fictional creations, the characters of the court and the rebellion are based on real historical figures. The following notes outline some of the known details of their lives.]

KING

Born in the same year as his cousin Richard ii, Henry iv (1367-1413) was eldest son to John of Gaunt. Known as Bolingbroke after the castle where he was born (spelt "Bullingbrooke" in Q0 and both "Bullingbrooke" and "Bullenbrooke" in Q1), he became Duke of Hereford in 1397, and Duke of Lancaster at his father's death in 1399. In 1398 Richard ii banished Henry from England for ten years; and when Gaunt died the following year, Richard seized his Lancastrian estates, declared Henry a traitor, and banished him for life. Henry responded by returning to England in July 1399 to reclaim his inheritance. With Richard in Ireland, he gathered powerful support and on Richard's return was able to capture the king and dictate terms. By the end of September 1399 Richard was forced to abdicate and Henry was acclaimed King. Richard died while imprisoned at Pontrefract castle a few months later. Henry was well-traveled, devout, and a capable king. While he was initially a popular monarch, the fact that he was a usurper and not Richard's proclaimed heir meant that his reign was never secure. His later years were marked by debilitating bouts of illness and he had to rely heavily on his sons for support in both military and administrative affairs. He died in 1413.

PRINCE

Prince Henry (1386-1422) was born in Monmouth, Wales, the eldest of six children produced by Henry iv and his first wife Mary Bohun. He was a seasoned warrior by the time he succeeded to the throne in 1413. His military career began at the age of 12 when he accompanied Richard ii to Ireland, possibly taken into the king's household as a hostage (see Mortimer 168). During his father's reign Prince Henry led several military campaigns and was Constable of Dover and Warden of the Cinque Ports. He was only fifteen at the time of the battle of

Homildon Hill ("Holmedon" in QF) discussed in the opening speeches of the play. At sixteen he took part in the Battle of Shrewsbury where he was wounded in the face by an arrow. (It is unlikely that he killed Hotspur.) Reports of friction between the prince and his father relate mainly to disagreements that arose in the later years of Henry IV's reign when his son was shouldering much of the responsibility of rule. Though stories did circulate about Prince Henry's riotous behavior in his youth, as king he was known for his piety and serious commitment to duty. Henry V is remembered especially for his victory against the French at the Battle of Agincourt, dramatized by Shakespeare in *Henry V*. In 1420 he became Regent of France and was recognized as heir to the French throne, but he died of illness just two years later, leaving a baby son as his successor.

LANCASTER

Henry IV's third son, John (1389-1435), is called "Lancaster" after the place of his birth. He was only thirteen at the time of the battle of Shrewsbury, and there is no record of him taking part. He was, however, made constable of England and Warden of the East March when he was just fourteen, and in 1405, along with the Earl of Westmorland, he was instrumental in quelling the Yorkshire Rising instigated by Northumberland and Lord Bardolph, and in capturing the Archbishop of York and the Earl of Norfolk. These events are dramatized in *Henry IV, Part Two* which may explain Shakespeare's decision to introduce him in *Part One*. The portrayal in *Part One* does not, however, foreshadow John's ruthlessness in *Part Two*.

WESTMORLAND

Ralph Neville, Earl of Westmorland (c. 1364-1425), was married to Joan Beaufort, Henry Bolingbroke's half-sister, and he joined his brother-in-law in his push against Richard II in 1399. He was created Marshall of England for life on the day Henry became king. Along with his rivals, the Percys, he was a key defender of England's northern borders, but unlike them he remained loyal to the Henry IV. Joan was his second wife, and one of their children, Cecily, became the mother of Edward IV and Richard III.

Sir Walter Blount (d.1403) was a nobleman who had been a loyal Lancaster family retainer for many years before the events in *Henry IV*, *Part One*. He accompanied John of Gaunt on several military expeditions abroad and was named an executor of his will (DNB). He joined Henry Bolingbroke when he landed at Ravenspur in 1399 and later served him as an ambassador and diplomat. Blount was one of the men wearing the king's armor at the battle of Shrewsbury. He died in the battle.

NORTHUMBERLAND

Henry Percy (1341-1408) became first Earl of Northumberland at the accession of Richard II and by the time of the events depicted in this play was a powerful and experienced politician. He was closely associated with John of Gaunt for many years as both fellow campaigner and rival magnate, and he and his family were engaged in ongoing struggles over control of England's border territories. Disillusioned with Richard II's hostility to his family's interests, Northumberland and his son, Hotspur, were among the first to join Henry Bolingbroke against Richard in 1399. The Percys' claim that Bolingbroke swore an oath to them at Doncaster that he did not intend to seize the crown was compromised somewhat by Northumberland's pivotal involvement in the capture of Richard II. Northumberland's rewards included the Isle of Man and the offices of Constable of England and Warden of the West March (DNB). Within three years of Henry's coronation, however, tensions between the Percys and the king culminated in the rebellion depicted in this play. Northumberland was not present at the battle of Shrewsbury and afterwards claimed that he was not involved in the conspiracy and was granted pardon. He launched another rebellion in 1405 and he was finally killed in battle in 1408.

HOTSPUR

Unlike the character created by Shakespeare in this play and in *Richard II*, Northumberland's son Sir Henry Percy (1364-1403) was older than the king. He was nearly 23 years older than Prince Hal and had probably acted as a mentor to the young prince when they campaigned together in Wales in 1401. By the time of the events depicted in this play, Percy had earned renown as a fearless soldier and an emblem of chivalry. His nickname, Hotspur, reflected his readiness for battle. His death during the battle of Shrewsbury was the decisive factor in Henry's victory. To quell rumors that he was still alive, his corpse was exhumed and put on display in the Shrewsbury marketplace.

WORCESTER

Northumberland's younger brother, Thomas Percy (1343-1403), was a soldier who served with the Black Prince and with John of Gaunt. He became an important diplomat and courtier during the reign of Richard II and was steward of the royal household from 1393 to 1399. Richard made him Earl of Worcester in 1398. He was in Ireland with Richard when Bolingbroke arrived in England in 1399, and although he is reported to have later broken his staff of office to join forces with his brother against the king, he did not play a prominent part in Richard's deposition. He served Henry IV in various roles, but joined his nephew Hotspur in rebellion in 1403. Worcester was captured at the battle of Shrewsbury and executed two days later.

LADY PERCY

Called "Kate" in this play and "Elianor" in Holinshed, Hotspur's wife's real name was Elizabeth (1371-1417). She was closely linked to the royal family: her mother, Philippa, was the daughter of Edward III's second son, Lionel. She was sister to the Edmund Mortimer portrayed in this play. Elizabeth and Hotspur had two children: a son who later became Earl of Northumberland, and a daughter whose second husband was Earl of Westmorland, son to the Westmorland portrayed in this play.

MORTIMER

Sir Edmund Mortimer (1376-c. 1408) was the youngest child of Edmund, the third Earl of March, and brother to Elizabeth, Hotspur's wife. His elder brother, Roger, the fourth Earl of March, was proclaimed Richard II's heir in 1385. When Roger died in 1398, his title and status as heir to the throne passed to his seven-year-old son, Edmund.

Henry IV kept the young Earl of March and his brother in custody throughout his reign. Shakespeare follows Holinshed in treating the two Edmund Mortimers—uncle and nephew—as one in this play. In reality the Edmund Mortimer who married Glendower's daughter and rebelled against Henry IV did not claim to be Richard's heir, and instead initially announced his intention to restore the crown either to Richard if he were still alive, or to his nephew, the Earl. Sir Edmund Mortimer died while under siege in Harlech Castle during the winter of 1408/09.

GLENDOWER

Shakespeare's Glendower is based on the Welsh leader Owain ap Gruffydd (c. 1359-1416). His estates included the lordship of Glyndyfrdwy from whence he took the name Glyn Dŵr (DNB). Territorial disputes escalated into a major Welsh rebellion in the early years of Henry IV's reign with Glyn Dŵr at the head. His supporters proclaimed him Prince of Wales in 1400, a direct challenge to Henry IV's investiture of the young Prince Henry as Prince of Wales in October 1399. The king, Prince Henry, and many English nobles, including Hotspur, mounted a series of campaigns to try to end the Welsh revolt, but Glyn Dŵr proved elusive. Glyn Dŵr's alliance with Edmund Mortimer and the Percys against the king posed a significant threat, deflected by the swiftness of Henry's response in meeting Hotspur's forces at Shrewsbury before the rebels could join with Glyn Dŵr. After Hotspur's defeat, Glyn Dŵr entered into an alliance with Charles VI of France and in 1406 was reported to have signed a tripartite indenture dividing England and Wales among himself, the Earl of Northumberland, and Sir Edmund Mortimer. Glyn Dŵr continued to wage guerrilla warfare against the English throughout Henry's reign, but by 1415 the rebellion was over. It is not known exactly when or how he died.

LADY MORTIMER

Glyn Dŵr's daughter Catrin (d. 1413) married Sir Edmund Mortimer in 1402. Her mother was an English woman—Margaret Hanmer—so it seems unlikely that Catrin would not have been able to understand English as portrayed in 3.1. She was captured by the English, probably at Harlech in 1409, and was held in the Tower of London along with her children, her mother, and a sister. Catrin and her daughters died in London in 1413.

DOUGLAS

Archibald, the fourth Earl of Douglas (1369-1424), was a magnate who owned extensive estates in southern Scotland. His wife Margaret was a member of the Scottish Royal family, and he also established strong connections in France (Charles VII granted him the Duchy of Touraine in 1424). Douglas followed his father, Archibald the Grim, in mounting several attacks on England, and in 1400, when Henry IV invaded southern Scotland, Douglas led the Scottish forces against him. He defeated an English army led by Hotspur in 1401, but his own army was crushed by Hotspur's at the battle of Homildon Hill in 1402. Taken prisoner after being blinded in one eye by an arrow, Douglas sought to retrieve his estates and power by agreeing to join with the Percys in rebellion against Henry IV in 1403. He and his soldiers fought fiercely at the battle of Shrewsbury, but after Hotspur was killed Douglas's soldiers fled and he was captured. He was kept prisoner for the next five years in London but had his own household there and some lengthy periods of parole. During the reigns of Henry V and of his son, Henry VI, Douglas lent important military support to the French. He was killed while battling an English force led by John of Lancaster (by then the Duke of Bedford) at Verneuil in 1424 (*DNB*).

VERNON

Sir Richard Vernon (d. 1403) belonged to a landed family from Cheshire, a region hostile to Henry IV. Sir Richard fought with the Percys against Henry IV at the battle of Shrewsbury, was captured, charged with treason, and beheaded.

ARCHBISHOP

Richard Scrope (c. 1350-1405) came from a powerful northern baronial family and had a distinguished career in the church and as a diplomat, drawing on his academic background in civil and canon law (*DNB*). He represented Richard II in Rome in his attempt to secure the canon-ization of Edward II and was made Archbishop of York in 1398. He led the commission that received Richard II's abdication in 1399. It is not certain at what stage he joined the Percys in their rebellion, or whether he was closely allied with them, but in 1405 Scrope led an ill-fated uprising from York against the king. He was taken prisoner by Westmorland and John of Lancaster at Gaultree Forest, imprisoned at Pontefract, and summarily executed by order of Henry IV.

ROYAL FAMILY TREE SHOWING THE MORTIMER CLAIM TO THE THRONE

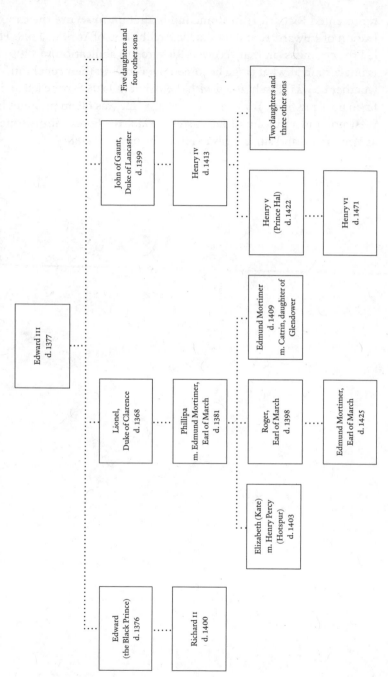

WORKS CITED AND BIBLIOGRAPHY

Aaron, Melissa D. "The Globe and *Henry v* as Business Document." *Studies in English Literature 1500–1900* 40.2 (2000): 277–92.

Addenbrooke, David. *The Royal Shakespeare Company: The Peter Hall Years*. London: William Kimber, 1974.

Bakhtin, Mikhail. *Rabelais and His World*. 1965. Trans. Hélène Iswolsky. Bloomington: Indiana UP, 1984.

Baldo, Jonathan. *Memory in Shakespeare's Histories: Stages of Forgetting in Early Modern England*. New York: Routledge, 2012.

Baldwin, William, ed. *A Mirror for Magistrates*. 1559. *Early English Books Online*. Web.

Barber, C.L. *Shakespeare's Festive Comedy: A Study of Dramatic Form and its Relation to Social Custom*. 1959. 2nd ed. Princeton, NJ: Princeton UP, 1972.

Barker, Roberta. "Tragical-Comical-Historical Hotspur." *Shakespeare Quarterly* 54.4 (2003): 288–307.

Beauman, Sally. *The Royal Shakespeare Company: A History of Ten Decades*. Oxford: Oxford UP, 1982.

Bell, John. *The Time of My Life*. Sydney: Allen & Unwin, 2002.

Belsey, Catherine. "Making Histories Then and Now: Shakespeare from *Richard II* to *Henry v*." *Uses of History: Marxism, Postmodernism and the Renaissance*. Ed. Peter Hulme, Francis Barker, and Margaret Iverson. Manchester: Manchester UP, 1991. 24–46.

Berger, Harry, Jr. "The Prince's Dog: Falstaff and the Perils of Speech-Prefixity." *Shakespeare Quarterly* 49.1 (1998): 40–73.

Bevington, David, ed. *Henry the Fourth Parts I and II: Critical Essays*. New York and London: Garland, 1986.

———, ed. *Henry IV, Part 1*. The Oxford Shakespeare. Oxford: Clarendon, 1987.

Billington, Michael. "Kate and the King." *Guardian Weekly*. 19 April 1992. Web.

Bloom, Harold. *Shakespeare: The Invention of the Human*. New York: Riverhead, 1998.

Bogdanov, Michael, and Michael Pennington. *The English Shakespeare Company: The Story of "the Wars of the Roses" 1986–1989*. London: Nick Hern, 1992.

Bowers, Fredson. "Establishing Shakespeare's Text: Poins and Peto in *1 Henry IV*." *Studies in Bibliography* 34 (1981): 189–98.

Bradley, A.C. "The Rejection of Falstaff." *Shakespeare Henry IV Parts I and II: A Casebook*. Ed. G.K. Hunter. Houndmills, Basingstoke: Macmillan, 1970. 56–78.

Bristol, Michael. *Carnival and Theater: Plebeian Culture and the Structure of Authority in Renaissance England*. London and New York: Routledge, 1989.

Bullough, Geoffrey, ed. *Narrative and Dramatic Sources of Shakespeare*. Vol. 4. London: Routledge, 1962.

Bulman, James C. "Performing the Conflated Text of *Henry IV*: The Fortunes of Part Two." *Shakespeare Survey* 63 (2010): 89–101.

Caius, John. *A Boke, or Counseill against the Disease Commonly Called the Sweate, or Sweatyng Sicknesse*. 1552. Appendix to *The Epidemics of the Middle Ages*. Ed. Justus Friedrich Carl Hecker. London: Trubner & Co, 1859.

Calderwood, James L. *Metadrama in Shakespeare's Henriad: Richard II to Henry V*. Berkeley: U of California P, 1979.

Caldwell, Ellen M. "'Banish All the Wor(l)d': Falstaff's Iconoclastic Threat to Kingship in *1 Henry IV*." *Renascence: Essays on Values in Literature* 59.4 (2007): 219–46.

Campbell, Lily B. *Shakespeare's "Histories": Mirrors of Elizabethan Policy*. 1947. 3rd ed. London: Methuen, 1968.

Clare, Janet. "Medley History: *The Famous Victories of Henry the Fifth* to *Henry V*." *Shakespeare Survey* 63 (2010): 102–13.

Cohen, Derek. "History and the Nation in *Richard II* and *Henry IV*." *Studies in English Literature 1500–1900* 42.2 (2002): 293–315.

Collick, John. *Shakespeare, Cinema and Society*. Manchester: Manchester UP, 1989.

Colman, Adrian. *Shakespeare's Henry IV, Part One*. Sydney: Sydney UP, 1990.

Corbin, Peter, and Douglas Sedge, eds. *The Oldcastle Controversy: Sir John Oldcastle, Part 1 and The Famous Victories of Henry V*. Manchester: Manchester UP, 1991.

Daniel, Samuel. *The First Four Books of the Civil Wars*. 1595. *Early English Books Online*. Web.

Davies, Michael. "Falstaff's Lateness: Calvinism and the Protestant Hero in *Henry IV*." *The Review of English Studies* 56.225 (2005): 351–28.

de Jongh, Nicholas. "Long Day's Journey into England's Nightmare." *Evening Standard*. 17 August 2007: 9. Web.

Dent, R.W. *Shakespeare's Proverbial Language: An Index*. Berkeley: U of California P, 1981.

Dillon, Janette. *Shakespeare and the Staging of English History*. Oxford: Oxford UP, 2012.

Dollimore, Jonathan, and Alan Sinfield, eds. *Political Shakespeare: New Essays in Cultural Materialism*. 2nd ed. Manchester: Manchester UP, 1994.

Draudt, Manfred. "Shakespeare's English Histories at the Vienna Burgtheater." *Shakespeare's History Plays: Performance, Translation and Adaptation in Britain and Abroad*. Ed. Ton Hoenselaars. Cambridge: Cambridge UP, 2004. 196–209.

Dromgoole, Dominic, dir. *Henry IV, Part 1*. 2010. Screen dir. Robin Lough. Globe Theatre on Screen. Opus Arte, 2012. DVD.

Dutton, Richard, and Jean Howard, eds. *A Companion to Shakespeare's Works: The Histories*. Malden, MA: Blackwell, 2003.

Edelman, Charles. "Shakespeare's *Henry IV, Part 1*." *The Explicator* 6.4 (2005): 5–7.

Empson, William. "Falstaff and Mr Dover Wilson (1953)." *Shakespeare Henry IV Parts I and II: A Casebook*. Ed. G.K. Hunter. Houndmills, Basingstoke: Macmillan, 1970. 133–54.

Evans, Lloyd. "Force of Nature." *Spectator*. 14 May 2005: 74. Web.

Eyre, Richard, dir. *The Hollow Crown: Henry IV, Part 1*. Neal Street, NBC Universal and Thirteen for BBC, 2012. DVD.

The Famous Victories of Henry the Fifth. 1598. *The Oldcastle Controversy: Sir John Oldcastle, Part 1 and The Famous Victories of Henry V*. Ed. Peter Corbin and Douglas Sedge. Manchester and New York: Manchester UP, 1991.

Gelber, Bill. "Review of *Henry IV Parts I and II*, by the Royal Shakespeare Company at the Courtyard Theatre in Stratford-upon-Avon." *Early Modern Literary Studies* 13.3 (2008) 21: 1–9. Web.

The Geneva Bible: A Facsimile of the 1560 Edition. Madison, Milwaukee, and London: U of Wisconsin P, 1969.

Gildersleeve, V.C. *Government Regulation of the Elizabethan Drama*. New York: Burt Franklin, 1961.

Goldberg, Jonathan. "Hal's Desire, Shakespeare's Idaho." *Theory in Practice: Henry IV Parts One and Two*. Ed. Nigel Wood. Buckingham (UK) and Philadelphia: Open UP, 1995. 35–64.

Grady, Hugh. "Falstaff: Subjectivity between the Carnival and the Aesthetic." *Modern Language Review* 96.3 (2001): 609–23.

Greenblatt, Stephen. "Invisible Bullets." *Shakespearean Negotiations: The Circulation of Social Energy in Renaissance England*. Oxford: Oxford UP, 1988. 21–65.

Grene, Nicholas. *Shakespeare's Serial History Plays*. Cambridge: Cambridge UP, 2002.

Hall, Edward. *Union of the Two Noble and Illustrious Families of Lancaster and York*. 1548. *Early English Books Online*. Web.

Hall, Jonathan. *Anxious Pleasures: Shakespearean Comedy and the Nation-State*. Cranbury, NJ: Associated UP, 1995.

Hammond, Antony. "Encounters of the Third Kind in Stage-Directions in Elizabethan and Jacobean Drama." *Studies in Philology* 89.1 (1992): 71–99.

Hatchuel, Sarah, and Nathalie Vienne-Guerrin, eds. *Shakespeare on Screen: The Henriad*. Rouen: Publications Univ. Rouen Havre, 2008.

Hattaway, Michael, ed. *The Cambridge Companion to Shakespeare's History Plays*. Cambridge: Cambridge UP, 2002.

Hawkes, Terence. "Bryn Glas." *Post-Colonial Shakespeares*. Ed. Ania Loomba and Martin Orkin. London: Routledge, 1998. 117–40.

Hazlitt, William. "From *Characters of Shakespeare's Plays* (1817)." *Henry IV Parts One and Two*. Ed. Ronald L. Levao. New York: Pearson Longman, 2007. 353–56.

Henderson, Diana E. "Performing History: *Henry IV*, Money, and the Fashion of the Times." *A Companion to Shakespeare and Performance*. Ed. Barbara Hodgdon and W.B. Worthen. Malden, MA, and Oxford: Blackwell, 2005. 376–96.

Hertel, Ralf. "Mapping the Globe: The Cartographic Gaze and Shakespeare's *Henry IV Part 1*." *Shakespeare Survey* 63 (2010): 49–62.

Hewison, Robert. "Review of *Richard II, Henry IV, Parts 1 and 2*." *Sunday Times*. 26 August 2007: 20. Web.

Highley, Christopher. "Wales, Ireland, and *1 Henry IV*." *Renaissance Drama* 21 (1990): 91–114.

Hinman, Charlton, and W.W. Greg, eds. *Henry the Fourth Part I, 1598: Shakespeare Quarto Facsimiles No 14*. Oxford: Clarendon, 1966.

Hodgdon, Barbara. *The End Crowns All: Closure and Contradiction in Shakespeare's History*. Princeton, NJ: Princeton UP, 1991.

———, ed. *The First Part of King Henry the Fourth: Texts and Contexts*. Boston and New York: Bedford, 1997.

Hoenselaars, Ton, ed. *Shakespeare's History Plays: Performance, Translation, and Adaptation in Britain and Abroad*. Cambridge: Cambridge UP, 2004.

Holderness, Graham. *Shakespeare Recycled: The Making of Historical Drama*. New York and London: Harvester Wheatsheaf, 1992.

———, Nick Potter, and John Turner. *Shakespeare: The Play of History*. Houndmills, Basingstoke: Macmillan, 1988.

Holinshed, Raphael. *Chronicles of England, Scotland, and Ireland*, rev. ed. 1587. Furness Collection. *Schoenberg Center for Electronic Text & Image*. U of Pennsylvania. Web.

Holland, Peter. *English Shakespeares: Shakespeare on the English Stage in the 1990s*. Cambridge: Cambridge UP, 1997.

Hopkins, Lisa. *Shakespeare on the Edge: Border-Crossing in the Tragedies and the Henriad*. Aldershot, UK: Ashgate, 2005.

———. "Welshness in Shakespeare's English Histories." *Shakespeare's History Plays: Performance, Translation, and Adaptation in Britain and Abroad*. Ed. Ton Hoenselaars. Cambridge: Cambridge UP, 2004. 60–74.

Howard, Jean E., and Phyllis Rackin, eds. *Engendering a Nation: A Feminist Account of Shakespeare's English Histories*. London and New York: Routledge, 1997.

Humphreys, A.R., ed. *The First Part of King Henry IV*. The Arden Shakespeare. 1960. London and New York: Routledge, 1989.

Hunt, Maurice. "The Hybrid Reformations of Shakespeare's Second Henriad." *Comparative Drama* 32 (1998): 176–206.

Jackson, MacD. P. "The Manuscript Copy of the Quarto (1598) of Shakespeare's *1 Henry IV*." *Notes and Queries* 7.33 (1986): 353–54.

Jackson, Russell. "Shakespeare at Stratford-upon-Avon: Summer and Fall, 2000." *Shakespeare Quarterly* 52:1 (2001): 107–23.

Jenkins, Harold. "The Structural Problem in Shakespeare's *Henry IV* (1956)." *Shakespeare Henry IV Parts I and II: A Casebook*. Ed. G.K. Hunter. Houndmills, Basingstoke: Macmillan, 1970. 155–73.

Kastan, David Scott, ed. *King Henry IV Part 1*. The Arden Shakespeare. London: Thomson Learning, 2002.

————. "'Killed with Hard Opinions': Oldcastle, Falstaff and the Reformed Text of 1 *Henry IV*." *Textual Formations and Reformations*. Ed. Laurie E. Maguire and Thomas L. Berger. Newark: U of Delaware P, 1998. 211–27.

————. *Shakespeare after Theory*. London and New York: Routledge, 1999.

Kelly, Henry Ansagar. *Divine Providence in the England of Shakespeare's Histories*. Cambridge, MA: Harvard UP, 1970.

Kennedy, Dennis. "Foreword: Histories and Nations." *Shakespeare's History Plays: Performance, Translation, and Adaptation in Britain and Abroad*. Ed. Ton Hoenselaars. Cambridge: Cambridge UP, 2004. 1–8.

Krims, Marvin B. "Hotspur's Antifeminine Prejudice in Shakespeare's 1 *Henry IV*." *Literature and Psychology* 4 (1994): 118–32.

Lander, Jesse M. "'Crack'd Crowns' and Counterfeit Sovereigns: The Crisis of Value in 1 *Henry IV*." *Shakespeare Studies* 30 (2002): 137–61.

Leggatt, Alexander. *Shakespeare's Political Drama: The History Plays and the Roman Plays*. London: Routledge, 1988.

Levao, Ronald, ed. *Henry IV, Parts I & II*. New York: Pearson Longman, 2007.

Levine, Nina. "Extending Credit in the *Henry IV* Plays." *Shakespeare Quarterly* 51.4 (2000): 403–31.

Lloyd, Megan. "'To Speak Welsh': Nonsense and Subversion in Shakespeare's *Henry IV, Part One*." *North American Journal of Welsh Studies* 2 (2002): 7–14.

Loehlin, James N. *Henry IV: Parts I and II*. The Shakespeare Handbooks. Houndmills, Basingstoke: Palgrave Macmillan, 2008.

Longstaffe, Stephen, ed. *1 Henry IV: A Critical Guide*. London and New York: Continuum, 2011.

Lyons, Bridget Gellert, and Dorothy Remy, eds. *Chimes at Midnight, Orson Welles, Director*. New Brunswick, NJ, and London: Rutgers UP, 1988.

Magelssen, Scott. "Henry IV." *Shakespeare Bulletin* 22.3 (2004): 99–101.

Mayer, Jean-Christophe. "The Decline of the Chronicle and Shakespeare's English History Plays." *Shakespeare Survey* 63 (2010): 12–23.

McAlindon, Tom. *Shakespeare's Tudor History: A Study of Henry IV, Parts 1 and 2*. Aldershot, England: Ashgate, 2001.

———. "Swearing and Forswearing in Shakespeare's Histories: The Playwright as Contra-Machiavel." *Review of English Studies* 51.202 (2000): 208–29.

McMillin, Scott. *Henry IV, Part One*. Shakespeare in Performance. Manchester and New York: Manchester UP, 1991.

McMullen, Gordon, ed. *1 Henry IV*. 3rd ed. New York: Norton, 2003.

Merlin, Bella. *With the Rogue's Company: Henry IV at the National Theatre*. London: Oberon Books, 2005.

Morgann, Maurice. "An Essay on the Dramatic Character of Sir John Falstaff." London: Wheatley and Adlard, 1825.

Mortimer, Ian. *The Fears of Henry IV: The Life of England's Self-made King*. London: Jonathan Cape, 2007.

"New Theatrical Bills." *New York Times*. 20 March 1896. Web.

Norwich, John Julius. *Shakespeare's Kings*. Harmondsworth, UK: Penguin, 1999.

Odell, George C.D. *Shakespeare—From Betterton to Irving*. 1920. 2 vols. New York: Benjamin Blom, 1963.

Ornstein, Robert. *A Kingdom for a Stage: The Achievement of Shakespeare's History Plays*. Cambridge, MA: Harvard UP, 1972.

Ostovich, Helen, Holger Schott Sym, and Andrew Griffin, eds. *Locating the Queen's Men, 1583–1603: Material Practices and Conditions of Playing*. Farnham, Surrey: Ashgate, 2009.

Palmer, T. "Master John Fletcher his dramaticall Workes now at last printed." 1647. *The Works of Francis Beaumont and John Fletcher in Ten Volumes*. Vol. 1. Project Gutenburg, 2004. Web.

Partridge, Eric. *Shakespeare's Bawdy: A Literary & Psychological Essay and a Comprehensive Glossary*. London: Routledge, 1947.

Patterson, Annabel M. *Reading Holinshed's Chronicles*. Chicago: U of Chicago P, 1994.

Peat, Derek. "Falstaff Gets the Sack." *Shakespeare Quarterly* 53.3 (2002): 379–85.

Pendleton, Thomas A. "'This Is Not the Man': On Calling Falstaff Falstaff." *Analytical and Enumerative Bibliography* 4.1 (1990): 59–71.

Pepys, Samuel. *The Diary of Samuel Pepys: A New and Complete Transcription*. Ed. Robert Latham and William Matthews. London: Bell, 1970.

Pilkington, Ace G. *Screening Shakespeare from Richard II to Henry V*. London and Toronto: Associated UPs, 1991.

Pugliatti, Paola. *Shakespeare the Historian*. New York: St Martin's, 1996.

Rackin, Phyllis. *Stages of History: Shakespeare's English Chronicles*. London and New York: Routledge, 1991.

Ribner, Irving. *The English History Play in the Age of Shakespeare*. 1957. Rev. ed. London and New York: Routledge, 2005.

Ruiter, David. *Shakespeare's Festive History: Feasting, Festivity, Fasting and Lent in the Second Henriad*. Aldershot, England: Ashgate, 2003.

Ryan, Kiernan. "The Future of History in *Henry IV*." *Henry IV Parts One and Two*. Ed. Nigel Wood. Buckingham and Bristol: Open UP, 1995.

Salgado, Gamini. *Eyewitnesses of Shakespeare: First Hand Accounts of Performances 1590–1890*. New York: Harper & Row, 1975.

Shaheen, Naseeb. *Biblical References in Shakespeare's History Plays*. Newark: U Delaware P, 1989.

Shaughnessy, Robert. "Falstaff's Belly: Pathos, Prosthetics and Performance." *Shakespeare Survey* 63 (2010): 63–77.

———. "'I do, I will': Hal, Falstaff and the Performative." *Alternative Shakespeares 3*. Ed. Diana E. Henderson. London and New York: Routledge, 2008. 14–33.

———. *Representing Shakespeare: England, History and the RSC*. Hemel Hempstead, UK: Harvester Wheatsheaf, 1994.

Shrimpton, Nicholas. "Shakespeare Performances in Stratford-upon-Avon and London." *Shakespeare Survey* 36 (1983): 149–55.

Shurgot, Michael W., and Peter J. Smith. "The 2010 Season at London's Globe Theatre." *The Upstart Crow* 29 (2010): 82–98.

Stewart, J.I.M. "The Birth and Death of Falstaff (1949)." *Shakespeare Henry IV Parts I and II: A Casebook*. Ed. G.K. Hunter. Houndmills, Basingstoke: Macmillan, 1970. 127–34.

Stow, John. *Chronicles of England*. 1580. *Early English Books Online*. Web.

Strype, John. *Annals of the Reformation*. Vol. 4. Oxford: Clarendon, 1824.

Tatspaugh, Patricia. "Shakespeare Onstage in England: March to December 2005." *Shakespeare Quarterly* 57.3 (2006): 318–43.

Taylor, Gary. "The Fortunes of Oldcastle." *Shakespeare Survey* 38 (1985): 85–100.

Taylor, Mark. *Shakespeare's Imitations*. Newark: U of Delaware P, 2002.

Thomson, Peter. *Shakespeare's Theatre*. London: Routledge, 1983.

Tiffany, Grace. "Puritanism in Comic History: Exposing Royalty in the Henry Plays." *Shakespeare Studies* 26 (1998): 256–87.

———. "Shakespeare's Parables." *Reformation* 16 (2011): 145–60.

Tillyard, E.M.W. *Shakespeare's History Plays*. 1944. London: Chatto and Windus, 1980.

Traub, Valerie. "Prince Hal's Falstaff: Positioning Psychoanalysis and the Female Reproductive Body." *Shakespeare Quarterly* 40.4 (1989): 456–74.

Traversi, Derek. *Shakespeare from Richard II to Henry V*. Stanford, CA: Stanford UP, 1957.

Tropea, Silvana. "Ron Daniels Finds the Space Inside Shakespeare." *American Theatre* 11.4 (1994): 40–41.

Ulrici, Hermann. *Shakespeare's Dramatic Art: And His Relation to Calderon and Goethe*. Trans. A.J.W.M. London: Chapman Brothers, 1846.

Vickers, Brian, ed. *Shakespeare: The Critical Heritage*. 6 vols. London: Routledge and Kegan Paul, 1974–81.

Walker, Alice. "The Folio Text of *1 Henry IV*." *Studies in Bibliography* 6 (1954): 45–59.

Weil, Herbert, and Judith Weil, eds. *The First Part of King Henry IV*. Cambridge: Cambridge UP, 1997.

Wells, Stanley, Gary Taylor, John Jowett, and William Montgomery. *William Shakespeare: A Textual Companion*. Oxford: Clarendon, 1987.

West, Gilian. "'Titan,' 'Onyers,' and Other Difficulties in the Text of *1 Henry IV*." *Shakespeare Quarterly* 34.3 (1983): 330–33.

Wharton, T.F. *Henry the Fourth Parts, 1 and 2: Text and Performance*. London and Basingstoke: Macmillan, 1983.

Wilders, John. *The Lost Garden: A View of Shakespeare's English and Roman History Plays*. London and Basingstoke: Macmillan, 1978.

Wiles, David. *Shakespeare's Clown: Actor and Text in the Elizabethan Playhouse*. Cambridge: Cambridge UP, 1987.

Wilson, John Dover. *The Fortunes of Falstaff*. 1943. Cambridge: Cambridge UP, 1979.

——, and T.C. Worsley. *Shakespeare's Histories at Stratford 1951*. Freeport, NY: Books for Libraries Press, 1970.

Wiseman, Susan. "The Family Tree Motel: Subliming Shakespeare in *My Own Private Idaho*." *Shakespeare, the Movie: Popularizing the Plays on Film, TV, and Video*. Eds. Lynda E. Boose and Richard Burt. London: Routledge, 1997. 225–39.

Wolf, Matt. "Sly yet sweet Falstaff in 'Henry IV, 1 and 2'." *New York Times*. 11 May 2005. Web.

Wood, Nigel, ed. *Henry IV, Parts One and Two*. Buckingham and Philadelphia: Open UP, 1995.

Yachnin, Paul. "History, Theatricality, and the 'Structural Problem' in the *Henry IV* Plays." *Philological Quarterly* 70 (1991): 163–79.

Zimmerman, Susan. "The Uses of Headlines: Peter Short's Shakespearian Quartos *1 Henry IV* and *Richard III*." *The Library* 6.7 (1985): 218–55.

from the publisher

A name never says it all, but the word "broadview" expresses a good deal of the philosophy behind our company. We are open to a broad range of academic approaches and political viewpoints. We pay attention to the broad impact book publishing and book printing has in the wider world; we began using recycled stock more than a decade ago, and for some years now we have used 100% recycled paper for most titles. As a Canadian-based company we naturally publish a number of titles with a Canadian emphasis, but our publishing program overall is internationally oriented and broad-ranging. Our individual titles often appeal to a broad readership too; many are of interest as much to general readers as to academics and students.

Founded in 1985, Broadview remains a fully independent company owned by its shareholders—not an imprint or subsidiary of a larger multinational.

If you would like to find out more about Broadview and about the books we publish, please visit us at **www.broadviewpress.com**. And if you'd like to place an order through the site, we'd like to show our appreciation by extending a special discount to you: by entering the code below you will receive a 20% discount on purchases made through the Broadview website.

Discount code: **broadview20%**

Thank you for choosing Broadview.

Please note: this offer applies only to sales of
bound books within the United States or Canada.